HOW TO KEEP YOUR
CAR ALIVE
THE COMPLETE GUIDE TO LOW-COST MOTORING

LINDSAY PORTER

This book is dedicated to my Dad. What now seems like many years ago, we taught ourselves, by trial and error, to become the fastest Morris Minor engine and gearbox quick-change act in the West. We had a lot of laughs – thanks, Dad!

First published 1993

Published by:
Haynes Publishing Group
Sparkford, Nr Yeovil, Somerset
BA22 7JJ, England

Haynes Publishing Inc.
861 Lawrence Drive,
Newbury Park,
California 91320 USA

British Library Cataloguing in Publication Data

A catalogue record for this book is available from the British Library

ISBN 1 85010 868 4 (Book Trade)
ISBN 1 85010 869 2 (Motor Trade)

Printed in Great Britain by J. H. Haynes & Co. Ltd.

While every effort is taken to ensure the accuracy of the information given in this book, no liability can be accepted by the author or publishers for any loss, damage or injury caused by errors in, or omissions from, the information given.

Contents

Foreword

by David Bowler, IEng, CEI, MIMI, AMIRTE, MSA, Cert Ed, Senior Lecturer in Automobile Engineering

Whilst there are undoubtedly many amongst us who are knowledgeable about automobiles, there are even more who would like to extend their armchair enthusiasms into more practical and rewarding areas, but lack the confidence to 'give it a go'. This book will encourage them to do exactly that!

Lindsay Porter's informal and relaxed method of writing is such that interest is created immediately and sustained until the end. Straightforward, clear and logical, it explains how to carry out all tasks, from the most simple, such as changing a wheel, through to the more complex, like thief-proofing your car.

As a senior lecturer in automobile engineering and the author of a few books, I have spent most of my life in explaining the intricacies of motor vehicles to students of all ages and backgrounds. This book combines explanations of specific procedures with basic common sense, to assist and guide you through the methods of repairing, checking, maintaining, purchasing and indeed, keeping your vehicle.

You can quickly establish your own limits in relation to the work you feel able to cope with, and then progress from the known to the unknown at a pace to suit you and your pocket. As your confidence and skill increase you will be able to delve ever deeper into the complexities of the motor car.

You can browse through the pages, and plan long and short-term strategies for maintaining your vehicle and keeping it on the road. And better still, a degree of smugness will undoubtedly be felt when, having completed a job, you contemplate how much money you have saved, and how well the job has been done.

This is a book for coffee-table and work-bench. I hope you enjoy both reading and learning from it as much as I did. The best of luck to those of you who decide to grasp the spanners and have a go – I am certain that with the invaluable assistance of this book, you will succeed.

Introduction and acknowledgements

Some people take in stray dogs, cats or donkeys. I have a strong urge to take in stray cars. I suppose it comes from my formative years, really. My wife and I were quite young when we married but it never crossed either of our minds that we wouldn't run a car! In those days, the early 1970s, MOT tests were much less strict and it was easier to keep a 'banger' on the road. One of the best cars we ever owned was a 1952 Morris Minor which had been owned from new by a doctor and his wife. We paid £45 for it and ran it for three years, unchanged. Unchanged, that is, apart from the engine (uprated three times for a bigger unit), gearbox (only twice), differential (whenever it failed), new body panels (whenever the local scrapyard had better ones in stock), seats (Rover 2000 seats fitted surprisingly woll), and the colour scheme. It was painted out of doors using something resembling a garden sprayer – and the results were so good that it took me years ever to repeat the standard of finish! When we started earning 'real' money, we chose to run a whole succession of cheap, interesting and crazy cars, from MGB special to E-type Jaguar, with dozens of others, too numerous to mention, to fill in the gaps. If nothing else, those days proved to me that you don't have to spend a fortune to run a car, provided you're not snobbish about what you drive.

This book is intended as a self-help guide for all those people who may, as we did, have no choice but to run a cheap car, and all those who are sensible enough to want to do nothing else. You *can* run a cheap car, save money and have reliable motoring, all at the same time. There's no great mystique about it, just an accumulation of experience and common sense. I hope the book proves useful to you and that you are able to have as much fun mixed in with the frustration of running older cars as we have had!

I have dedicated this book to my dad, Doug, because of all the help he gave me in learning as we went along. His accountant's training turned out to be quite useless when it came to Morris Minor gearboxes, but his patience and logic often did the trick. My mum, Doris was pretty helpful too! Once, when my wife and I lived in the Shropshire countryside, my parents allowed us to sell our Morris Minor from their house, well situated in a West Midlands town. There was such a good response to my advert that people were queuing up at the door to buy. So insistent were the callers that I ended up selling one of them my mother's Morris Minor as well as our own. She was very good about it when my father and I told her about it later. Well *quite* good about it, considering... She felt better when Dad found her a replacement.

I always make a point of mentioning my wife Shan in the introduction to my books, and as ever there's a lot of her in this one. She has taken a good many of 'my' photographs over the years and her experiences in helping to keep old cars going have provided a lot of the insights used in this book.

Sean Niescior proved himself to be an able and intelligent young mechanic when he helped with many of the 'how to' sections, and my assistant Zoe Palmer has worked hard and long in her usual efficient and determined way to ensure that the complicated 'coming together' that goes into the production of a manuscript all 'came together' in the right manner. She also showed off her wheel-changing skills in the relevant section of the book!

A number of individuals and companies were helpful in supplying invaluable advice and materials used in the book and to all of them I am extremely grateful. They are all listed in Appendix 4 at the back of the book. In particular, I am indebted to the guys at Potter's Car Dismantlers in Stourport-on-Severn, Worcestershire. They're great characters, and completely opposite to the scrapyard owner stereotype. (But then, most car dismantlers are...) To me, breakers' yards are fascinating places, full of interesting stuff among the dross, just waiting to be discovered.

My grateful thanks are also due to David Bowler, a Senior Lecturer in Automobile Engineering at, appropriately enough, the nearest technical college to Rover Group's main assembly plant, for his kind assistance with checking the contents of this book for safety and accuracy, and for making several useful and constructive additions. The points he raises about the relatively recently discovered dangers of fluoroelastomers and the insides of electronic ignition modules are required reading for anyone: see the appendices of this book!

Last but not least, I'd like to thank someone who doesn't even know he helped. In the 1970s, Robert Persig wrote a 'cult' book called *Zen and the Art of Motorcycle Maintenance*. In 1992, he wrote an almost equally brilliant sequel entitled *Lila*. If you want a fascinating, difficult, incredibly challenging read, I can recommend nothing better. If some of the processes he encourages have found their way into this book, I'd be delighted. If his ideas take one a little further than mere auto repair, so much the better...

Lindsay Porter
Bromyard, Herefordshire.

Chapter 1

KEEPING YOUR CAR GOING

At its worst, your car can be your enemy. This chapter shows you how to make it your friend! It will be your enemy when it lets you down, when it stops you doing the things you want to do and even worse, the things you really *need* to do! Everyone who has driven a car that's not 100 per cent reliable knows those main dreaded moments:

– You **have** to get to work on time; perhaps you've taken time off and you need to create an impression, or there's something important that you need to get done. But will the car start when you want it to?

– You go out for the evening with some friends. Is the car going to play up when it's time to drive home? And will it restart if it stalls or if you stop for petrol?

– It's time to put the car through the annual MOT test. There's no way you can afford a replacement car, but will it pass?

To many people, a problem car is just another of life's curses, something to put up with like bad weather or thoughtless neighbours. But that need not be true. It's worth remembering that no matter what goes wrong **car faults can *always* be fixed!**

This chapter will show you how you can drastically reduce unreliability, fix minor faults and turn your car into something you can enjoy – a real pal, instead of an enemy!

Section 1 Making sure it starts

– and keeps going all the way to work and back.

Your car's engine might be worn, it might look as though it's past its sell-by date, and it might be prone to clunks, groans and wheezes when it's on the move. But in the vast majority of cases, none of this will prevent your car from starting. In almost every case, cars suffer from starting problems because of problems with the electrical/ignition systems. Fortunately, these areas are the easiest to work on and simple to put right at home. You **don't** need to be a qualified mechanic although you **do** need to follow the safety rules. Unfortunately, it's also true that the vast majority of car fires are caused by faulty electrics, so make sure you follow instructions carefully. On the other hand, unless you know what to look for, you won't know whether or not your car already has the potential for a fire. In other words, this chapter is doubly useful!

The check-and-repair jobs shown below can be used in one of three ways:

1. Go through your car methodically to get rid of the potential for problems before they occur.
2. Go through the car to get rid of persistent problems.
3. Carry out emergency repairs to areas of the car giving problems.

Engine won't turn over: more power needed!

'Ye cannae have more power Captain; she'll bloow...'

Once an engine starts running, it generates enough electrical power for all its own needs. (Theoretically – see later!) To get it started, you need a good, healthy amount of stored power in your car's battery and a clear route for the power to get to where it is needed. Therefore you need to check two separate items:

1. The battery.
2. The wiring, connections and clamps.

SYMPTOMS: The power supply is probably at fault if:

– The engine turns over slowly when you turn the key.

– The battery loses its power overnight or over a period of a few days when the car is left standing.

– The starter works fine on some occasions, but on others everything goes 'dead' when you turn the key. For example, the ignition light dims and perhaps the fuel gauge goes down to zero.

If all of the wiring and battery checks shown in this chapter have been made, the problem is probably a faulty starter motor. However, problems occur most often with the power supply side of things, so don't despair!

The battery

EQUIPMENT: Sand paper, basic workshop tools, hydrometer (cheap to buy from motorists' shops), rubber gloves, goggles, battery charger.

SAFETY:

– Before beginning work on or near any battery, be sure to extinguish all cigarettes, matches, and lighters. Never expose a battery to an open flame or electric sparks. Batteries give off a gas which is highly flammable and explosive.

– For safety, in case an explosion does occur, wear eye protection or shield your eyes when working near any battery. Never lean over a battery.

– Do not let battery fluid contact eyes, skin, fabrics, or paintwork because battery fluid is corrosive acid. If battery fluid gets on your skin or in your eyes, immediately flush the area with water thoroughly. Seek medical help immediately if acid has entered the eyes.

– To lessen the risk of sparks, remove rings, metal watchbands, and other metal jewellery.

– Never allow metal tools to contact the positive battery terminal and anything connected to it while you are at the same time in contact with any other metallic portion of the vehicle because a short circuit will be caused.

– Keep everyone including children away from the battery.

– Always disconnect the battery earth (negative) lead before working on the battery or the electrical system.

– Charge the battery in a well-ventilated area.

1.1 *Corrosion on terminals will reduce the amount of power that can get through and can cause the power to disappear altogether when you turn the key. The contact is good enough to turn on ignition lights, fuel gauge and so on; try to start the car though and the extra demand causes the contact to disappear altogether. Sand the vertical part of the terminal. You must get rid of any hard, dull deposit that may have formed – use a file if necessary – until you can see clean, bright metal.*

1.2 *Badly corroded terminals are best dealt with by replacing them. Cut off the end of the cable and bare a new section, taking care that the insulation comes right up to the edge of the terminals. Screw new terminals in place; they're cheap and are guaranteed to give a better contact. Pinch clamps are better than the cap type.*

1.3 *Use Vaseline or, better still, CopperEase, a copper impregnated paste, that prevents corrosion and transmits electrical current.*

1.4 *To wash off the 'furry' corrosion that builds up on poorly maintained battery clamps, you need nothing more exotic than hot water.*

1.5 *A hydrometer measures the amount of 'charge' held in the battery electrolyte. The better the charge, the higher the float will go. Insert the tube into the battery, one cell at a time. (Each cell has its own access, through the filler caps.) Draw some fluid into the hydrometer and write down the reading you get. The reading should be at about 1.25 volts, or on the green coloured part of the scales if a green-to-red range is shown. If one or more cells are a lot worse than the others, you have the reason for poor battery performance – one or more of the cells will have failed. This Sykes-Pickavant tester works on the floating ball principle. If they all float, the battery is fully charged.*

1.6 *One very temporary solution is to use 'battery tablets', revitalisers that help to overcome the chemical changes that spell the end of a battery's life. They might keep you going while you shop around for the cheapest replacement. Don't pay garage forecourt prices – unless you find one doing a special deal – and do make sure that you receive a guarantee in writing.*

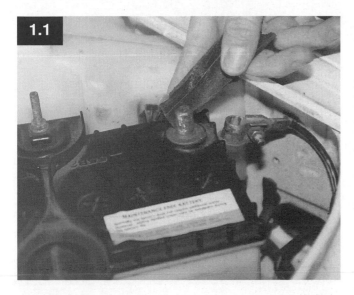

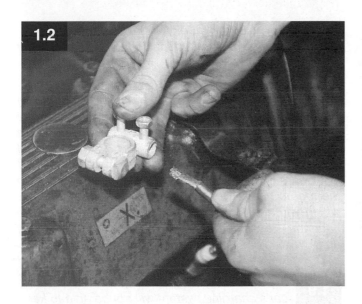

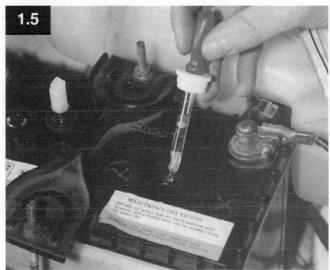

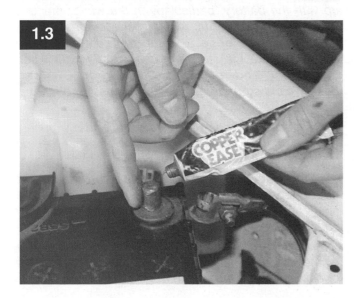

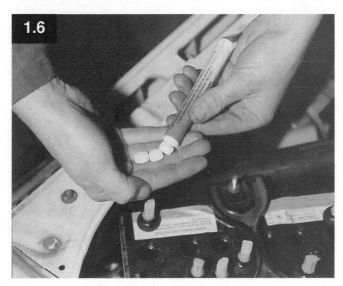

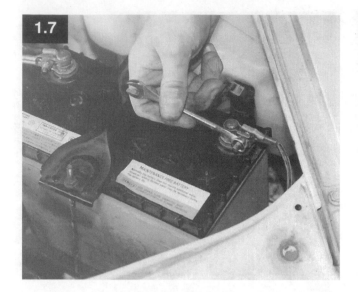

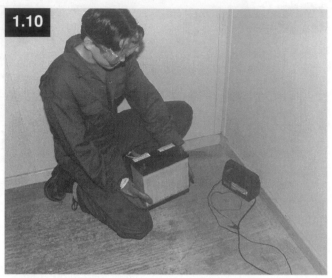

1.7 Don't overtighten battery terminals. You might twist the terminal in the case, causing it to crack.

1.8 If the battery has not been topped up with distilled water for a long time, the electrolyte level will fall too low and this will also cause the battery to operate below par. If there is no level indicator on the battery, top up the electrolyte so that it just clears the plates inside the battery, visible through the top-up holes. Use distilled water, never tap water which will shorten the life of the battery. NB Some batteries are 'sealed for life' and will not need topping up.

1.9 If your car is used for very short drives, the car's charging system will not be able to keep up with the battery, particularly in the winter months. Charging the battery up with a trickle charger over a 24-hour period once a week should restore the balance. Note the following important points when connecting and removing the charger. Unscrew battery caps so that gas can escape as the battery is charged.

Connecting: Fit the crocodile clamps to the battery terminals before turning on the power, so that they do not touch each other and short out.

Disconnecting: Turn the power off and re-fit the battery caps before removing the crocodile clips. A spark may conceivably ignite the hydrogen created by charging the battery.

Always disconnect the car's battery leads before connecting the charger so that there is no risk of fire or damage to the car's electrical system.

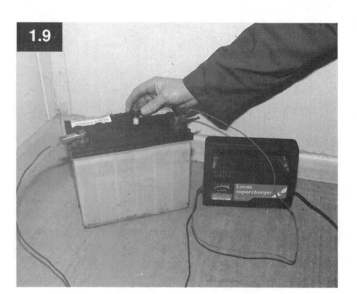

1.10 Most car batteries are very heavy and contain enough sulphuric acid to cause a lot of problems if dropped. Handle with care, always ensuring that they are carried and stored in an upright position. Wear rubber gloves and, ideally, a pair of goggles.

If the battery still gives problems there is another way to check its efficiency. Charge it up fully and then take it to a garage who will be able to put a discharge tester across the main terminals. The results will not be definitive, but will give you another clue as to whether the battery is still able to pull its weight.

Wiring, connections and clamps

Having established that the battery is sound and that the terminals to the battery are doing their job, it is now essential to ensure that the power is getting to where it's needed. The biggest drain on the battery occurs when you start the engine, so the biggest cables on the car are those which carry the power directly from one side of the battery to the starter motor, and from the other side of the battery to the car's bodywork which acts as an 'earth' cable.

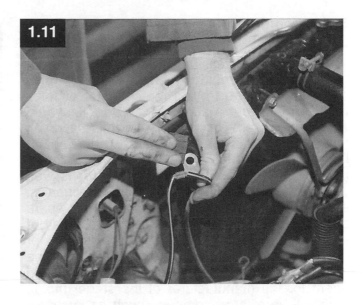

1.11 Unbolt the cable that goes from the battery to the bodywork, clean the metal on the clamp and on the car's body until it is shiny and bright in that area, coat it in CopperEase to prevent corrosion and reassemble.

1.12 Do the same with the clamp that is bolted to the starter motor. In this way you will have ensured that the power flowing to and from the battery is getting through. N.B. DISCONNECT THE BATTERY NEGATIVE LEAD FIRST! This terminal leads directly to the battery: if that spanner touches any part of the bodywork a massive short will result!

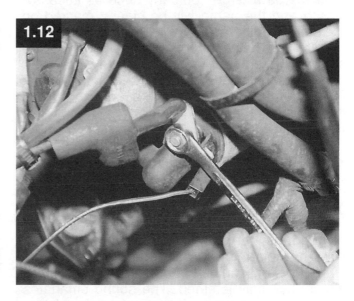

1.13 It is often forgotten that although the car's bodywork is an effective 'earth', the engine is insulated from the bodywork by the rubber engine mounts. Somewhere, either on your car's engine or gearbox, there will be another fat cable bolted through a clamp at one end and passing to the car's bodywork where it will again be bolted into place. As with the previous stage, remove both ends, clean until all connections are bright and re-fit with a protective coating such as CopperEase. Tip: If the throttle or choke cables on your car become hot when you attempt to start the car, it means that the earthing system has broken down and the cables are trying to give the engine the earth connection it needs.

Starter motor

If the starter motor still operates feebly it may be time – gulp! – to fear the worst and to consider exchanging this relatively expensive item for a reconditioned one from a motor factor or for a replacement from a scrap-yard. (See *Section 3 Recycled spares – scrap-yards* for information on how to check out a second-hand starter motor.) Despite what the Haynes workshop manual might say, rebuilding a starter motor is well beyond the capabilities of most home mechanics, even if they were able to get hold of the spare parts required. The simplest and surest way of finding out whether your starter motor is faulty or not is to remove it from the car (and here the manual is helpful!) and to take it to the main agent for the manufacturer of the starter motor. This will be a large company such as Lucas or Bosch and the name will be clearly marked on the starter motor. Ask them to test the unit for you to tell you whether or not it is faulty. If you are seriously interested in saving money, however, don't even consider buying a replacement unit from them! Motor factors are able to supply inexpensive reconditioned (recycled?) units at a fraction of the cost of the main agent's parts. Exchange items should also come with a worthwhile guarantee – check it out when you are shopping around.

If when you turn the key the starter motor makes its usual noise but almost instantly stops with a 'clunk', it may have jammed. Wait a couple of seconds, then try again. If the result is a whirring noise with an absence of the normal trying-to-start, engine-turning-over sound, it has almost certainly jammed. The sound emanates from a gear known as the starter dog which is shot along a pinion shaft, turning as it goes, until it comes into contact with a large ring gear, typically 18 in (450 mm) in diameter, on the engine flywheel. This gear is *supposed* to turn the flywheel and thus the engine until it starts. The trouble is that when the gears wear, the starter dog can stick in the flywheel gears like a piece of celery between the teeth. Unfortunately, a toothbrush is no help...

There are three self-help steps you can take:

1.14 *Some starter motors have a squared pin on the end of the motor housing. Turn this with a spanner and you can wind the stuck dog back down the pinion shaft. Try starting up again – it won't stick every time.*

1.15 *You could hit the starter motor on the side of the casing or on the solenoid with a hammer. This might also help to free a starter dog that has gone 'sticky' on the pinion shaft or a sticking solenoid (but be careful not to crack the starter motor case!).*

1.16 *Put the car in a low gear and 'rock' it backwards and forwards (ignition OFF!) until the dog comes free.*

The real cure for a starter that regularly sticks is, unfortunately, replacement of the ring gear on the flywheel – an engine-out job.

A starter dog that sticks on the pinion only needs you to remove the starter motor and thoroughly clean the pinion shaft, checking for wear and a broken spring. On the other hand, a scrap-yard or 'exchange' unit will be needed if the motor has become slow and lazy – but *do* remove, clean and re-fit all electrical connections before leaping to conclusions.

Leaking voltage

If you are certain that your car's battery is in good condition and that it is being properly charged, it may be that your car is 'eating' electricity of its own accord! Prime suspects include a sophisticated alarm system which may well flatten a car's battery over a period of about a week if it is not used, courtesy light switches which can corrode and cause a slight, slow drain of power and a faulty alternator diode pack.

1.17 *A simple way of checking whether there is any current draining from the battery is to disconnect one of the battery terminals and then to touch it lightly and repeatedly on to the battery post.*

Do so in the dark with the light turned off and you may well see a small spark created as you make and break the contact between the terminal and battery post. If you do see sparks, try disconnecting the electric clock and pull the wiring plug out of the back of the alternator and try again. Do ensure that nothing is turned on in the car, including ignition switch and courtesy lights.

SAFETY: Do not do this immediately after charging the battery. Ensure that the battery caps are properly screwed down and that the area around the battery has been ventilated for some time such as by leaving the bonnet open.

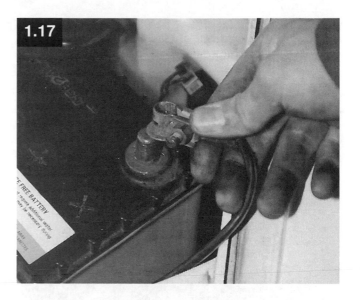

1.17

An alternative to the sparking method is to remove the non-earth terminal, and connect a bulb between battery post and terminal. If the bulb illuminates with everything switched off then there is a leak to earth. Each circuit on the vehicle can be disconnected in turn, and when the bulb goes out, the faulty circuit is located.

If you discover a wiring fault in a wiring loom or another place where access is difficult, for example within the rooflining, then simply replace the complete circuit by taking new wires along a more convenient route – not forgetting to disconnect the original faulty wiring.

If by connecting and disconnecting the alternator you find that this is the source of the sparking (see caption 1.17), take your car to an auto-electrician who can test the amount of current loss using a multi-meter. It may be that the current lost in this way is within accepted tolerances and is built in to the type of alternator you have and is not likely to cause a problem in which case you will have to continue to look elsewhere.

By using your car's manual, you'll be able to find out where the fuse box is situated and by disconnecting the fuses one at a time you will establish which area of the car is providing the current loss. Each fuse covers in most cases a group of electrical components. Once you have established in which group the current loss is being suffered, you can check out each item one at a time or have an auto-electrician do the work for you. For instance, you may wish to pull out the courtesy light switches from the door pillars and to clean the contacts if you have narrowed your investigations down to that part of the car. Anything more complex will undoubtedly require the services of an auto-electrician

1.18 *A course of action that might seem defeatist but could save you an awful lot of money might be to fit a Dis-car-nect battery isolator to the battery, so that when you leave the car you turn the power off. This could also be an effective anti-theft device, and there is no doubt that fitting it could be a lot cheaper than having an auto-electrician spend many hours looking for the needle in a haystack of a current loss in some obscure part of your car. In fact, this device cost about two-thirds of the average charge for one hour of an auto-electrician's time!*

Check charging circuit

Another reason for a battery failing to maintain its charge can be that the car's dynamo or alternator is not working efficiently. Many manuals show you how to overhaul an alternator or dynamo, but quite frankly it's just not worth it. It could take quite a long time to do, you may very well need specialist tools which the average home workshop does not possess, and in the end you may find that some special bushes and bearings are simply not available on the open market. Far more cost-effective is to exchange the alternator or dynamo for a specialist reconditioned unit or to buy one from a scrap-yard. Compare prices from both sources and shop around for the best price you can get for a reconditioned unit. Do bear in mind, however, that the cheapest of them may have had the bare minimum of work done to them. Ensure that you receive an adequate

guarantee and that you obtain and hang on to your receipt.

Before assuming the worst remember the good old saying:

– Check the obvious things first!

– Ensure that the drive belt is to the correct tension (see handbook). With some alternators, the belt has to be tighter than you might expect. If someone has fitted an incorrect belt in the past, you may not be able to move the alternator or dynamo sufficiently to put the belt under enough pressure. Alternators can consume a lot of power when under load and a little belt slippage can lead to a lot of lost electrical energy! Check also that the unit is tightly and correctly clamped so that it can't move and come loose, and also that the pulley is not loose (pretty unusual but worth checking).

– Check each of the terminals and especially the wires as they enter the terminals themselves. Over a period of time, the wires will tend to shred at this point and that will also lead to a drop in the amount of current they can carry.

– If the ignition warning light stays on all the time it suggests that either there has been a major wiring breakdown or the alternator or dynamo itself or its ancillary components are at fault.

– The ignition warning light should go out at anything over tick-over speed. Some alternators are efficient enough to make the light go out even at such low speeds.

– An excellent way of checking whether a dynamo is working is to turn the headlights on full at night, then raise the engine revs from tick-over. You should see the intensity of the lights increase. Once again, alternators are so efficient at low speeds that the difference may not be noticeable.

– An electrical specialist should be able to check whether your alternator or dynamo is putting out a charge in a matter of moments. (Ask first what the cost will be – it should be very little.) Once you've checked that everything is connected up correctly, it's well worth having an auto-electrician carry out this test for you.

1.19 *It is most important that an alternator's drive belt is kept tight as shown in the manufacturer's instructions.*

1.20 *If wiring connections to an alternator or dynamo become frayed, the result can be a serious drop in the amount of power transmitted.*

You will now be sure that there is enough power to spin the engine, but what if it still won't start? *Beam me up, Scottie*? No – just read on!

Fire first time!

It can be most frustrating when the engine spins away on the starter but it still won't fire. You always wonder just how long to sit there, churning away the starter in the hope that it *will* fire up, but in the knowledge that all the time the battery is getting flatter and flatter.

Once you have established that there is plenty of power on tap (see previous section), it only takes a series of simple, logical steps to ensure that your engine will fire up every time. Quite simply, all you have to do is to ensure that the spark plugs are receiving a good, hefty spark (over 90 per cent of starting problems are in this area) and that fuel is getting through (less than 10 per cent) and you're away – literally!

You may have noticed that starting problems are at their worst in cold, damp weather. Cold weather reduces the efficiency of the battery, so there is less power to churn the starter and less left over for the sparks; damp weather is even worse because it allows the electric current 'carrying' the sparks to the plugs to shoot off in all directions, rather like a leaking hose.

The best 'type' of electricity for creating a fat spark is high voltage. It is the job of the coil to supply the very high voltage required, so this is a key component, of which more anon. The trouble is, this high voltage is extremely difficult to insulate. As everyone knows, water and dampness conduct electricity extremely well. But 'everyone' is wrong! Water *doesn't* conduct electricity; it's the particles it carries that conduct. This isn't just a matter of being a clever dick; the point is that the inside of an engine bay always has a fine, invisible oil mist in it. The oil settles on the plug leads and distributor cap and dust sticks to the oil like flies to treacle. So when moisture attaches itself, it makes a wonderfully conductive soup which could be purpose made for draining current out of spark plug leads. And how does the water get there? In cold weather and especially during the night, moist air gets inside the engine bay which then condenses out as water on the engine and electrical ancillaries. The shape of the engine bay, with an opening at the bottom and a sort of bubble shape above, could have been purpose made for all the wrong things to happen. There are one or two simple steps that you can take to reduce the problem without even getting in to the mechanical side of things:

– Never park the car over bare earth or grass, unless you really can't avoid it. Tarmac or concrete will release far less moisture from beneath the car.

– Park under cover if you can.

– Before trying to start the car in the morning, open the bonnet and wipe the battery, plug leads, distributor cap and coil with a dry, clean cloth. Spray on aerosol moisture repellent if leads are damp – most releasing fluids are fine; check the instructions on the pack.

– Don't forget that condensation can often form inside the distributor cap, too. Wipe it dry; don't spray inside the cap.

– Don't place a blanket over the radiator. It won't keep the engine warm; it will cut out even the little air that otherwise would have circulated to help keep the engine bay drier. If you're worried about freezing up, use the correct concentration of anti-freeze.

Many people put up with poor starting unnecessarily. It's just not something you should tolerate, especially when it will be so simple to put right. Remember that, when it comes to starting difficulties:

The simplest things cause the biggest problems.

After dark checks

WARNING: Do not run the engine in a confined space such as a garage without ensuring adequate ventilation.

If your car is a poor starter – or even if it's not this could be illuminating! – wait until night time and drive it into a garage or some other place that can be made dark, lights out. Start and run the engine for a few minutes and look into the engine bay. Especially in winter or in damp weather, you may well see sparks flickering around the plug leads and the distributor cap. This is electricity that should be reaching the spark plugs but is, in fact, getting out and being wasted. When the battery is at its most stretched and when the engine is cold and the weather against you, this is when the loss will be too great and the car refuse to start. Here's what to do to put it right or prevent it from happening:

Spark plugs and leads

TIP Before removing plug leads, wipe them with thinners or white spirit to get rid of grease then put 1, 2, 3 or 4 (or more...) dots of paint on them, starting with '1' at the front. You may *think* you'll remember which is which later...

SAFETY: If you touch a spark plug lead or the coil or distributor cap whilst the engine is running, you can receive enough of an electric shock to give you a severe jolt. A very few cars' ignition systems produce enough power to kill a healthy person, but all can cause damage if there should be a heart problem – you may not know about it, so don't take chances! If nothing else, the violent reaction to the shock has often been known to cause injury to head or hands. **Do not touch anything to do with the car's ignition system when the engine is running!**

1.21 *Several items in a car's ignition system are so notorious for giving starting problems that they should be changed regularly, say, every two years, if you want to be sure to escape starting difficulties. What's more, they are very cheap. A new distributor cap (try motorists' shops or a motor factor, such as Partco, see Yellow Pages, rather than a main dealer for substantial price savings) and new plug leads will go a long way towards improving starting.*

1.22 *Spark plugs don't really need changing quite as often as the makers would have you believe, in my view: not unless your car has a high performance engine, in which case spark plugs do come in for a hard time. Clean them, check that the gap is correct (see your handbook) but do renew them if you are experiencing starting problems. The trouble is that when they do go wrong you can't usually see the problem. Either the fault lies inside the plug, or the insulation cracks and breaks down. If the plug has got to the stage where the electrode is worn down, it is probably in dire need of replacement. We used plugs supplied by the UK's biggest manufacturer, Champion.*

Distributor and coil

The distributor does three jobs, not one as many people imagine. As the word suggests, it distributes the pulse of energy from the ignition coil to the spark plugs. In particular:

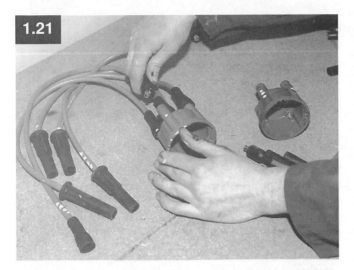

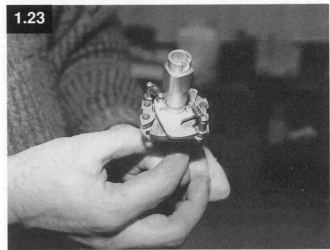

- It carries 'bursts' of electric current to the spark plugs.

- It breaks the circuit to the ignition coil, which then releases the powerful burst of electricity to be supplied to the plugs.

- It makes sure that the engine fires at exactly the right time and it changes the timing to suit the needs of the engine, depending on whether it is ticking over, running along a level road or accelerating hard.

Look after your distributor and it'll look after you! First of all, here's a brief explanation of why the distributor is so important.

1.23 *A mechanism inside the distributor advances the ignition timing as the car's engine speed picks up, while another mechanism retards it as you put your foot hard down on the throttle pedal. When you open the accelerator, the flow of fuel and air*

mixture through the inlet manifold creates a partial vacuum. A pipe is run from the inlet manifold to the distributor so that as you accelerate, an amount of 'suck' is transmitted to the distributor which pulls the base plate around, retarding the ignition. If this mechanism fails – and it depends on the diaphragm in the large ring mounted on the side of the distributor being in good condition – your car will run less efficiently.

1.24 *Check it out by pulling the pipe off the inlet manifold end – engine not running – and sucking quite hard on the pipe. As you let go, you should hear the base plate inside the distributor return back to its original position with a click. (It's spring loaded.) If you can suck freely with no resistance, or you don't hear a click from the base plate, then either the diaphragm has failed completely or the mechanism inside the distributor has seized solid. A breaker's yard replacement might be the ideal solution but check the replacement carefully before buying it.*

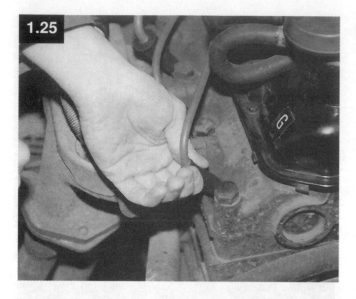

1.25 *Check that all the high tension leads are securely in place on the spark plugs, distributor and coil. Don't hesitate to replace them all if they appear damaged, if the connectors look insecure, if you are suffering from starting problems, or if you haven't replaced them for a couple of years. Champion make high-quality lead sets with full radio suppression for virtually all cars. They're guaranteed for life. Keep your receipt in case of problems!*

1.26 *Quite commonly corrosion takes place where leads push into the distributor cap. You could clean it but it's better replaced. Also, check for a tight fit where the lead fits into the cap.*

1.27 *If your car is already refusing to start, take out all the spark plugs, fit one of them to the end of its HT (high tension) lead (don't forget what was said earlier about numbering each HT lead so that it goes back in its correct place) and rest the threaded part of the spark plug against a bare metal part of the engine. Now, WITHOUT TOUCHING ANY PART OF THE IGNITION SYSTEM, have someone turn the ignition key until the engine turns over. You should see a spark at the end of the sparking plug. In very bright light, you may have to rig a shade over the plug with a piece of cardboard. If no spark occurs, the problem lies with one of the items in 1.28 to 1.31 below, or in the coil. If it does spark, either there is a problem with the fuel supply or (just as likely!) there is still a problem with the rest of the ignition system. Unfortunately, it is possible for the sparking plug to spark when out of the engine but when it is placed back into the engine, the stresses placed upon the system mean that the spark is inadequate. A strong spark should be a sharp blue colour while a weak spark will be difficult to see and could tend towards yellow or white in colour. If you can see a really good crack of a spark it is unlikely that the HT system is at fault.*

The Engine fires but won't run

If the engine fires and sounds keen to start when the starter motor is operating, but dies as soon as you release the key, it could be that a component called the ballast resistor is faulty. This resistor is bypassed when starting so that the coil can produce a fatter spark, but is then brought back into circuit to prevent overloading of the coil and contact breaker points. Ballast resistor systems were common in cars produced in the late 1970s and throughout the 1980s. The workshop manual for your car will tell you if you

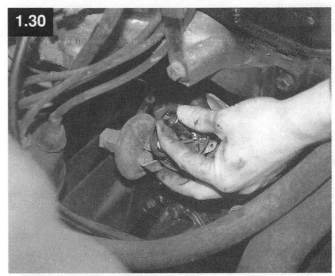

have a ballast resistor system, and where the resistor is to be found.

The next five pictures refer to cars with non-electronic ignition.

1.28 With the sparking plugs out, the car out of gear and the ignition now turned off, it will be easy to turn the engine over by hand by grasping the fan belt – or the fan itself if the belt is tight enough – with both hands. Be careful that you don't trap your fingers between belt and pulley! Alternatively, use a spanner on the bottom pulley nut on the front of the engine.

1.29 Turn the engine so that the cam turns on the distributor until the heel on the points is at the top of the cam. The points should be clearly open and

you should check the gap with a feeler gauge. It is common for the heel on the points to wear down so that the points gap closes up. It's the points that supply the coil with its 'trigger' shot of electricity.

1.30 Try moving the cam from side to side. If you can feel any play, the distributor is worn and in need of replacement. A worn bush in the top of the distributor, allowing the cam to move, means that the points gap – and therefore the ignition timing – will be constantly changing.

1.31 Turn the engine over again until the points are closed. Now turn on the ignition and flick the points open and closed with a screwdriver or with your finger tip. There should be a small blue or white spark; if not, or if you see a large yellow spark and the points are becoming rapidly pitted, the low tension circuit may be faulty.

distributor cap. Hairline invisible cracks will allow current to flicker away to earth (see After Dark Checks mentioned earlier) while the carbon contact that presses down on top of the rotor arm can wear away and the brass contacts inside the distributor cap can pick up contamination and pitting. If the contacts are bright because they are badly worn through the rotor arm rubbing against them you've probably got a worn distributor which is ripe for replacement. You can easily check a scrap-yard distributor to see if it works properly (see next section, entitled Recycled spares) or you can shop around between the motor factors for an exchange unit. The top bush in the distributor can wear which allows the shaft to move around causing the rotor arm to rub against the contacts in the distributor cap. New caps are cheap; new distributors are not. Don't rush to replace the distributor unless you really have to.

1.32 *If the points are particularly badly pitted or burnt and 'blued' a prime culprit will be the condenser. This is another item that is cheap to replace. Another symptom of failure – especially if the car has been standing for a long time, when the condenser is particularly prone to giving up and going home – is that the engine starts but then runs horribly when you try to accelerate it.*

The only other low tension faults will be in the wiring – check all connections – or in the coil itself which can only be remedied by bolting on a replacement.

Electronic ignition

1.34 *According to Ron Hull of XL Components reconditioners of a vast range of distributors, there are two major faults that can beset cars that are fitted with electronic ignition. Unfortunately, the symptoms for each are well nigh identical!*

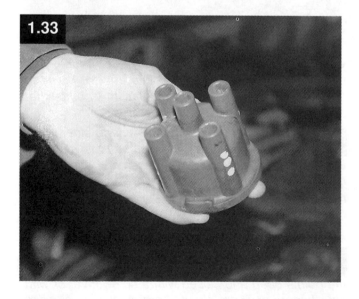

1.33 *Here's another item that's cheap to replace but a prime source of problems if ignored: the*

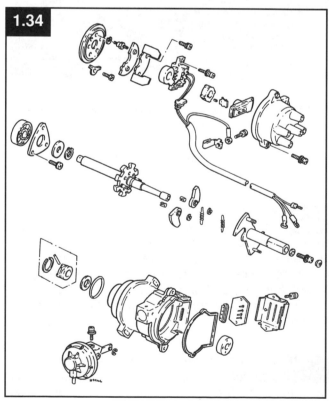

The trigger mechanism module can fit on the side of the distributor or on the bulkhead inside the engine bay. The other common failure point is the pick-up unit (which replaces the function of the contact set on non-electronic ignition cars). Both units display symptoms ranging from 'missing' at high revs, erratic running at low revs and cutting out, failure to start when the engine is hot, or just plain failure to start at all!

Replacement of the module costs more than half the price of a complete reconditioned distributor and may be tricky to carry out, while replacement of the pick-up unit would involve extensive dismantling of the distributors internal mechanism. The obvious moral is to check every other part of the ignition system to see if the faults you are experiencing can be found outside the distributor; if not, buy an exchange overhauled distributor. The added advantage of buying an overhauled distributor is that all the wear points described earlier will have been eliminated at the same time. XL distributors are available from most motor factors and if not 'on the shelf' can usually be obtained the same day.

Coil

The coil converts the steady trickle of 12 volt power to something with much higher voltage in short, sharp bursts. As previously mentioned, the distributor triggers it off. It's a simple piece of equipment but the wound coil of wire inside it that gives it its name can sometimes go haywire, especially when it gets hot. If you have intermittent starting problems, combined with intermittent spluttering or loss of power when accelerating, try replacing the coil. Once again, shop around for the cheapest on offer; it's not terribly sophisticated!

your motorists' shop and a handful of connectors.

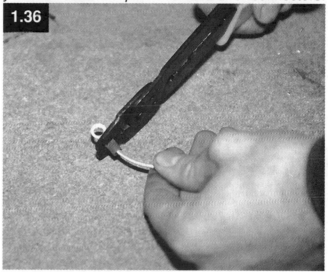

Before cutting off the old ones, make sure that you are able to obtain exactly the correct size – they can differ somewhat and your local shop might not have 'your' size in stock when you want them.

1.35 *Keep the body of the coil clean, replace the rubber sealing boot if the makers fitted one from new (they must have known something about potential problems) and concentrate on keeping it dry. Remember to check and dry the inside of the boot; moisture often gathers there, making things even worse. Also check that all low tension terminals (the ones other than the centre one, which is like a spark plug lead) are (a) tight, (b) clean, and (c) free from loose or breaking wires.*

1.36 *Remake the low tension connections if they look poor. Buy a crimping tool (cheap) from*

SAFETY: Never try opening up the casing of an electronic ignition module. None of the parts can be DIY serviced, and some makes of module are said to contain cancer-causing agents. Don't risk it!

Fuel system

> SAFETY: It is essential that you read the safety notes in the Appendices before working on the fuel system. See especially (but not exclusively) 'Fire', 'Fumes' and 'The Battery' on pages 181 and 182.

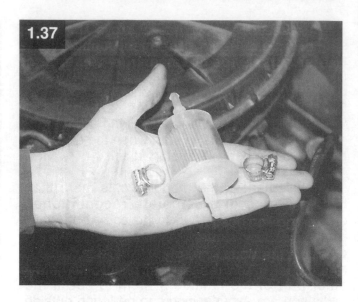

Once you have ensured that the ignition system is giving of its best, you'll want to ensure that the fuel system is fine. As I said at the start of this chapter, most problems with starting have nothing to do with the fuel system, even though it is often unfairly blamed.

One way in which the fuel system is prone to delivering starting difficulties, especially with older cars, is if it pumps contamination into the carburettor along with the petrol. You will only know if this is the case if you often have to clean out the carburettor and blow out the jets in order to get the car started up, only to find that the problem comes back time and again. Fortunately, the problem can be beaten by sneaking round the back of it and hitting it on the head while it isn't looking. It may be difficult to remove the contamination at source. Instead:

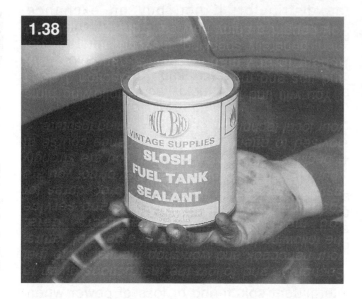

1.37 *Try buying an in-line fuel filter from your local motorist's shop. Ours came from the motor factors, Partco. You may need flexible fuel line and a number of clamps. Find out whether the line on your car is plastic or metal, as well as its size, and buy accordingly. Fit it just before the pipe enters the carburettor. Cheap to replace at each service, it will keep tiny particles out of the carburettor.*

1.38 *If you are certain that the fuel tank contains lots of 'bits' that you can't be sure of getting out, or if it is corroding and flakes are getting into the petrol, either buy a scrap-yard replacement (it will probably be better than yours – this is not a very common problem, although you may want to know how long the tank has been in the yard) or use 'Slosh Fuel Tank Sealant' from one of the specialist vintage car suppliers such as Holdens, Paul Beck or Woolies (see a classic car magazine). You remove and empty the tank (see vital safety points in your Haynes manual), then pour in the sealant. 'Slosh' it around the tank until it coats the inside, where it will seal any pin holes and grab all the particles in a permanent pin-down.*

As for the rest of it, you must find out if the fuel system is carrying out its simple task. Your car

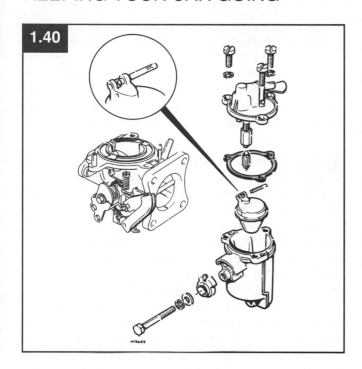

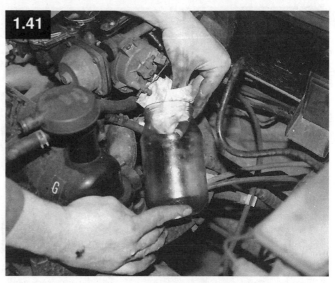

constant smell of petrol. Also, the float could be punctured. Shake it, and listen for petrol inside. If in doubt, submerge the float in a bowl of water, and look for air bubbles emerging from the float body, as you would with a cycle innertube. Any bubbles indicate a punctured float so replace the unit preferably with a new needle valve at the same time.

won't start properly if:

- There is no petrol getting through to the carburettor

- The carburettor's air intake is blocked (unlikely).

- The choke isn't working, or is not working properly.

- The carburettor becomes blocked (often suspected but not all that common).

1.39 *In order to get at the rest of the carburettor you'll need to remove the air filter housing. This will tell you whether there is any blockage in there preventing the air from getting through and you should also check whether the air filter itself is clogged although that should not prevent the car from starting. It will, however, prevent it from running properly.*

1.40 *Every carburettor has a float bowl containing a small reservoir of fuel. If when you remove it it turns out to be empty, petrol is clearly not getting through. While there, clean out sediment from the bottom of the fuel bowl. If petrol leaks from the carburettor in normal use, replace the needle valve and seating above the float. See your manual for details. If the needle valve has worn, allowing too much petrol to come through, it might give you a problem with starting the car when the engine is hot, as well as giving high fuel consumption and a*

1.41 *If there's no petrol in the float bowl you must check that the pump is operating correctly. Disconnect the fuel line from the back of the carburettor and place the flexible end in a jar with a rag around the top to prevent splashing. In the case of this Escort, the crimped clip had to be cut off and replaced with a screw-on clamp. If your car has an electric fuel pump (see manual), turn on the ignition and the electric pump should pump fuel through into the jar. But note that if your car is one of those whose electric fuel pump only operates with starter motor or even engine running, you will not be able to carry out this test. Check your workshop manual or with your main dealer. As soon as petrol appears, turn the ignition off. It's best to work with an assistant so that you can look after the petrol pipe without spilling petrol. If the car has a mechanical fuel pump driven by the engine, you will have to crank the engine over on the starter. It would be best to remove the spark plugs so that the engine turns over more freely, but then take the low tension leads (the two smaller cables) off the end of the coil – the large one that leads to the distributor – so that there is no spark being produced which might ignite the petrol. Once again, take careful note of the appendices and especially page 181 and 182 relating to 'Fire' risks.*

usually even simpler to remove and replace and once again replacement is the only practicable option. Do check that the filter in a mechanical fuel pump is not clogged, and also that the fuel line from the tank at the rear of the car has not accidentally been flattened. When they become very old, flexible fuel lines, especially of the rubber type, can collapse internally.

1.43 *When an engine is cold it needs a higher proportion of petrol to air than once it has warmed up. The choke closes off part of the air supply giving a richer mixture with more petrol in it. With the air filter removed, check that the so-called butterfly flap at the opening to the carburettor operates as the choke knob is pulled and pushed. It should be fully open when the choke is pushed in; almost fully closed when completely pulled out. On some cars, you can't actually see the flap working, but check the mechanism visually at the carburettor, and listen for the flap opening and closing. With an automatic choke, you may be able to see the flap in operation (or otherwise!) by attempting to start the car and then removing the air filter. Don't peer down into the top of the carburettor with the air filter removed whilst attempting to start the engine. There might be a backfire which could cause flames to spurt up through the top of the carburettor. You should try to start the car, turn off, then take a look to see if the choke has operated. Some automatic chokes need the ignition to be turned on; others need you to have operated the throttle pedal.*

If you still suspect that particles have got into the carburettor causing problems, you will have to strip it down and remove the jets and clean them out by blowing through with an air line. You'll also have to blow through the passages inside the carburettor. Wear goggles. If like most people you don't possess a compressor you can always use the tyre pressure gauge available at your local petrol station if you strip the carburettor at home and take it with you! See your workshop manual.

Flooding

They say you can have too much of a good thing and where petrol is concerned it's certainly the case! If you have tried to start your car with no success for too long you will end up with neat petrol in the cylinders which will prevent the sparking plugs from firing. It may seem odd but the simplest way of putting matters right is to push the choke back in, push the throttle pedal

1.42 *If your car has an electric fuel pump but you did not hear it clicking when you turned the ignition on, try hitting the casing smartly with a hammer – but take more care if it's made of plastic! If it then starts up, the points inside the pump are burnt and it would be best to buy a replacement pump. A good temporary cure is to disconnect the feed wire to the pump and remove the plastic cover. Beneath it, you will see a pair of contact points, similar to those in the distributor. One set has a neat little toggle mechanism that opens and closes the points to give the pumping action. It is worth giving this a gentle prod to ensure it is free. Use an emery board rubbed back and forth between the points, until you have cleared away any pitting from the surfaces. Replace the plastic cap and try again. Mechanical fuel pumps which bolt on to the side of the engine block are*

right down to the floor and hold it there without pumping the pedal and then spin the engine for anything up to ten seconds – quite a long time if you look at your watch! Holding the throttle pedal right down in this way has the effect of forcing a blast of air through the cylinders which should get rid of the excess petrol. You might find that towards the end of the ten seconds, the engine fires up spontaneously in which case you should pull the choke back out again to keep it going.

If this simplest step fails you will have to resort to taking the sparking plugs out of the engine, cranking the engine over a good few times to expel the unwanted fuel, before cleaning the sparking plugs and putting them back in ready to try again. To clean wet spark plugs, hold them over a gas ring in the kitchen. Take care as they get very hot, but this will help in re-starting.

Engine cuts out and restarts; cuts out and restarts; cuts out and restarts....

For a whole variety of reasons to do with modern engine design and modern fuel, as well as the immutable law of physics, carburettors have a tendency to act as mini-refrigerators. In weather that is both cold and damp it is quite possible for water vapour to freeze as it enters the carburettor, blocking everything up solid. To counteract this, many manufacturers fit a pipe that runs from the exhaust manifold to the air cleaner, along with a flap – which may be operated manually but is more likely to be operated automatically – to switch the air supply to this hot pipe in cold weather. If the pipe is missing or blocked or the thermostatic valve for switching the supply is damaged, the result will be a car that behaves in the most irritating manner: it starts and runs perfectly, but then on a journey it mysteriously loses its power, becoming less and less powerful until it conks out entirely. The owner gets out of the car, walks round it twice kicking the tyres as he/she passes, curses a few magic spells, gets back in and the car starts up and runs normally until the process starts all over again. If you were to look for the problem you would never see the symptoms because by the time the air filter is removed the ice around the carburettor has melted from the heat of the engine and the evidence has disappeared. Many is the owner who has been persuaded to fit a new fuel pump and even a new carburettor and distributor to cure a problem that isn't there.

1.44 *If you are a victim of your car's engine icing up, all you need to do is to make sure that the hot air supply pipe is in place and that the thermostatic valve (if fitted) is operating successfully. You'll find that a vacuum pipe runs from the manifold to a temperature sensor and from there to the air flap that directs hot air either into the air filter or into the engine bay. Check the temperature sensor – it sometimes fails – by connecting the pipe from the manifold direct to the flap mechanism. If the engine stops icing up (because the flap is now permanently in the position that allows hot air in to the air filter housing), you've found the problem. On the other hand, do check that the flap itself has not seized. Either free the flap as necessary or purchase a new thermostatic valve.*

Section 2 Maintenance

Don't underestimate the importance of correctly maintaining your car. Once it has been brought into ship-shape trim, carrying out a regular and *thorough* maintenance schedule can turn an unreliable car into a little gem! There will always be the odd unforeseen snag for your car to catch itself on; that's just life! But the number of breakdowns will be drastically reduced just by carrying out the steps shown here. And there are other terrific benefits to carrying out your own maintenance:

– You will spot problems before they occur: that is part of the point of maintenance – just changing the oil isn't even the half of it!

– You will come to understand your car – even to become part of it, if that isn't too fanciful. It's only in this way that you can feel at one with the beast when things go wrong. Then you will have a good feeling for what needs doing and a good fund of knowledge about the car to enable you to put it right.

— You'll save a fortune in servicing charges.

— You will carry out the work better than 90 per cent of all known mechanics. Some are conscientious, involved and thus excellent, of course. But only you can do the job and be sure that it has been done properly.

There is one golden rule to carrying out your own maintenance; a rule that you will find in no workshop manual on earth: take pleasure in the work you do. This doesn't mean that you must skip with joy at the thought of going outside on a cold evening to lie beneath your car – although some people do feel like that! I mean that you have to *want* to do the work properly, if for no other reason than the great benefits it will bring you in practical terms. And you should then feel pleased when you have done your best. It may seem weird to harp on about the toolbox in your brain, but without getting that straight *you won't carry out a satisfactory standard of work*.

Watch a modern athlete before a big event: he or she will be concentrating, emptying the mind in readiness for doing 'the job' properly. I'm not suggesting that you adopt the lotus position beneath the sump – in any case, oil running down the back of your neck is useless for achieving a good state of mind! But I do, very strongly, recommend the following:

— Allow yourself lots of time to carry out a job – more than you need, if possible. One of the biggest causes of getting things wrong is in trying to finish a job. Just be content to be doing the job, until it is done. You can't do anything else, anyway, so resign yourself to it. Otherwise, you'll rush and make mistakes.

— If things go horribly wrong and trying harder only makes them worse, walk away from the car for a while. You'll come back to it afresh and the problem will have shrunk. Any mechanic will tell you of trying for ages to get an awkward nut in place only to come back to it later and do it first time.

— Decide what sort of person you are. If you tend to leave things not properly done, calmly insist

to yourself that you finish each job properly. If you are a perfectionist, be pleased with doing your best. Whichever type, be content with what you have finished because it won't be perfect. Feel that sense of quiet contentment and you'll have the right frame of mind next time a job needs doing.

— Set your limitations according to your circumstances. If you have to work outside, ensure that you only carry out a 'completable' job at a time. In the winter, cold weather can drive you indoors before you have finished anything major, while wet weather can intervene at any time. Don't tackle major jobs until you have become proficient at smaller ones.

— Don't be stopped in your tracks by problems; use them to your advantage, like a wrestler uses judo techniques. Don't know the first thing about mechanics? Read up all you can (even if you don't understand every word) and have a trained mechanic come to you and pay him to do the work on condition that he lets you lend a hand. You'll learn a lot! Is something totally stuck or totally broken? So what! Hire the aforesaid mechanic to work while you learn and/or buy another part, perhaps a second-hand, cheap replacement.

— Don't be afraid of making mistakes. Turn the whole dread of getting things wrong completely on its head! If you don't make mistakes, how can you learn from them? Ergo, mistakes are a Good Thing; aren't you lucky! (You almost never think so right at the time the nut drops inside the rocker box or you assemble some stupid part upside down; but it's useful to bring it to mind later.)

Now that the mental toolbox has been put in order, you can start getting out the physical one full of spanners and your last car's rust flakes. Which brings me on to the subject of where, with what and how...

Weekly checks

You probably know this much already, but here's a reminder of the vital checks which need to be performed on any car at frequent intervals. The maker's handbook for your car probably says 'daily', but being realistic, once a week (or before a long journey) will be enough.

Every time you lift the bonnet it's worth glancing at the level of brake fluid in the master cylinder reservoir. Any sudden fall is cause for concern. The other important checks are easy to remember if you realise that their initial letters spell out the word 'POWER':

Petrol: Do you need to fill up with fuel?

Oil:Check the engine oil level and top up if necessary. (You'll get used to the rate at which your car uses engine oil, but remember that any engine can suddenly spring a leak. Catching it before the level gets too low could mean the difference between a new oil seal or gasket and a new engine.)

Water:Check the level in the radiator or expansion tank. If frequent topping-up is necessary, look for leaks. While you've got water on the brain, so to speak, top up the screen washer bottle.

Electrics:Check the operation of all the electrical equipment (especially the exterior lights). Glance at the alternator drivebelt and maybe check the battery electrolyte – old batteries can get thirsty.

Rubber:Check the tyre pressures (not forgetting the spare) and have a quick look at the tyre treads and sidewalls. If any tyre is consistently losing pressure, find the reason without delay.

Service your own car

Please refer to the reliability checks shown in Section 1, and follow the instructions given in your handbook and workshop manual. Note that the following instructions are of a general nature: you must refer to manufacturers' data, specifications, service intervals and service instructions so that the detailed procedures for your car can be followed. Whether or not you are a beginner at car maintenance, you are strongly advised to attend a car maintenance course at your local technical college or evening institute.

You will find that many of the following hints and tips and many of those in Section 1 don't appear in any manufacturer's handbook. But then, generally speaking, they would prefer that you bought a shiny new car from them, at vast expense, rather than Keeping *Your* Car Alive...

1.45 *Many of us have carried out some of the biggest car repair jobs that you can imagine out of doors! If you raise the car on ramps or a jack, only do so if the ground is level and firm; never on a soft surface such as soil. If you have no option, invest in a sheet of block board or plywood 8 ft x 4 ft (2.4 m x 1.2 m) and at least ¾ in (18 mm) thick – don't use chipboard because it's not strong enough – and drive the car up on to that. Place another stout piece of timber underneath the base of the jack just in case that part of the board is over a hollow. With the car driven on to the board, you'll also have a clean surface for lying on if you have to get beneath the car.*

1.46 *Never work on a car supported only by a jack. Use the jack to lift the car on to axle stands or drive it on to ramps, and firmly chock the wheels still on the ground.*

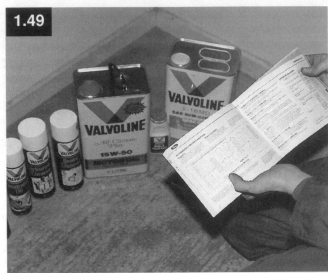

1.47 *You'll often need a source of extra light but mains voltage can be very dangerous when working on the ground, especially out of doors. Buy yourself an inexpensive 12 volt lead lamp or, if you must use mains voltage, buy one of those special trip switches made to go between plug and socket when you're using an electric mower. FOR A FULL LIST OF SAFETY DOS AND DON'TS SEE APPENDIX 1 AT THE BACK OF THIS BOOK.*

1.48 *Another life saver (in every sense) if you're working away from a power supply is the range of rechargeable power tools now available, such as this drill and power screwdriver made by Bosch. Fortunately you don't need many power tools when servicing your car, but on the few occasions that you do, this could be the answer.*

1.49 *Regular lubrication will ensure that all the mechanical components on your car last for very much longer, and you'll also guard against unexpected breakdown of items such as gearbox, differential and engine main bearings. It is essential that you use your car's handbook and service schedule – obtain one from a main dealer if you didn't receive one with your car. These days, many components on a car are 'sealed for life' so lubrication should not be an arduous job. We used Valvoline lubricants and a selection of Champion servicing components. Thanks are due to both for their kind assistance with this section.*

1.50 *Before you start work, you'll need to obtain a complete set of basic service materials. Take a look at your vehicle registration document and jot down your car's chassis number or VIN identification* number and take it with you when buying parts to ensure that you buy the correct ones. Also note down the exact make, model and year of first registration – some manufacturers' parts lists are laid out in this way. Typically, you will have to buy:

– A good quality motor oil of correct viscosity: see your handbook. You can make large savings by shopping around for the best price.

– Oil filter.

– New washer for the oil drain plug. These are designed to be used once only, and unless you replace them each time your car will be likely to drip oil. They cost next to nothing but may only be available from the main dealer for your model of car.

– Air filter.

– Grease: check with your handbook to see which type or types.

– New gasket for the rocker cover or camshaft cover. (Once again, this may only be available from your main agent if the car is not one of the most popular.)

– Thin oil and, possibly, releasing fluid.

– Spark plugs, if required.

– Contact breaker points for cars not fitted with electronic ignition.

– Distributor cap and HT leads, which should be changed about every two years.

– Brake fluid (which can also be used for topping up hydraulic clutch reservoirs)

1.51 The following parts may not need changing so regularly but you should check them on the car before buying the parts for the service. There

may be other service parts required, too. See the typical service check list at the end of this section and refer to your car's service requirements in the handbook.

– Fan belt. If the existing one is showing signs of cracking or fraying replace it without delay.

– Overhead camshaft drive belt (for cars with an overhead camshaft only, of course!). This should be replaced at around 40,000 miles or sooner if your handbook recommends it, whether you think it needs it or not. If the belt breaks, severe damage will be caused to your engine. Follow the workshop manual for details of how to carry out this work on your car.

– Brake shoes or disc brake pads for both front and rear. Use your manual to see how to carry out a check on what are acceptable thicknesses of brake shoes or pads, and replace if you are not certain that they will run through to the next service. SAFETY NOTE: Avoid inhaling asbestos dust – purchase an aerosol of brake 'damping spray' from your local accessory shop or parts store.

– Water and heater hoses. Pinch hard the ones on the car: any signs of cracking and they should be replaced. On some cars, hoses are also visible where they run to the heater beneath the dash. Check there as well because they can easily be forgotten.

1.52 SAFETY NOTE: Oil drain plugs are often over-tightened and the effort in loosening them could easily disturb a car not properly supported

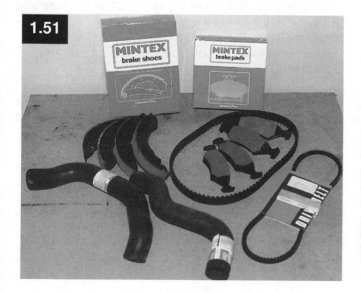
1.51

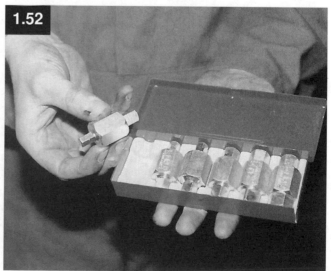
1.52

on axle stands. Take care, use ramps for preference, and ensure that the wheels remaining on the ground are tightly chocked. Ideally, and so that you drain the *maximum amount of oil out of the sump*, after slackening the sump nut remove the axle stand so the car is back on level ground before fully removing the oil drain plug.

Before you start, check which type of oil drain plug you have got on your car. It will be situated either on the bottom of the sump, at the lowest part of the engine seen from beneath or on one side of the sump very close to the bottom. Some just require the correct size of spanner; others need a special recessed square or six-sided socket. Sykes-Pickavant sell a set of drain plug keys for those engines that have internal hexagons or squares. Alternatively you could try making your own from a piece of hexagonal steel stock in an appropriate size. Bend one end over to make a 'handle'.

1.53 The Escort simply needs a 13 mm spanner. You should warm up the engine thoroughly before draining the oil so that it flows out much more completely. Roll up your sleeve. Take out the drain plug, but be careful because as you remove it the hot, dirty oil will come gushing out. Cut the side out of an old plastic oil can to act as a receptacle.

1.54 There are several different types of oil filter fitted to cars, but by far the most common is the screw-on, disposable canister. Place a drain tray beneath the filter, drive a screwdriver through the middle of it and lever the filter anti-clockwise to free it, after which it can be removed by hand. Oil may gush out of course, where you drive the screwdriver in. If you can, lower the car to level ground to allow the last of the oil to drain out but ensure that the drain tray is carefully placed because quite a lot of oil may still follow. It helps to have lots of newspaper to hand! We used a Sykes-Pickavant chain-link oil filter remover which tightens on the oil filter canister as you turn the spanner.

1.55 When fitting the new oil filter, we placed a smear of oil around the sealing ring and then screwed it in firmly but only hand tight.

1.56 After carefully wiping the seating around the oil drain plug, you must fit a new washer and tighten the plug, but not excessively. With the car standing on level ground, pour engine oil in through the filler cap – rags at the ready! – until the oil is at 'full' on the dipstick; allow time for oil to run into the sump. Run the engine for a couple of minutes, leave it

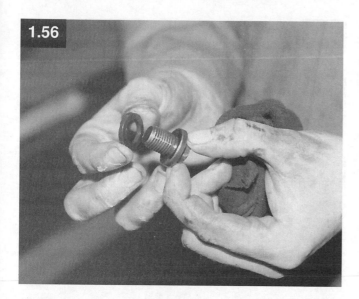

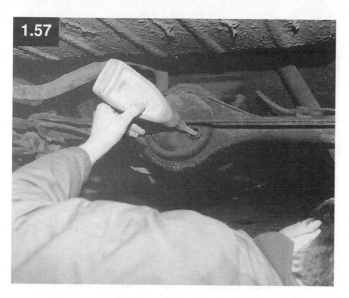

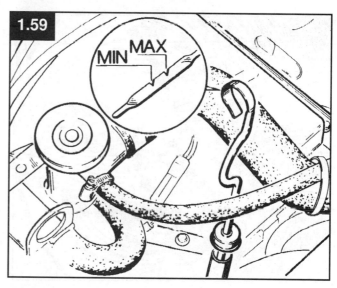

for a few minutes longer for the oil level to settle down again, then check the level once more before finally topping up if necessary. Tip on pouring oil from the can into the filler: hold the can with the oil outlet uppermost – the air can enter easily and the oil will not 'glug' out all over the engine!

1.57 Rear-wheel drive cars have their differential gears in the rear axle. If a drain plug is fitted, it is a good idea to change the oil if the car has reached 50,000 or 60,000 miles, whether or not it is recommended in the manual. (Check, however, for the correct type to use – this is most important!) Otherwise, simply use a squeezy bottle in which the oil can be purchased to fill up the differential casing to the correct level. Crudely enough, the correct level is almost always indicated by the oil starting to dribble out of the filler hole. Wipe around the filler plug to remove dirt before removing it.

1.58 Use your manual to determine how often the gearbox oil should be changed and exactly which type of oil to use. Some gearboxes have to be topped up until oil dribbles out of the filler hole; others have a dipstick. Consult your car's handbook. Some can't be drained at all, in which case these's not a lot you can do about it except check the level, unless you are prepared to remove an inspection plate to allow the oil out – check visually and check your Haynes manual. Here an Allen-type gearbox oil level plug is arrowed.

1.59 It is usually necessary to check the oil level in an automatic gearbox when the oil is hot – consult your manual. Carefully wipe the dipstick handle before checking the level as the smallest amount of dirt introduced into the automatic gearbox can cause problems. Never overfill the gearbox as this

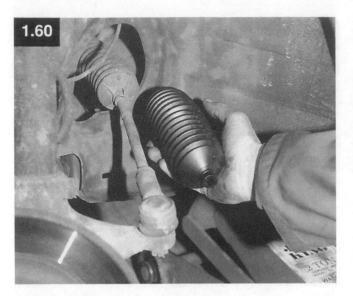

may lead to overheating. Also, be careful not to allow fluff or lint from the rag to get onto the dipstick.

When it is time to change the oil you will find that topping up to the correct level is slightly more involved than for a manual gearbox. Insert the oil through the dipstick/filler hole under the bonnet. Use a squeezy bottle in which you can buy the oil and dribble it in a little at a time because often the filler only tends to take oil in relatively slow, small quantities. When you have added most of the quantity of oil shown in your handbook as being the full capacity for the gearbox, start the engine up, fully apply the handbrake and with the engine idling, move the lever through all the positions at least three times before returning it to the 'P' (Park) position. Now, with the engine still idling, pull out the dipstick and wipe clean the marked end with a cloth. Refit the dipstick all the way and then pull

it out immediately. Top up to the required level if necessary.

Note that automatic gearboxes require the correct type of gearbox oil known as automatic transmission fluid or 'ATF' for short.

1.60 Steering racks are sealed for life but it is essential to check that the gaiters on the end of the steering rack are not damaged or split, because if they are the oil will run out and the life of your steering rack will then be measured in weeks rather than years. Replace them or have them replaced – it can sometimes be quite a tricky job – if there are any signs of splitting in the rubber. The best way to check is to look at the left-hand end of the rack with the steering in the fully turning-left position and at the other side with the steering pointing the other way.

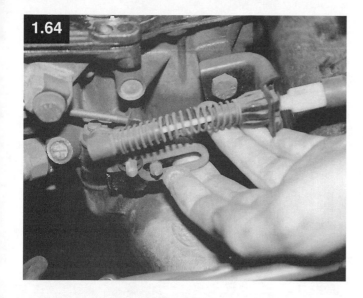

Obtain gaiters from Partco or other motor factors for the more popular cars, or from main dealers for less common models.

1.61 Many older cars have lever arm-type shock absorbers and these have a filler plug situated at the top on their top face into which special shock absorber fluid can be introduced. Clean the plug carefully before removing it so that bits don't drop inside the shock absorber.

The great majority of cars have the strut-type shock absorbers shown on page 75, sometimes encased in a coil-spring. If they leak, nothing can be done about it except to replace them. Shock absorbers have a large effect on the handling and therefore the safety of your car. They deteriorate slowly so you don't usually notice the difference. If you see any oil leaking from your shock absorbers, replace them. Do so in pairs, replacing both front or both rear shock absorbers at the same time. Your car will fail an MOT test if they leak.

1.62 Power steering top-up is simple enough. Clean around the cap, remove and check the level. Check your handbook for the correct type of fluid to use. If a great deal of topping up is required the system is leaking and needs investigation. Unfortunately, power steering pumps and power steering racks are expensive to replace. If necessary, investigate the cost of an exchange rack, an exchange pump, second-hand parts or, if your car is worth very little, look into the possibility of replacing the car, especially if it is an expensive import where the cost of replacement parts may be astronomical.

1.63 Engines fitted with SU and Zenith Stromberg carburettors should have oil in the dashpot in the top of the carburettor. Without it, the engine will run but will do so less efficiently. Unscrew the cap on the top of the carburettor and add thin lubricating oil (engine oil will do) to just below the level of the shoulder beneath the threads in the top of the dashpot. Re-fit the damper piston and rod, and screw down the cap to finger tight.

1.64 Remove the air filter if necessary. Check that the cables running to the carburettor are not kinked or sharply bent. Add a few drops of lubricating oil to the end of each cable. Smear high melting point grease over the contact areas of all cams and levers on the carburettor.

1.65 The internal parts of the distributor are often widely ignored and for that reason, many cars' distributors seize up over a period of years leading to poor running and poor fuel economy.

Remove the distributor cap and pull off the rotor arm. Place two or three drops (no more!) of thin oil on to the end of the centre shaft — it will work its way downwards from there. NB: This only applies to cars without electronic ignition — but consult your handbook.

1.66 Using a thin-bladed screwdriver, put the lightest smear of grease around the distributor cam.

1.67 If you suspect that your car's distributor has not been lubricated in years, use aerosol releasing fluid with an injector tube fitted – it usually comes strapped to the can. Insert the end of the tube beneath the distributor base plate and squirt away for no more than three or four seconds. If you like, repeat the process in about a week's time. This should help to free off any seized components inside the distributor.

Many distributors have an oil hole in the top of the base plate through which you should normally add two or three drops of thin oil. Check your handbook. Do not over lubricate the distributor and be very careful not to get any oil at all on the contact breaker points otherwise the car simply won't start! If you accidentally do so, clean the contact breaker points with a spot of methylated spirits or nail varnish remover (but not the oily type) on something like a cotton bud, opening up the points to ensure that the faces are perfectly clean. When you fit new points – do so each service – clean the new faces with methylated spirit because they are often coated with protective lacquer.

1.68 Check that the route of the cable is smooth and has not become kinked or trapped. (You would then probably know about it because the clutch or gear change action would be stiff). At each end of the cable or cables, if they can be reached, put a good size blob of grease at the point where the inner cable

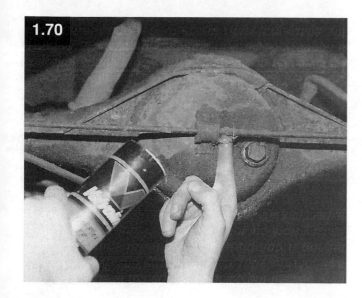

enters the outer. Use a grease gun if the manufacturers have been wise enough to fit a grease point – see your handbook for details. If your car is fitted with a hydraulically operated clutch, check fluid level. Check your handbook to see if your clutch is fitted with manual adjustment or whether it has automatic adjustment. If the cable is frayed, replace it with a new one. Ours came from the motor factors again.

1.69 Some cars have an external gear change linkage. If yours is one of them, clean all of the pivot points on the linkage and apply a generous coating of high melting point grease to each of them, working the grease in well.

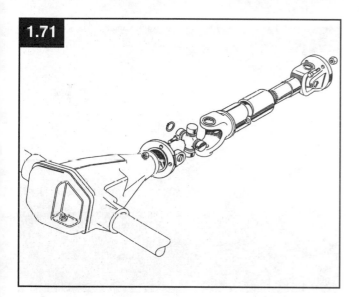

1.70 Find the route of the handbrake cable and any rods or linkages that may exist from the cable to the rear brakes. Apply the grease gun to any grease points on the cable; thoroughly clean all external linkages and apply a generous coating of grease to each of the pivot points. Where a cable passes through a channel or guide tube, work grease as far into the channel or tube as possible. Consult your handbook and adjust where necessary. As a rule of thumb, the handbrake should raise by three 'clicks' on the ratchet when the handbrake is fully on.

1.71 Check your workshop manual: most modern cars are not fitted with grease points at all on propeller or drive-shafts. Make sure that you clean each grease nipple before injecting grease – assuming any grease nipples have been fitted. Virtually none has been fitted to new cars, apart from Ladas, since the early '70s.

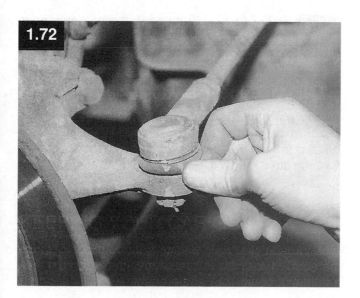

1.72 Follow methodically each part of your car's front suspension and steering and check each ball-joint and pivot to see if a grease point has been fitted. If so, clean the grease nipple and use the grease gun as recommended in your manual. If any wear is apparent, have the joints replaced immediately. Check carefully for wear in the track rod end joints. See Getting through the MOT later in this chapter for details. Take note of the safety notes with regard to working on a car supported by axle stands and never work on a car supported only on a jack.

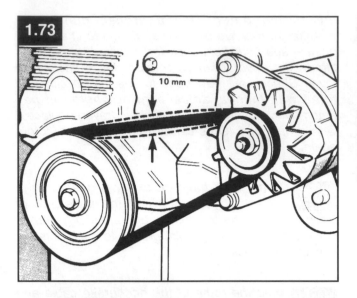

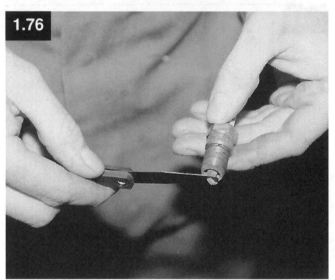

1.73 *Check the tension of drive belts. Most alternator belts should have about ½ in (1 cm) of movement in each direction at their longest point. Check your manual. Replace with new if you see any cracks or fraying. Try your local motor factors, as prices may be keener than at retail stores.*

1.74 *Check the air filter every 6,000 miles as a matter of course.*

1.75 *Every 24,000 miles (or sooner: check handbook) replace the oil filler cap if it contains a filter. Some cars have a filter incorporated in the air cleaner or elsewhere in the engine crankcase breather system; again, check your handbook.*

1.76 *6,000 to 12,000 miles is the recommended life of most spark plugs – check your handbook. If you park in 'dry' conditions (ie where damp is not likely to cause starting difficulties) and yours is a non-performance engine, you may get away with more. On the other hand, one breakdown and the saving will have been wasted. Gap plugs correctly, tapping the outer electrode towards the centre electrode – never move the centre electrode – or levering it open until the gap is right.*

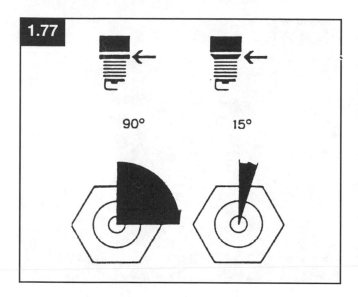

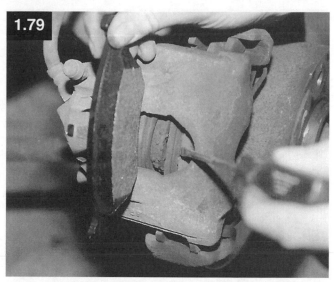

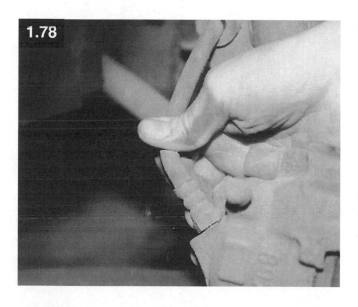

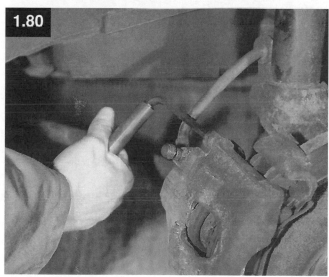

1.77 *Screw new spark plugs in by hand until seated correctly. New plugs with flat seats are turned a further 90 degrees with a spark plug wrench. If you are re-using a flat seat plug or fitting a conical seat plug, turn it a further 15 degrees with the wrench. (Courtesy Robert Bosch Limited)*

1.78 *Check brake hoses for damage. Bend near each end. If you see any cracks, have the hoses replaced or do it yourself, closely following the instructions in your manual.*

1.79 *Check front pads for wear. The new Mintex pad alongside shows how much 'meat' is there when the pad is new. With the front of the car safely supported on axle stands and the rear wheels securely chocked, remove each front wheel. If the pads have less than about ³⁄₃₂ in (2 mm) of friction material on either side replace all four – the complete front set. If your brake discs appear worn or damaged, ask your main dealer if they need replacing. Also, have them checked for thickness against the manufacturer's recommended minimum.*

1.80 *This Ford demands use of an 'odd' (7 mm) sized Allen key in order to remove the brake pads. Specialist motor factor Partco supplied this Sykes-Pickavant tool 'off the shelf'.*

1.81 Always clean road dirt and brake dust from the front callipers. It can make one or other of the pads seize and cause brake squeal. Only use a proprietary cleaner, such as this aerosol from Valvoline, and follow the instructions on the can. Do remember that the inhalation of brake dust can be lethal, particularly if the brake pads or shoes are of the asbestos type.

1.82 New pads will have to be bedded in so that they take on the contours of your worn discs, before you can expect the best from them. This can take several hours of driving. Add a thin smear of copper lubricant or brake grease to the back of each pad (not the friction material that presses on the disc!) to cut out brake squeal.

1.83 Raise the rear of the car (see 1.79 – chock the front wheels this time, of course!) and check the condition of the rear brake pads or shoes. If drum brakes are fitted, loosen the adjuster behind the back plate so that the drum comes off more easily. (You can't always do this when automatic brake adjusters are fitted – see your manual.) While you're in the area, look for the presence of lubricating oil or brake fluid, which could point to a leaking oil seal or wheel cylinder. See your manual for repair details.

1.84 Our 'project' Escort had leaking wheel cylinders and once again, Partco had them in stock.

1.85 *Replacing brake shoes and discs is not difficult if you follow the advice in your manual. But, if you're a novice or unsure of your car's brake layout have a trained mechanic check your work before trying the car on the road. Lives may depend on it!*

N.B. There are many different types of brake drum securing systems. It is essential that you use this section in conjunction with your workshop manual.

Brakes: safety notes

1. Only use asbestos-free friction materials. Insist upon them!
2. Wear an efficient face mask when working on brakes – the old components may contain lethal asbestos. Dispose of old components *and dust* in a sealed plastic bag. Clean away all traces of dust with cleaner – see 1.81.

1.86 *If steering rack gaiters or drive shaft gaiters (front wheel drive cars) are damaged, they will need replacing urgently. You'll have to remove the trackrod end – see your manual for how to. Remember to re-lubricate the rack as described in your manual. If you drive for long with split gaiters, the rack will rapidly wear out – an expensive replacement!*

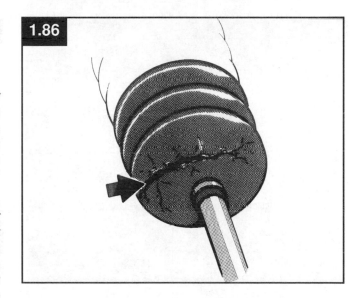

1.87 *Replace the brake fluid every three years or 36,000 miles. Here's why. Brake fluid slowly absorbs moisture from the air. This gradually corrodes brake components internally, causing them to fail. Worse still, brake fluid can heat up to over 100°C under heavy braking. This boils the water vapour in the fluid, turning it to steam at which point the brakes may completely fail, just when you most need them. You won't know until it's too late. If you can, syringe the fluid out of the master cylinder and top up with fresh. If you can't, just pump it through. You must pump all the old fluid out of the pipes and wheel cylinders in any case.*

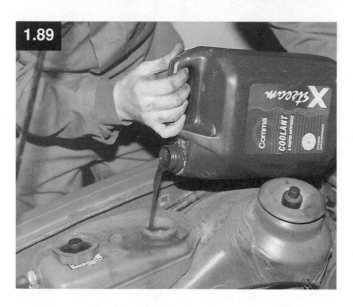

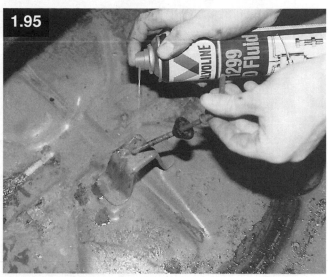

1.88 Using standard brake bleeding techniques, we pumped fluid out of the system via one wheel-cylinder at a time, topping up the master cylinder every few pumps with Valvoline brake fluid, until each one flowed only with fresh, clean fluid. IMPORTANT: Don't do this without following meticulously the procedure for bleeding brakes described in your Haynes manual. In particular, check the level of the fluid in the master cylinder regularly and do not allow it to fall so low that you introduce air into the system. If you have any doubts whatsoever, leave it to a trained mechanic. Don't round off the bleed nipple screws: manufacturers such as Sykes-Pickavant produce inexpensive spanners for freeing and tightening specific bleed nipple screws.

1.89 In order to prevent internal engine corrosion you should also replace coolant and anti-freeze every three years. Comma X – stream comes ready mixed with de-ionized water which, it is claimed cuts corrosion still further. Normal anti-freeze is just as effective for older cars, however.

1.90 Don't neglect the bonnet release cable and catch mounted on the bonnet shut panel. They can become stiff, awkward to use and eventually break, causing no end of inconvenience. Where the bonnet release mechanism is operated by a lever, apply grease to each of the pivots and supports and operate the linkage several times to work the grease in. Where a bonnet release mechanism operated by a cable has become stiff and difficult to use, it would be best to remove one end of the cable while having someone at the other end on standby with a rag. Drip thin oil or releasing fluid down the cable so that it runs between inner and outer whilst working the cable backwards and forwards. If the cable has become

frayed there might be no option but to replace it. The bonnet lock itself should be lubricated at each service point using plenty of grease.

1.91 Don't neglect to lubricate the door locks. If they have become stiff and are on the point of seizing, hold open the protective flap over the lock (if fitted) or half insert the key and squirt releasing fluid into the lock, then work it backwards and forwards many times with the key. Be very careful at first so that you don't end up breaking the key in the lock. A few spots of lubricating oil usually help matters along at each service, although the experts recommend special lock oil or graphite powder.

1.92 The problem with the door closing plate is that if you use grease you will be certain to get it on your clothing. Use Vaseline, or better still a clear silicone lubricant, wiping off the excess.

1.93 Don't forget to lubricate the door and boot or hatchback hinges as well as the fuel filler flap hinges and release mechanism. If the tailgate hinges are hidden behind trim panels, use aerosol releasing fluid with the extension tube fitted. Don't forget if you have an aerial to extend it fully, and clean and lightly lubricate each of the segments.

1.94 When you check tyres for pressure and tread depth don't forget the spare wheel. At the time of writing, the legal minimum is 1.6 mm depth over the centre ¾ of the tyre.

1.95 Lubricate the spare wheel retainers so that you can get out the spare wheel easily in an emergency...

1.96 ...and check that the jack works properly and is thoroughly lubricated.

To give you an idea of the extent of recommended service items (which don't include some of those shown on the preceeding pages) for a Ford Escort of the mid-eighties, here is the full service schedule. You'll notice that some of the items in the 6000-mile service are things that you do every week – this is for the benefit of owners who leave absolutely everything to the garage.

You will also notice towards the end of the schedule the instruction to renew the timing belt. The timing belt drives the camshaft; not all engines have one (some use a chain instead), but if it's there, it needs renewing every so often. *If the timing belt breaks while the engine is running, severe damage may result.* Consult your workshop manual for details. If you've just bought the car and you're not sure about the age or condition of the timing belt, don't gamble on it lasting indefinitely – renew it!

Every 6000 miles (10,000 km) or 6 months – whichever comes first

Engine
Renew the engine oil and filter.
On OHV engines remove and clean the oil filler cap.

Cooling system
Check the hoses, hose clips and visible joint gaskets for leaks and any signs of corrosion or deterioration
Check and if necessary top up the cooling system.

Fuel, exhaust and emission control systems
Visually check the fuel pipes and hoses for security, chafing, leaks and corrosion.
Check the fuel tank for leaks and any sign of damage or corrosion.
On RS Turbo models check the tightness of the exhaust manifold retaining nuts.
Check and if necessary adjust the idle speed and mixture settings.

Ignition system
Clean the distributor cap, coil tower and HT leads and check for tracking.
On contact breaker point distribution lubricate the distributor shaft and cam.
On contact breaker point distributors check and if necessary adjust the points gap (dwell angle), then check the ignition timing.
On RS Turbo models renew the spark plugs.

Braking system
Check the front disc pad and rear brake shoe lining thickness.
Check the condition and security of all brake pipes, hoses and unions including the servo vacuum hose (where fitted).

Suspension and steering
Check the tyres for damage, tread depth and uneven wear.
Check and adjust the tyre pressures.
Check the steering components for any signs of damage.
Check the security of the front suspension lower arm balljoint.

Bodywork
Check the seat belt webbing for cuts or damage and check the seat belt operation.
Carefully inspect the paintwork for damage and the bodywork for corrosion.

Electrical system
Check the function of all lights, electrical equipment and accessories.
Check the condition and adjustment of the alternator drivebelt.

Every 12,000 miles (20,000 km) or 12 months – whichever comes first

In addition to all the items in the 6000-mile (10,000 km) service, carry out the following:

Engine
On OHV engines check and if necessary adjust the valve clearances.

Fuel, exhaust and emission control systems
Check the underbody for signs of fuel or exhaust leaks and check the exhaust system condition and security.
On RS Turbo models check the tightness of the turbocharger-to-manifold nuts.

Ignition system
Renew the spark plugs.
On contact breaker point distributors renew the contact breaker points.

Manual transmission
Visually check for oil leaks around the transmission joint faces and oil seals.
Check and if necessary top up the transmission oil.

Automatic transmission
Visually check for fluid leaks around the transmission joint faces and seals.
Check and if necessary top up the automatic transmission fluid.
Check the operation of the selector mechanism.

Driveshafts
Check the driveshafts for damage or distortion and check the condition of the constant velocity joint bellows.

Suspension and steering
Check the condition and security of all steering gear components, front and rear suspension joints and linkages, and steering gear bellows condition.
Check the front and rear shock absorbers for fluid leaks.
Inspect the roadwheels for damage.
Check the tightness of the roadwheel bolts.
Check the wheel bearings for wear.

Bodywork
Lubricate all hinges, door locks, check straps and the bonnet release mechanism.
Check the operation of all door, tailgate, bonnet release and window regulator components.

Road test
Check the operation of all instruments and electrical equipment.
Check for abnormalities in the steering, suspension, handling or road feel.
Check the performance of the engine, clutch and transmission.
Check the operation and performance of the braking system.

Every 24,000 miles (40,000 km) or 2 years – whichever comes first

In addition to all the items in the 12,000-mile (20,000 km) and 6000-mile (10,000 km) services, carry out the following:

Cooling system
Renew the antifreeze in the cooling system.

Fuel, exhaust and emission control systems
Renew the air cleaner air filter element.
On CVH engines renew the crankcase emission control filter.
On fuel-injected engines renew the fuel filter.
On OHV engines clean the oil filler cap.

Every 36,000 miles (60,000 km) or 3 years – whichever comes first

In addition to all the items listed in the previous services, carry out the following:

Engine
On CVH engines renew the timing belt.

Braking system
Make a thorough inspection of all brake components and rubber seals for signs of leaks, general deterioration and wear.
Drain and refill the hydraulic system with fresh fluid.

Section 3 Save money on spares

The majority of new cars in Britain are sold to companies as 'company cars'. The majority of companies are far less cost-conscious than most individuals. Therefore, the majority of manufacturer's spares are priced for the majority of users; companies who will pay the list price, almost irrespective of how high it is. Car makers make big profits from car spares. Therefore car owners can make big savings by not buying from them. Having said that, there are certain categories of spares that are best bought from the manufacturer:

– Body parts are sure to fit properly if 'original equipment'; likely to fit badly if not.

– Safety related items are certain to be sound if they came from the same source as the car, although this is a rule that can be broken if you follow the advice below.

– Some parts are just not profitable for independent suppliers to stock, whereas the original manufacturers will be likely to do so. Or at least that's the theory. In practice, some manufacturers have a dreadful record in not stocking parts for models they no longer produce. Some are notoriously poor, while Land-Rover, Volkswagen, Audi and most very small manufacturers such as Morgan are excellent.

Recycled spares – scrap-yards

Once upon a time, scrap-yards were places where old cars sat and mouldered until just about everything off them had been sold. Today the emphasis is more on recycling, although the appearance of most yards is far from green!

Scrap-yards make their money from selling you and me, Mr and Mrs Public, the parts we want to buy, and then, at lower income to the yard, items such as alternators, steering racks, shock absorbers and the like to companies who set about overhauling and reconditioning the units for sale through motor factors and motorists' shops. Bodywork is crushed and the metal sold for scrap. Increasingly, plastic parts are being recycled and, led by the German industry, manufacturers in Europe are heading towards total 'recyclability' of cars. American and Japanese makers are following behind.

Scrap-yards are visited by private buyers galore; you won't stand out like a sore thumb, not unless you go in Burberry and green wellies! There are two types of scrap-yard and the preparation for your visit will depend upon which type it is. There is the 'organised' type of yard and the 'organic'. The organised yard will have removed and possibly cleaned the parts, placed them in a store and have a counter which, apart from the inevitable oil on the counter, will be much like a parts shop of the old-fashioned type. The organic type will have – a yard full of cars, nothing more!

The organised type of yard is much easier to use if you're relatively inexperienced, and much better if you don't like grovelling around dismantling bits of oily motor car. The parts are inevitably more expensive and you really must shop around and compare the cost of reconditioned parts from your local motor factor before buying parts from this type of yard.

The organic type is much more fun, if you like that type of thing, and likely to be much cheaper. It really is the place to go if you seriously want to save money. You may also spot other parts that will improve the appearance or comfort of your car while you are there. Things like catches and latches, switches and upholstery are usually cheap to buy, but a word of warning! Quite apart from the moral issue, don't try pinching bits and pieces from a scrap-yard. The people who run them may be pleasant if you play ball (although they sometimes emulate the scrap-yard dog and go around snarling for no apparent reason), but they tend to be somewhat tougher than the average nun or primary school teacher if they are crossed. Don't risk it! Also, do remember to take cash with you – cheques are not always popular – and ask for a receipt. There is invariably a guarantee, one that says 'if it doesn't work, bring it back and we'll change it'. Most yards are excellent in this area – they would soon lose custom if they didn't respect this basic code – but don't leave it more than a week to try the part out.

Some parts are well worth buying second-hand, some are not worth the hassle and others should be avoided like the plague, either because they're not worth having or for safety reasons. In order to describe what to look out for, we visited my favourite scrap-yard, Potters of Stourport-on-Severn in Worcestershire, where the proprietors are friendly and helpful, the yard is interesting, and the prices are right. Anyway, we ageing hippies actually like a bit of organic...

1.97 A replacement for a rusty door or tailgate can often be found in a breaker's yard. It would take far less time to search for a panel of the correct colour than it would to respray the right panel in the wrong colour. This way, you can make really big savings! Bonnets, boot lids and tailgates are often quite simple to remove.

1.98 Door removal is usually straightforward if the hinges are bolted on to the door or pillar. Unbolt them from the pillar if possible so that you get the benefit of spare hinges as well and most yards won't charge you extra. Many hinges, however, are welded to both the door and the pillar, and the only way to remove them is to drive the pin out of the centre of the hinge. Unfortunately, it's usually stuck solid. Either take with you a butane blow torch and heat up the hinge to make it easier to remove the pin, or take a hacksaw and cut through the hinge – on the door pillar side of course! Alternatively use a hammer and sharp bolster chisel to cut the hinge away from the door pillar.

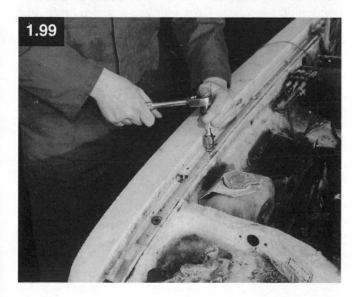

1.99 Bolt on body panels are less likely to be useful, although rust is funny stuff! Just because it has destroyed the panel on your car doesn't mean it will attack another panel in exactly the same place on another car – although to be fair, the chances are that it probably will have done so. Look to replace dented panels or rusty panels with those from a later model or a car that has been particularly well looked after in the body department, or has had new panels fitted to it in the years immediately prior to it being scrapped.

> BEWARE OF THE SHARP EDGES OF CUT STEEL. ALWAYS WEAR INDUSTRIAL STRENGTH LEATHER GLOVES.

1.100 Weld-on panels are far less likely to be of use to you. Rust is likely to occur along the welded seams and it would be extremely difficult to remove the panel from the car without causing damage. However, if you drive a rare vehicle or one for which spares are extremely expensive you may wish to consider this option. Remove the panel by chiselling or cutting through the bodywork to which the panel is fixed and then spend some considerable time in angle grinding the welded seam aiming to take away as much as possible of the unwanted metal while leaving the original panel untouched.

1.101 Interior trim can be a godsend. Compared with the cost of retrimming seats or door panels, replacements from the breaker's yard will usually work out far less expensive. Examine them carefully to look for rips and sags in the seat supports but don't be put off by dirty vinyl; it can easily be cleaned up. Dirty cloth seats may be a different matter and heavy staining can be difficult to remove. Don't try buying a passenger seat and fitting it on the drivers side; it rarely works. You might try buying a pair of front seats if the colour match is not exactly the same as those in your car, or you might even consider buying a complete set of interior trim. It doesn't usually work out too expensive. Needless to say, don't expect carpets to be reusable.

1.102 If your car insurance doesn't cover you for windscreen breakage, consider purchasing a replacement windscreen while you can. If yours is of the bonded type don't even try buying a breaker's yard replacement – even professionals can't guarantee to take one of these out without breaking it. However, if yours is held in with sealing rubbers, removal is a doddle. Take with you a sharp knife and a squeezy bottle with some soapy water in it. Squirt the soapy water on to the rubber and the knife will slice through like, well, a knife through rubber. (If you try to cut through it dry, the knife will bind horribly.) The screen can then easily be lifted out with the help of an assistant. Needless to say, try to select a screen which doesn't have cracks, scratches or windscreen wiper rub marks on it.

> SAFETY NOTE: WEAR THICK INDUSTRIAL TYPE GLOVES WHEN HANDLING GLASS. THE EDGES MAY BE VERY SHARP AND WILL CERTAINLY BE SO IF THE GLASS BREAKS!

1.103 Very occasionally you will be able to hear an engine running, but unfortunately that's not very common. Therefore what you must do is don your Sherlock Holmes hat and look for relevant evidence. Unscrew the oil filler cap and look at the inside of the cap and the inside of the rocker box or camshaft cover. Everything should look shiny and clean. If it's rusty, the engine has either been standing for a heck of a long time or the cap has been left off allowing the water to get in. Avoid. If you see yellow sludge it means that the engine is very badly worn. Avoid. Black sludge means that the oil is in disgusting condition. Probably avoid.

1.104 Pull out the dipstick and look at the condition of the oil. If the oil level is very low this suggests that the engine may have been poorly maintained, although to be fair if you knew you were going to scrap a car would you bother topping up the engine oil? If the oil is very black – as it probably will be – it doesn't bode particularly well, although that's not enough reason to avoid the engine. If it's clean, chalk it up as a plus point. If you see droplets of water in the oil It could mean that the head gasket has blown. Avoid.

1.105 Unscrew the radiator filler cap (if fitted), if everything has been left connected up and there is water in the radiator. If you see oil in the water once again you have evidence of a blown head gasket. Avoid.

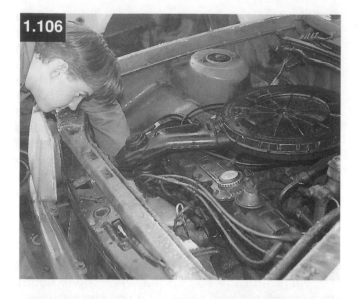

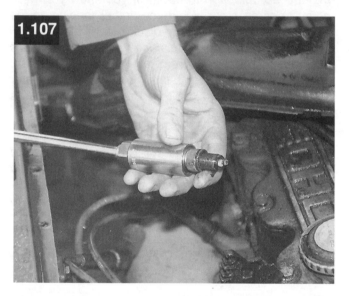

1.106 Look carefully at the sides of the block and examine for evidence of water leakage. Try to locate the core plugs which are fitted to 'blow' should the water in the block freeze solid. Are they seeping? If there is water in the engine, this just means that you will have to replace the core plugs – a straightforward job; see your manual. If all hoses are still connected up but there is no water in the radiator check to see if the water has frozen and drained itself by cracking the block. Have any of the core plugs been pushed out? Can you see any evidence that water has been dribbling through any parts of the block where it shouldn't have been? Look for tell-tale brown staining. Avoid. Look out also for leaks from around the water pump area.

1.107 Take the spark plugs out and have a look at the condition of the electrodes. If they are very black it suggests that the bores are badly worn, allowing oil to come up through them. Avoid. Don't confuse this with sooty black deposits that wipe off dry. This is caused by an over rich mixture setting. Don't forget to check all of the cylinders.

1.108 With all of the sparking plugs out, try grasping the fan belt with both hands and see if you can turn the engine over. Ideally use a spanner on the bottom pulley nut. (The gearbox must be in neutral.) If you can't, the engine may be seized, more likely through rust than anything else.

Take hold of the crankshaft pulley and try to lift or push and pull it in relation to the block in order to check for crankshaft end float. Use a screwdriver as a lever. You should not be able to lift and lower it at all; if you can then wear in the crank must be of astronomical proportions! If you find that the crank has any backwards and forwards movement (and some engines are particularly susceptible to this), it means that there is a lot more endfloat in the crank than there should be. Avoid.

The only occasions on which you may wish to accept some of these faults – but never a cracked block – would be if your engine is totally scrap and you are looking for another one to have it reconditioned. You may be able to negotiate an extra low price from the scrap-yard dealer. In purely economic terms, however, you would be better off looking for an engine that runs well.

1.109 *Manual gearboxes: unless you can actually drive the car, there is no way you can be certain that a gearbox is sound. Try to select all of the gears, although as everyone knows gears often balk when you can't run the engine. If the gearbox is out of the car, put the lever in neutral and turn the shaft at the engine end of the gearbox and the output shaft at the other end of the gearbox in opposite directions. The action should feel smooth with no graunching bearing noises. You can then put the gearbox into gear, one at a time, turning the input shaft and noting if the output shaft turns with that gear selected.*

1.110 *Almost all gearboxes have an inspection plate on them. Unbolt it but look out for detent springs, plungers or balls which are retained by the cover and you will be able to see the insides of the gearbox. Consult your workshop manual before getting to this stage. Peer inside with the assistance of a torch – it will be as black as the inside of a gearbox in there! – and look at all the gear teeth that you can see, as well as the selector forks. If you see any chipped teeth or severe wear on the selector forks, avoid. Look at the condition of the oil. If it's black, avoid. Undo the drain plug and let the oil run out of the bottom of the gearbox. If it comes out looking like metallic paint, either gold or silver, it means that bushes or bearings have broken up inside. Avoid. Check to see if oil is seeping past the seals at the front or back of the gearbox. Check your manual if you do find evidence of a leak although they are not usually difficult to replace.*

1.111 *Automatic gearboxes are virtually impossible to check without a test drive although the colour of the oil (automatic transmission fluid) gives some clues. It should be a semi-transparent red. Brown or black fluid indicates that the box has overheated at some time – avoid. Black bits floating in the fluid usually signal one or more of the bands in the gearbox beginning to break up – avoid. Consult your manual and don't forget to take the torque convertor as well as the gearbox. NB: If the oil has an unpleasant 'burning' smell, this also indicates the clutches and bands have been slipping – avoid.*

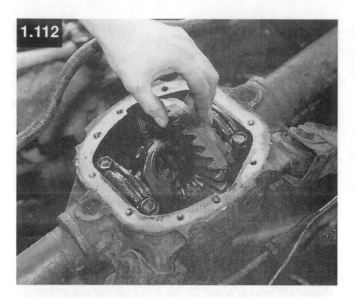

1.112 *Back axle and differential units should be inspected visually by removing the cover (if one is fitted) and peering inside at the gears. Try to turn the driveshaft and inspect all the teeth on the crown wheel and pinion, and the differential itself.*

1.113 *It is possible to buy a radiator which looks fine but which, when you fit it to the car, leaks when under pressure. All that you can do is look at the radiator core and the top and bottom header tanks for signs of leaks and heavy rust deposits. You may be able to find a tap in the yard which will enable you to fill the radiator and check for obvious leaks.*

1.114 *You can check the common pre-engaged and Bendix starter motors using a car battery and a couple of jump leads. There will undoubtedly be*

a few bangs and crackles from sparks to contend with, so make sure that you are well away from any fuel tanks and keep hands safely away from the starter dog (identify it in your manual). Hold motor firmly down to floor to stop it from leaping about! Connect one lead from the battery negative terminal to the starter body, well away from the plus or feed terminal. Connect the other to the positive battery connection and carefully touch the other end of this lead on to the plus or feed terminal. If the starter motor jumps and whizzes it's probably fine. With pre-engaged units, those with a separate starter solenoid, you will have to connect the positive feed from the battery to the main positive connection and the positive spade terminal on the solenoid, simultaneously.

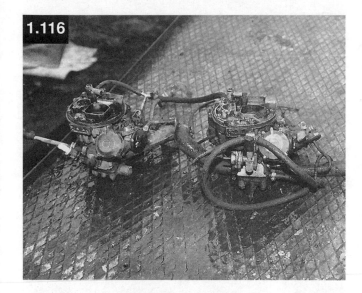

1.115 Never buy an alternator from a scrap-yard without the certainty of a money-back guarantee, and also check on the price of an exchange alternator from your local motorist shop – you may be surprised to find that the cost difference is not all that great! There's very little you can check on an alternator before purchasing it, but ensure that the mountings are not broken or elongated. If the unit is already off the car this may well have been the reason for discarding it.

1.116 Carburettors rarely fail; they just become old and fade away. Most of them – in fact almost all of them – work perfectly well in practice, however. Only consider buying a second-hand replacement if yours has somehow become broken or you have lost some of the parts out of it. If this is the case, simply check that the replacement does not appear to have been tinkered with and that it looks complete.

1.117 Steering racks, driveshafts and shock absorbers are items that may also be available from your local motorist shop or motor factors, at a price that is low enough to make it not worthwhile buying second-hand, although complete strut units can be very good value. However, at some yards the prices of these second-hand parts might be so low that you consider them anyway. If so, make absolutely certain that the vehicle from which the parts have been taken is sound and has not been involved in an accident. If there is any sign whatsoever of crash damage to the vehicle, avoid. Don't buy shock absorbers or a steering rack that you cannot see still on the vehicle. Any evidence of oil leaks reduces the parts to scrap value; you don't want to risk their having been cleaned up before you see them.

1.118 No one would buy second-hand tyres from a scrap-yard, would they? After all, you wouldn't be able to tell what sort of treatment they had received. But exactly the same is true of tyres fitted to a second-hand car and no one thinks twice about that! I really can't see what makes tyres from a scrap-yard any worse than those fitted on a car that you buy, and if you check the tyres carefully, there are some excellent savings to be made. It's best to buy a wheel that you can see still fitted to a car so that you can be reasonably sure that the tyre hasn't been involved in an accident.

Bear in mind the European legal minimum (at time of writing) of 1.6 mm over the centre ¾ of the width and all the way round the tyre.

1.119

1.122

1.120

1.123

1.121

1.124

1.119 Check the wheel rim with very great care to ensure that there is no evidence of damage to the edge of the rim either inside or outside. Also check the area around the wheel nuts for elongation, cracks or signs of damage.

1.120 Check the side walls inside and outside the tyre all the way round. If you encounter any splits or bulges, no matter how small, avoid. Check the tread to ensure that the wear is even. If it's not, avoid. Make sure that the tyre type is going to be exactly the same all the way round your car; don't mix steel belt radials with textile belt radials. Ask at your local tyre depot if you're not sure which make is which. Having done all of this, you've probably made a far more careful check on the tyres than you did when you purchased your last car!

1.121 Do make sure that tyres are the correct type and size for your car, and if you use the wheels to which the tyres are fitted make certain that they are the correct wheels for your car as well. Some may have the correct stud centres but the offset – the position of the tyre relative to the position of the hub – may be different. Don't take chances!

1.122 Take with you a tyre depth gauge and don't bother with anything that has less than 3 mm of tread at least – and ensure that the tread is even all around the tyre and right across its width. If the tyre has been removed from the rim, carefully run your hand all the way around the inside of the tyre and check that the internal surface is smooth and consistent. If you find any bulges or patches on the inside of the tyre, avoid. Look at the outside of the tyre for evidence of heavy scuffing, and in particular if any of the maker's marks, such as trade name or tyre size or tyre ratings, have been scuffed off or removed, avoid like the plague! Your best bet by far is to buy a tyre that is on a wheel and fitted to a car. A small number of faulty tyres, some of them with potentially lethal faults, are sold for use in Third World countries on horse-drawn vehicles and other non-demanding uses. It is not common but it has been known for such tyres to find their way on to the UK market. Be very suspicious of apparently new tyres at give away prices.

1.123 Light units either work or they don't; they're either rusty or they're not. Most yards have a battery lying around on which you can check their operation.

1.124 Many manufacturers have some very fancy ideas about the value of their replacement switches, and you can save a lot of money by buying scrap-yard replacements. Ensure that they click smoothly into each of the positions they are supposed to take and make absolutely sure that the unit you are offered is the right one for your car. For instance, there are several types of Lucas indicator switch that look to be identical at first but which operate differently and have different fittings. Ideally, take your old unit along with you to ensure that the new one will be the same. (Might be a good idea to show it to the scrap-yard owner before you go in. You don't want him to think that you have pinched it!)

Plan your visit

You can waste a lot of time if you don't plan your visit properly. Try to telephone a number of yards before setting out – find them in *Yellow Pages* or compile your own list when you visit, for future use. The person answering the phone will be able to give you an idea of whether the specific part you want is in the yard. Expect some optimism on the part of the yard representative if the part you want is on a car and you ask what condition it is in. If you're looking for a major part, such as engine or gearbox, you could ask if the car was recently driven in to the yard and, if so, what sort of state it was in. (Roger, the proprietor of Potters is one of the friendly, honest types who tells the truth.) But in general, this is the sort of information that is more readily given when you have established a good working relationship with 'your' yard, and this is easier with the smaller, friendlier variety. So, remember these key rules: learn to love your breaker, but don't say miaow to the dog!

Here's what to remember before you venture out:

- Take your oldest clothes, thick industrial leather gloves, strong boots, preferably with steel toe caps, and goggles. Take a plastic sheet for lying or kneeling: the ground will probably be filthy with oil.

- Put together a selection of suitable tools. Leave your best ones at home! Take a couple of hammers, including a large one and a sharp bolster chisel; a nut splitter if you own one; self-grip wrench; adjustable spanner, and range of open-ended and socket spanners; impact screwdriver; hacksaw; plastic boxes or plastic bags for carrying the fixings and accessories that go with the part you will be removing; penetrating oil; pliers, and, if you're into some heavy dismantling, a trolley jack and axle stands. (Don't under any circumstances work beneath a car supported only by a jack – or by a pile of bricks!) Don't forget to bring back with you all the fixing nuts and bolts, wiring plugs and sockets and anything else that might come in handy that form an ancillary part of the component you are purchasing.

IMPORTANT SAFETY NOTE: Some yards are not at all careful about safety. Cars are often left on their side or piled three or four high. If a tipped car looks as if it could be in any way unstable or if the part you want is at the top of a tottering pile, leave it alone. 'He gave his life for a second-hand starter motor' would not make a very moving epitaph.

– Before spending hours removing a part from a car, find out the price and whether there is any return guarantee. Also check the part over very carefully to ensure that it is in good condition.

– Do look all around the yard to find the best and most accessible part available to you.

– Take your workshop manual with you. You may not need to use conventional dismantling techniques, but you will need to know how things come apart.

– While you're there, look around for any other odds and ends that might save you money in future. Look out for replacements for broken switches and handles, as well as light bulbs, wiper blades and arms and other small components that won't cost you very much to buy from the yard.

– Before leaving the car you are working on and before leaving the yard, check that you have got all of your tools with you. They don't tend to stay in one place for long.

– Before leaving the car you have been working on, close the bonnet and replace a loose rocker cover or oil filler cap. It might be you who needs to go back in the future for another part!

– If there is a return guarantee, make sure that you fit and try out the part you have purchased within a week or so. Most yards won't want to know if you leave it too long.

The following items emphatically *don't* make good scrap-yard buys. Steering and suspension joints are not too expensive to buy new, they're an important safety item, it will be extremely difficult to remove track rod ends without damaging the rubber boot, and in general the grief factor outweighs the cost of buying new. If track rod ends come already fitted to a steering rack, check them carefully for wear and continue to use them if you wish. If they're serviceable, you have the same situation that you would have if you bought a second-hand car with track rod ends already fitted. Batteries are not often a good second-hand buy, unless you can work out the date of purchase from markings on the top. Exhaust systems might or might not make a good buy: it depends entirely on their condition. It's not unknown for a car to be scrapped having fairly recently been fitted with a new exhaust. On the other hand, a rusty system should stay where it is. Under no circumstances should you bother with minor ignition components such as plug leads, points, spark plugs, distributor caps because they are cheap to buy new and you are trying to build reliability into your car, not put it at risk. You should scarcely ever consider using second-hand clutch components unless you can see that the parts are fairly new and have a large amount of life left in them. In general, don't take chances; there's just too much dismantling involved should you get it wrong. Also give a miss to brake pipes, brake pads or shoes, seat belts, gaskets and filters.

Buy new, buy cheaply

You can save a lot of money by buying spares carefully. It's unlikely that you will find a single source of inexpensive spares for your car, so be prepared to spend time shopping around.

– Write down the correct name of the part you need, the make and model of your car, its date of first registration, and the chassis number. (See the chassis plate, usually under the bonnet, or your Vehicle Registration Document)

– Compile a list of suppliers (see below).

– Telephone each one in turn. Write down the name and telephone number of each as you call. If you don't, you'll forget who's who later on!

– Against each, write down i) the price; ii) availability – is it in stock; when will it be coming in; is that certain; iii) extra details such as 'Ours comes complete with the widget flap' (does everyone's?), and opening times of the store or postal charges and delivery times, if ordered by post; iv) whether or not the price included VAT/sales tax.

If you drive one of the more popular makes and models of car, finding spares at every motorists' shop will be no problem. But don't leave your search there. Look in *Yellow Pages* where you will find Motor Factors listed. They supply parts to the motor trade, but almost without exception they will also sell to you. When asking for price/availability, check on whether VAT is included; it usually isn't.

Motor factors can usually obtain parts for even the most obscure makes of car, even if they haven't got them in stock. But be prepared to look further. If the car is particularly old or of special interest, there may be an owners' club where you can buy spares cheaply or find advertisements from specialist suppliers. This applies to specialist cars such as Jaguar or Audi Quattro and also older Ford Cortinas and Ford Capri. Buy a magazine such as *Practical Classics*, and every few months you will see all the clubs listed.

One of the best sources of cheap spares in the UK is *Exchange & Mart*. Look under 'Car spares' and also under the 'Spares' column for your make of car. For instance, Lancia, Citroen and Audi owners will find suppliers of parts that cost a fraction of main dealer prices. Good quality Audi brake pads at around 40 per cent of the main dealer price are available, and lower quality parts are available for even less. But when it comes to buying spares, a general rule is to fight shy of the cheapest of the cheap unless you have been able to inspect the part, and you have what seem to be good assurances regarding quality.

Among the best bargains in the spares department come from companies which advertise in *Exchange & Mart*, selling second-hand engines for Japanese cars imported direct from Japan. I bought an engine for a Datsun light truck a few years ago that was at least as good as they described it: only two years old; scarcely worn; ready to go in, except for some very strange-looking emission control connections that were not then common to European cars; and an air filter that had been flattened by the weight of another engine on top of it on the voyage. It

seems that the Japanese 'throw cars away' with gay abandon, well before they have been worn out. These engines have been stripped from those cars and are only a fraction of the cost of manufacturers' replacement and can be much less than the cost of reconditioning your own. I doubt if you could find a well worn engine for less cash at your local scrap-yard. And you'd probably have to take it out for yourself... On the other hand, note that situations can change and you must check out the options (reconditioned; UK second-hand; Japanese second-hand) before leaping in.

Safety note: Many synthetic rubber-like materials used in motor cars contain a substance called fluorine. These substances are known as fluoroelastomers and are commonly used for oil seals, wiring and cabling, bearing surfaces, gaskets, diaphragms, hoses and 'O' rings. If they are subjected to temperatures greater than 315°C, they will decompose and can be potentially hazardous. Fluoroelastomer materials will show physical signs of decomposition under such conditions in the form of charring of black sticky masses. Some decomposition may occur at temperatures above 200°C, and it is obvious that when a car has been in a fire or has been dismantled with the assistance of a cutting torch or blow torch, the fluoroelastomers can decompose in the manner indicated above.

In the presence of any water or humidity, including atmospheric moisture, the by-products caused by the fluoroelastomers being heated can be extremely dangerous. According to the Health and Safety Executive, 'Skin contact with this liquid or decomposition residues can cause painful and penetrating burns. Permanent irreversible skin and tissue damage can occur.' Damage can also be caused to eyes or by the inhalation of fumes created as fluoroelastomers are burned or heated.

There are several other hazards associated with fluoroelastomers. For further information on fluoroelastomers and their hazards to health, **it is most important that you read carefully the safety section of the appendices of this book.**

Section 4 Safety

This section could just as well be called 'Keep yourself alive!', because in the end that's what car safety is all about. We all become far too blasé about blasting along without giving the risks a second thought. Even older cars are far more reliable than ever they used to be; cheap tyres grip far better than they did; everyday cars handle like sports cars used to. As a result, and without always meaning to, we take greater risks – and usually get away with it. But what we tend to forget, all of us, is that if we *fail* to get away with it, the consequences are not trivial but often horrific. Shattered limbs, lives and families are the result of not taking enough care with our driving – and with our cars. If we see a youngster driving too fast we shake our heads or our fists and blame modern youth. But what about the oldster with under-inflated tyres? Or the hard-driving rep with brakes that are dangerous because the service interval has been missed? Or the person running his or her car so far 'on the cheap' that it is badly neglected? All are equally dangerous and equally foolish. This book is not about safe driving but it is about keeping your car alive – and that also means keeping it safe. So here are the main areas to be checked, either as part of the service schedule shown in *Section 2 Maintenance*, or as part of a daily or weekly routine.

Wheels and tyres

The area of the tyre in contact with the road is often called the 'footprint', appropriate enough because that's the size of the tread area that keeps your car on the road. The maintenance of correct tyre pressures enables the contact patch to operate at maximum efficiency, allowing the tread pattern to disperse water rapidly on wet roads, giving you more grip. Incorrect tyre pressures will inhibit this water dispersal and will also adversely affect vehicle handling and stability, ride comfort and tyre wear.

However, as the tread pattern depth decreases through wear less water can be evacuated, so that wet grip decreases and stopping distances increase. That being the case, you should check your tyres on a *very* regular basis:

CHECK ONCE A WEEK AND BEFORE EVERY LONG JOURNEY.

Do remember that you need to check *both* sides of wheels and tyres. A tyre blowout at 70 mph is just as dangerous if it is the inside of the

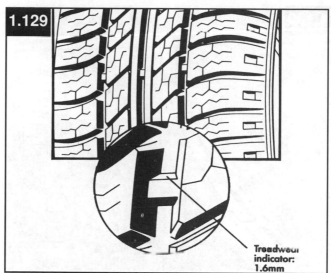

tyre that has failed – and you can almost always tell in advance when one is likely to happen by careful checking.

1.125 *Check tyre pressures weekly. Do so at home with a reliable brand of DIY pressure gauge such as this Sykes-Pickavant tool available from most motorists' shops or use your nearest garage. Remember that you will take a false reading if tyres are warm and that they warm up as you drive the car under normal conditions. If a tyre loses pressure to a notable degree or by a small, constant amount each week, have a tyre repair shop take the tyre off the rim, inspect it and make a permanent repair.*

1.126 *Check the side walls of the tyre for splits, bulges or cracks. If you find evidence of any of these, don't hesitate – scrap the tyre! It can be frustrating to do so if there is plenty of tread left on the tyre but it is very unsafe to drive a tyre in this condition. If you're unsure as to what is or is not safe, have your main dealer or tyre centre take a look.*

1.127 *Check the tyre tread, particularly of the front tyres. National regulations are prone to change – check with your local tyre centre for the minimum tread depth allowed – but most experts recommend that you should never depend on tyres with a tread depth of less than 2 mm. Buy a tread depth gauge from your local motorists' shop – they cost very little.*

1.128 *Bibendum says there's another way to ensure that at least your tyres aren't near or below the 1.6 mm legal minimum.*

1.129 *New tyres now have tread wear indicators built in to them. When the level of the tread reaches the level of the wear indicator, it's time to change the tyre! Once again, if you are in any doubt, play safe and seek expert advice from your local garage or tyre dealer. (Courtesy Michelin)*

If the tread depth varies over the width of your front tyres, it probably means that the tracking needs to be set – a job that has to be carried out by a garage. Remember that if the tread depth is below the permitted level on any part of the tyre, you should replace it. While you're at it, look for the heads of nails or tacks that are the usual cause of punctures. If you find anything embedded in the tyre, fit the spare straight away and have your local tyre centre carry out a repair.

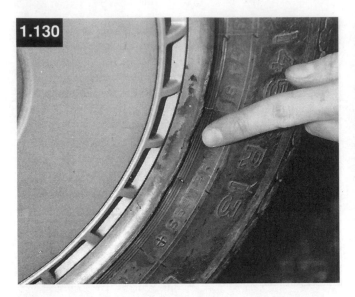

1.130 *If the wheel rim is damaged, inside or outside, the tyre beading can fail to seat properly which will allow air to escape. Very slight damage should not be a problem, but if you have any doubts get your local tyre centre to give their advice. For most cars fitted with steel wheels, replacements from a breaker's yard will be cheap and a far safer alternative to driving around on damaged rims. Check second-hand replacements to ensure that they have no rim damage and also that there is no rust present inside the rim of the wheel which may prevent a tyre from seating properly. Also check the area around the wheel nut holes for elongation, cracks or signs of damage.*

1.131 Make *absolutely certain that your car is fitted with tyres of the same type all round. Some tyres have textile reinforcements within them and others have steel reinforcements. The two types should not be mixed but you cannot readily tell from the markings on the tyres which type you have fitted. If all your tyres are of the same make, there should be no problem. If they are not, drive down to your local tyre centre and ask for their advice.*

You should also ensure that all tyres are of the same size other than in a few rare cases where the manufacturer recommends different sizes of tyres to be fitted front and rear. These are normally tyres fitted to very high performance cars and keeping them alive *is often a different sort of problem altogether!*

As time goes by tyres are fitted with an increasing number of identifying markings on the side wall, and if you have difficulty in interpreting those on your tyres, your friendly local tyre centre should, once again, be prepared to help. You will find a group of numbers and

letters which may look as follows: 175/70 R 13. The first numbers indicate that the tyre has a width of 175 mm. The 'R' stands for a radial ply tyre. The '13' means that the wheel is 13 inches in diameter while any succeeding letters and numbers indicate the maximum loading to be placed on each tyre and its maximum speed rating. The number after the '/', ie the number '70' in this example, means that the tyre is a lower profile tyre. In other words, the distance between the rim of the wheel and the outside of the tyre is 70 per cent of the width of the tyre.

Whether or not you are interested in what the details of the tyre markings mean, you should at the very least check that all of your tyres have exactly the same markings and that they comply with the speed and load rating recommended in your handbook or by your main dealer. Your local tyre centre will also be able to advise.

Tyre safety is paramount!

– If your tyre suddenly deflates at speed, your car will almost certainly go totally out of control. Check for tyre side wall damage or rim damage as shown above.

– If you fit tyres of different types around the car its handling will be badly impaired. You may not notice the difference whilst driving around town, but you can get badly caught out on the open road, particularly in wet weather and especially whilst cornering or under heavy braking.

– An acceptable tread depth and the existence of sipes (the small slits that run sideways from the main treads) are both essential if your car is to retain its grip in wet weather. Each tyre acts as a pump, pushing thousands of gallons of water to one side to enable the tyre to grip the road surface beneath. If it can't do so, the tyre will aquaplane on the surface of the water. The first thing you will know about it will be when you go straight on at a corner or when braking hard.

Thanks to Michelin Tyres for checking through the foregoing for technical accuracy. For any specific queries, you can contact Michelin on 081 861 2121.

Brakes

Brakes usually get worse and worse without the driver noticing, until it is too late! Here are some of the warning signs to look out for both at every service and on a regular basis when the car is in use:

– Can you hear a rubbing, graunching or squealing sound when you apply the brakes? Any of these imply that *they are* dangerously worn. Check them as shown below and, if you feel competent, replace with the help of your manual, or take the car to a garage to have the work carried out. Check that the problem isn't caused by jammed grit or an accumulation of brake dust.

– With the car stationary, press down the brake pedal. If it slowly but surely descends to floor level, you have a serious problem with the hydraulic system. Either the master cylinder is faulty, or there is air in the system, or, conceivably, the fluid is leaking away. In any of these cases, *don't drive the car!* Have a garage or a qualified mechanic come out to you to either fix the car on the spot or trailer it away. The latter could be rather expensive – get a quote first.

– Does the car pull to one side when you brake? Try it out – but never when there is any traffic around you – on a level stretch of road, gripping the steering wheel lightly. If the car pulls towards the gutter, try again on a one-way stretch of road, on the opposite side to the one you normally drive on. That way, you will rule out the pull of the camber in the road. If the car now pulls the other way, you're probably OK. If it regularly pulls one way, you either have a seized brake or there is oil on one of the brakes, front or rear, or one of the brake pads or shoes

is worn beyond the point of usefulness. In the latter case, you'll probably encounter some of the noises mentioned above.

– With the car stationary, pull on the parking brake. Attempt carefully, not too vigorously, to drive off. If the car 'takes off' as usual, the rear brakes could be seized, the brake shoes oiled, or the handbrake mechanism seized. If the car feels as though a big hand is holding it back – and don't get out of first gear or attempt to drive more than a few yards because of the strain placed upon the system – the rear brakes are probably fine. The car will appear to stop almost as well with front brakes only under light braking, so you may not otherwise notice rear brakes that are failing – until it is too late and your car skids in an emergency stop.

Carrying out simple maintenance to the braking system is within the reach of home mechanics, provided that they have had some experience and training – a chicken and egg situation, on the face of it! How do you gain experience if you're not supposed to do the work until you have experience? There are two ways out. One is to hire a *trained* mechanic – not just someone who likes working on cars – to come and do the work for you, on condition that he lets you help and explains what he is doing and why he is doing things. The other is to attend a course at a local evening school where you can learn the skills of car maintenance from a trained instructor. Almost all local colleges offer such courses at a very modest cost.

Whichever route you choose, always work with a high quality workshop manual. A Haynes Owners' Workshop Manual provides full information specific to your car and would be a good investment. You will be able to buy one for your car from your local motorists' shop or borrow one from your public library. In a few cases, a DIY manual may not be available, in which case visit your local main agent and see if they can recommend an alternative. There may be a manual produced by an obscure publisher, or overseas, or by the manufacturers of the car. If yours is a special interest car, ask the owners' club: reprints of 'factory' manuals are almost always available. But in the end, if you don't have access to all the information and training you need, DON'T WORK ON THE BRAKING SYSTEM YOURSELF!

Steering and suspension

In this area, there is a limited amount that you can check with precision for yourself, but there are a number of symptoms that will tell you if your car's suspension or steering is in need of attention. Like faulty brakes, problems with steering and suspension can creep up on you without your noticing. In fact, when such problems are fixed the car can feel strange at first because you find that you have been driving to compensate for the problems in your car. But make no mistake about it: defects in these areas can be just as lethal as any others. In fact, because they only show up at their worst in an emergency, they can be a real danger.

- If your steering feels 'woolly' and the car meanders a little, check: Front and rear tyre pressures; front track (the amount the front tyres are set pointing in or out – a professional garage or tyre centre job); check the tightness of the bolts holding the steering box, steering idler or steering rack to the car. See workshop manual; check the condition of front and rear springs. Is the car 'down' on one side relative to the other? Springs could be worn or broken. Is the steering rack or steering box badly worn? With the car stationary, you should only be able to turn the steering wheel up to a couple of inches one way or the other without turning the road wheels. (The actual acceptable amount of free movement in the steering wheel varies from model to model – check your manual or main dealer). Have a garage check this out for you if in any doubt. If there are any graunching noises or stiffness as the steering is turned, suspect worn steering gear.

- 'Bounce' the car at each corner. If there is any more than one rebound suspect faulty dampers. Check them for fluid leakage or to see if they have come loose on their mountings, or for worn bushes. Consult your manual.

- Replace dampers in pairs (both fronts or both rears, never singly), and replace bushes or tighten mountings as necessary.

- There are many different ways of checking worn steering swivel pins, ball joints and track rod ends. In some cases, the suspension load has to be in place; in others, the load has to be removed. Take careful note of your manual, but do carefully check each swivel and joint in the system. If the worst comes to the worst, a broken ball joint would lead to a catastrophic steering failure. A garage or service centre will carry out a safety check at very low cost, and sometimes free of charge.

- Other items to check include the top mounting bolts of a MacPherson strut type of suspension (see manual), and anti-roll bar bushes and mountings

- Some cars, such as some Rover Group cars, Austins, Minis and Metros, have hydraulic, pressurized suspension. Check the hydraulic lines for any signs of damage. Problems are usually seen when the system loses its pressure and the suspension settles downwards. Sometimes an individual wheel displacer gives up. Measure the distance between wheel and wheel arch with a ruler, comparing opposite sides of the car. On other occasions, suspension settles slowly and unnoticed, so consult your manual and check the height against the manufacturer's figures. You will have to use a main agent or specialist to have work carried out, such as pumping up the pressure or letting it down in order to carry out repairs. UNDER NO CIRCUMSTANCES SHOULD YOU ATTEMPT TO DEPRESSURIZE THE SYSTEM YOURSELF!

Lights, indicators and wipers

It might seem that the safety requirements for this section are obvious: either things work or they don't work. But in practice, there's a bit more to it than that. Taking your car to a garage to have the wiper blades changed can make a very nasty hole in your pocket. You'll be charged full labour rates and a full and apparently very wicked price for new wiper blades. You can do it far more cheaply by buying carefully and carrying out the work yourself. Similarly, problems with lights and indicators on a new car are usually overcome by changing a bulb. Not so with older cars where wiring and earthing problems can give some pretty strange symptoms, such as brake lamps flashing with the indicators. See 1.152 – 1.155 for information on how to overcome the problem!

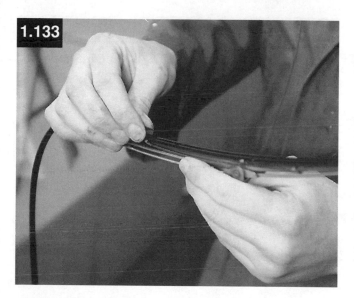

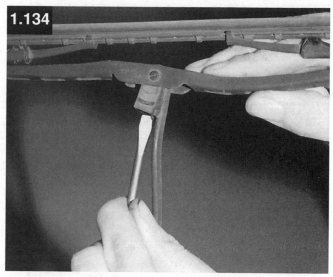

1.132 Wiper blades don't have to look like this before they're changed. If one leaves lines across the screen, the edge of the blade is worn and it should be changed. For safety's sake, regard wiper blade changes as a service item.

1.133 Don't be duped into buying a complete new wiper blade assembly because a new rubber can almost as easily be fitted to your existing wiper blades at far lower cost. If you can avoid it, don't buy from a main agent but shop around from your local motorist shops for the best price. The differences can be staggering! With these Champion replacement blades, instructions are included on the pack.

1.134 Wiper blade removal can appear mysterious at first. Probably the most common nowadays is the U-type fixing. Use a small screwdriver to relieve the tension of the spring clip that holds the pin in place...

1.135 ...and slide the blade backwards and off the wiper arm.

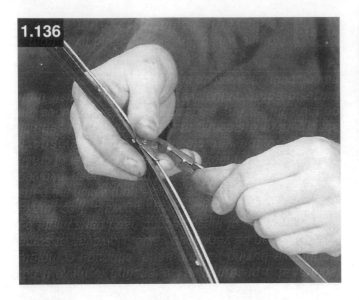

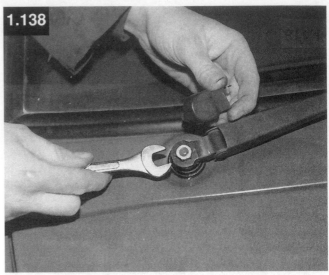

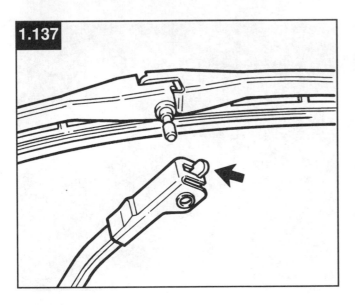

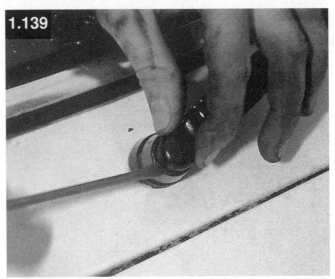

1.136 Another type is also removed by relieving the pressure on the spring clip, although this time the blade just slides forwards off the arm.

1.137 A third type has a pin that is locked by a spring into a hole in the arm. Turn the blade on the arm to break the rust seal, if one has formed. Pull the blade away after pushing down the small clip with a screwdriver.

1.138 Wiper arms are straightforward to change. Mark the position of the wiper on the screen with a wash-off felt tip pen before removing the arm. This will help you to reposition the arm correctly later. Some arms have a hinged cover which has to be lifted up before the nut beneath can be undone with a spanner...

1.139 ... others have a plastic cover concealing a screw which is removed with a crosshead screwdriver...

1.140 ... while others simply have to be levered off the splined spindle. Use as large a screwdriver as you can find and start the arm moving by carefully twisting the screwdriver between arm and spindle mounting nut. Then lift the arm right away from the car's bodywork, grip the arm with one hand, and the end of the arm where it goes over the spindle with the other hand, and 'wiggle' the thing off. In some cases there will be a spring clip at the base of the arm assembly where it goes over the spindle. Check first, levering the spring clip out of the way if necessary.

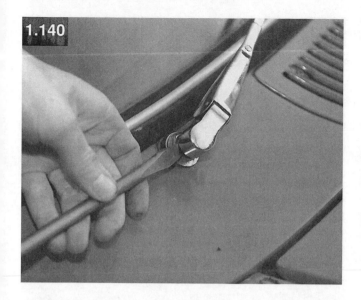

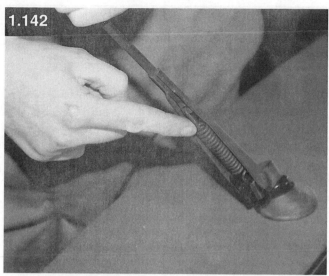

1.141 Juddering windscreen wipers are an annoyance but are very simple to put right. The problem is usually caused by the wiper arm becoming twisted so that the blade fails to flip over as the direction of the travel of the wiper arm changes. This will be the case if the arm judders only in one direction but not the other. If you can't tell properly what is happening as the wipers are running normally, try switching the wipers on (wet the screen first) and turn off the ignition first when the wipers are moving in one direction and then again when the blade is moving in the opposite direction. The blade should trail the direction of travel so that it is, in effect, pulled along behind the wiper arm. If it fails to do so, take an adjustable spanner and tighten so that the jaws are a good fit on the wiper arm towards the blade end. Twist the arm so that it lies parallel to the screen and allows the blade to flip over as the direction of travel changes.

If the wipers judder in both directions, it could be time to change the blades, or it may be necessary to clean grease off the windscreen using methylated spirit.

1.142 Another fault could be a broken spring inside the wiper arm – easily checked.

1.143 If the wipers don't seem to cover the full extent of the screen it is probably because the wheelboxes beneath the wiper spindles have become loose where they clamp to the guide tube. This would only apply to the rack-and-wheelbox type of wiper mechanism fitted to very many cars. Tighten up the wheelbox fixing nuts as necessary.

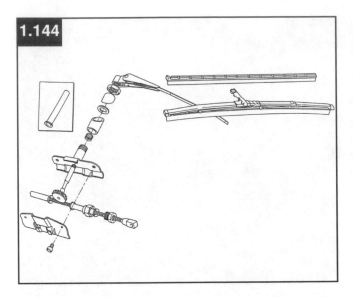

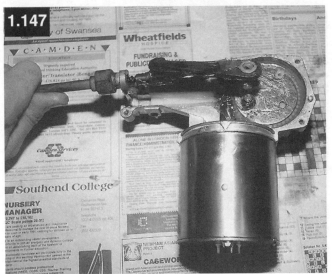

1.144 It could also be that the wiper motor – or in the case of wipers with a solid pushrod linkage the whole wiper assembly – has come loose. Once again, check the mounting nuts. Alternatively, the motor may be seriously worn.

1.145 A worn wiper motor could easily be replaced by one from a breaker's yard. They're very expensive new! With this Lucas type, you first remove the motor cover...

1.146 ... take off the circlip holding the wiper motor cable rack to the crank...

1.147 ... and then remove the cable and crank mechanism (if necessary) from the old motor, and reassemble the cable on to the new motor.

1.148 Changing a faulty bulb is theoretically simple – see your handbook for details – but in the real world, there are often problems such as the light unit being found to be corroded and in need of replacement, or the bulb being rusted into the light unit itself. If you find a seized bulb, start by squirting in releasing fluid and leaving it to soak for a day, if possible.

1.149 Take a clean rag, place it over the bulb to give yourself extra grip and to protect your fingers in case the glass breaks, and try working the bulb clockwise and anti-clockwise. If the glass starts to come loose, don't give up straight away although your chances of getting the bulb out will of course be a little diminished.

1.150 If the glass breaks, clear as much of it out of the way as you can with a screwdriver and try pressing and turning on the shank of the bulb still left in place with a cork out of a bottle.

1.151 If all else fails, push the bulb shank inwards with a screwdriver and grasp it with a pair of pliers, twisting, turning and encouraging it to come loose until it does so. If the inside of the bulb holder is equally badly corroded, you may have to cut your losses and buy a replacement lamp either new or from a breaker's yard. If you use the latter source, go to the trouble of stripping the bulb out of the lamp and inspecting its insides before bothering to remove it from the car. Place a smear of Vaseline or Copperease lubricant around the bulb shank before pushing it back into the bulb holder.

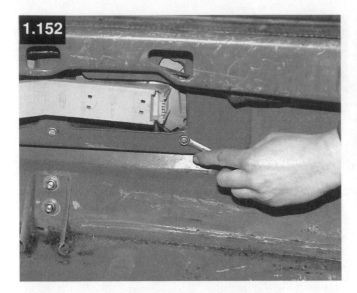

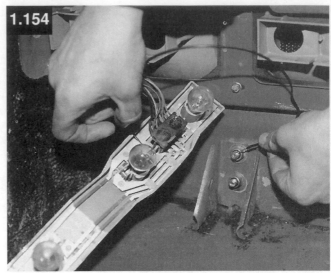

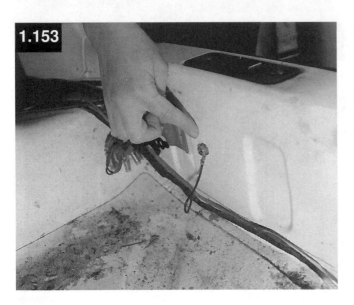

1.152 *You will notice that most of the lights on your car have just one wire going to them, even though electricity needs a feed and a return in order to work. This is because the return 'wire' is always (or almost always) taken to be the car's bodywork. If the connection between the lamp structure and the bodywork breaks down because of corrosion, some pretty weird things can happen to your lights! For instance, if when you indicate a turn other lights flash on and off in a dull fashion, or if when you apply the brake light say, one indicator lamp and one tail lamp flicker fitfully to life, it is likely that you've got earthing problems. Take off each lamp, clean up the point where the lamp is mounted to the bodywork, including the fixing screws and washers, protect the surface with Vaseline or Copperease and you will notice an appreciable difference.*

1.153 *Some components are earthed with a separate (usually black) cable that is screwed to a point on the bodywork through a special type of flat washer soldered on the end. Unscrew; remove; clean up; protect; refit. Simple!*

1.154 *In order to check out whether you do have any earthing problems, take a length of wire bared at each end and make your own definite earth between a bright and shiny part of the car's bodywork (scraping the paint off the head of a bolt inside the boot would be ideal) and the body of the lamp, whilst operating the indicator or brake lights that's giving the problem.*

1.155 *If the test wire makes the problem go away, you've found your culprit! One solution might be to make up a separate earth wire.*

If the indicator switch and its close cousins used for operating headlamps, dip switch, horn and all the other things that manufacturers like to put on the same operating stalk should fail, it's not likely that you will be able to carry out any sort of repair. On the odd occasion, you will find that one of the wires soldered to the tags on the switch will have broken – sometimes they move around with the operation of the switch which tends to make them fatigue and break – in which case you can carry out a very simple soldered repair. In most other cases, it will be necessary to replace the switch with another one. This is another good example of a breaker's yard replacement costing far less than a new item. Test the second-hand replacement while it is still on the car if you can, ensuring that it goes into all of the positions it is supposed to go into without jumping back. Broken catches and springs inside the switch are not uncommon.

Section 5 Getting through the MOT test

About one quarter, maybe more, of all cars entered for the annual MOT test in Britain fail. Over the past few years it has become increasingly strict, but it should be possible for you to check over most of the areas to be tested before you take the car into the testing station. Putting right faults before the examiner finds them could save you a re-test fee and could prevent you unexpectedly being without the car while repair work is carried out.

This British annual car test has gradually been amended with the aim of standardizing it with the test in most other EC countries by 1996. As a result, it's a lot tougher than it used to be. It can be annoying for a car to fail, but obviously it is in all of our best interests that only cars in good, sound condition are on the road. If you want to be absolutely sure of not being without your car should it fail the test, simply have the test about a month before the old certificate runs out. Then if the car passes the unexpired portion will be added on to the new certificate, giving you 13 months on your new certificate. If it doesn't, you've got time to put things right.

Do note that as things stand at the time of writing and for the foreseeable future, MOT testing stations can charge the full fee, or as little

as they like. Do be warned, however, that some garages who carry out both tests and repairs – the majority of them – may be tempted to offer low test fees as an inducement to 'find' more cars with faults in order to supply the garage with more work. In theory this shouldn't be possible, but in the real world there will always be grey areas, where the tester's personal interpretation will be required. If the test is too cheap for the garage to pay its overheads, suspect the worst...

Having said that don't be put off finding a garage with a more competitive price, and do remember that costs can escalate alarmingly because in many circumstances, a re-test costs the same as a full test! Once again, shop around to see if your favoured test station carries out re-tests either free or at reduced charge. *All* test stations are obliged to carry out a re-test free of charge provided that the car is taken back and re-tested before the end of the next working day, but only for the following items:

– Horn

– Direction indicators

– Headlamp aim

– Lamps

– Rear reflectors

– Seat belts (but not their anchorages)

– Windscreen washers and wipers

They are also obliged *not* to charge for a re-test if the vehicle is left at the garage for repair and re-test (big deal!). But under any other circumstances, the testing station is entitled to charge you the full amount for each and every re-test they carry out. It is clearly in your interests to:

– Find out if re-tests are charged for, and if so how much.

– if re-tests are free or at a lower price, find out how long you have got before the garage feels obliged to charge the full rate.

– Best of all, do all you can to ensure that everything is right before even taking the car to the testing station. Here's how.

Lighting

In general, if you ensure that all the lights fitted to the car as standard when it was new (now including even number plate lights and rear fog lamps) are working correctly, you should have no problem. Rules regarding vehicle lighting have rarely applied retrospectively, certainly not for many, many years. If your original lights are fine, you should pass. But do bear in mind that this includes all tell-tale lights on the dash, informing you if items such as indicators, fog lamps and so on are operating. And do remember to check stop lights and indicators and ensure that all rear lights (in particular) are capable of operating properly at the same time. If one or more of the lamps goes dim when others are operated, suspect earthing faults (see *Section 4 Safety*). One of the exceptions to the retrospective rule applies to hazard warning lights when fitted to vehicles first used before 1 April 1986, the date when they became obligatory. If they have later been fitted to earlier vehicles, the MOT test rules say that they should work properly and with the interior warning light operating, too. Fair enough!

If the testing station you are using is known to be a stickler, ask if they will adjust the headlamps as part of the fee if they find the alignment to be wrong. If they don't, you could end up with a fail certificate and a re-test fee. Have them adjust the headlamps separately beforehand, just to be on the safe side – it's not something that you can do for yourself with total accuracy.

If your indicators flash particularly quickly or slowly, your car will fail. Time them: they should flash between 60 and 120 times per minute. Check the earth connections to the lamp units (see *Section 4 Safety*), and if that doesn't do the trick replace the flasher unit. They're usually cheap enough.

Corroded lenses are a fail point. Nothing for it but to replace.

Other main reasons for failure

– A lamp does not light up as soon as it is switched on.

– It flickers when you tap it.

– It is affected by the working of another lamp (best to check the light with everything turned on).

– A lens is missing or broken.

– A switch is faulty.

Testing headlamps

It is difficult to test headlamps precisely at home, but this is how the Vehicle Inspectorate recommend that you set about it. (All diagrams here courtesy HMSO.)

Park your car with the headlamps about 12 ft 6 in (3.8 m) away from a wall. Check that your tyres are correctly inflated and the car is on level ground. The test may best be carried out when it is dark or inside a garage.

1.156 *Draw a horizontal line on the wall about 6 ft 6 in (2 m) long and at same height as centre of headlamp lens, and two vertical lines about 3 ft 3 in (1 m) long, each forming a cross with the horizontal line and the same distance apart as the headlamp*

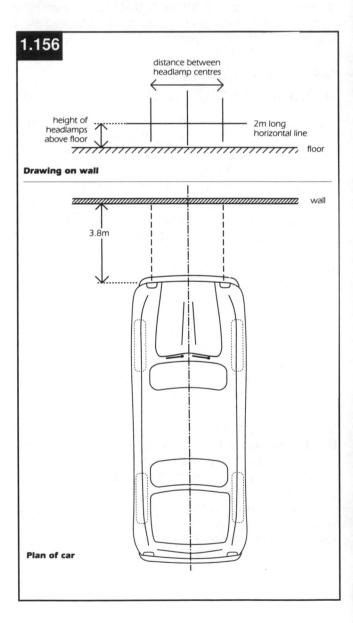

centres. Then draw another vertical line to form a cross on the horizontal line midway between the others.

Position car so that it faces wall squarely and its centre line is in line with centre line marked on wall, the steering is straight and the headlamp lenses are 12 ft 6 in (3.8 m) from the wall.

Switch on the headlamps' main and dipped beams in turn. One of the beams will match one of the three images shown in the diagrams that follow. Check that the boundaries of the beam image are not outside the limits given in the appropriate diagram.

1.157 This is how British and American lamps should appear on main beam when in the UK.

1.158 This is how they should look on dipped beam. Note that with the car parked this distance away from the wall, each 1º of variation equals 2·5 in (66 mm).

1.159 European headlamps' glasses are marked like those shown here – and should appear like this when in the UK, on dipped beam.

Other electrical equipment

Wipers must cover the full area in front of the driver's line of vision, and the blades and arms must be good and serviceable. Windscreen washers, whether manual or electric, must squirt both sides of the screen. Manual systems must work on no more than two pushes of the pump, so make sure that the system is fully primed before you go in! Problems frequently occur from:

– Blocked jets. Clean out with a pin.

– Plastic tube coming loose or age hardening and splitting at the connections, or connections breaking.

– Blockage inside the washer bottle.

– Faulty pump. This is cheap enough to replace with a universal part from your motorists' accessory shop.

The horn must work properly. If it doesn't, consult your manual. The fault can easily lie in the horn switch, the wiring in the steering wheel (affected by movement), the wiring to the horn (vulnerable to the elements), or the horn itself.

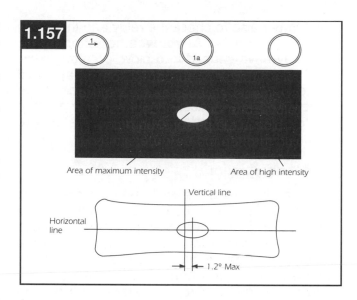

1.157

Area of maximum intensity   Area of high intensity

Vertical line

Horizontal line

1.2° Max

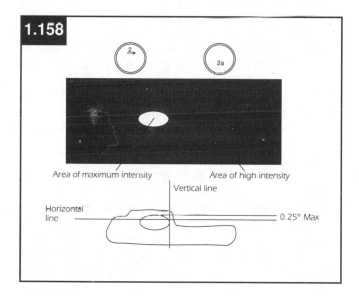

1.158

Area of maximum intensity   Area of high intensity

Vertical line

Horizontal line

0.25° Max

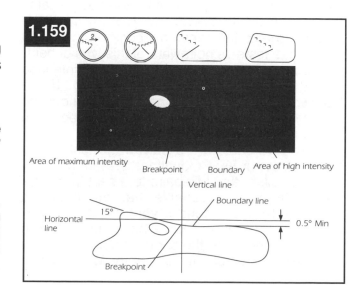

1.159

Area of maximum intensity   Breakpoint   Boundary   Area of high intensity

Vertical line

Boundary line

Horizontal line   15°   0.5° Min

Breakpoint

Don't forget also to check the relay and the wiring to it, and the fuse. A wet weather short in the horn may have caused it to blow, or, more likely, the horn has failed internally. Scrap-yard replacements are cheap and ideal. You can have fun testing your replacement if you have a spare 12 volt battery and a strong sense of the ridiculous!

Interior equipment

Your car has to have at least two rear view mirrors, one inside the car and the other on the driver's side (not necessarily the offside – please note if you drive a left-hand drive car!). All the mirrors must be visible from the driver's side, secure and in good condition. Broken exterior mirrors are expensive to replace with new in many cases, especially if they are electrically operated. Accessory store replacements are cheap; breaker's yard replacements are sometimes cheap; stick-on replacement plastic 'glasses' have to be cut to size with a saw and file – it can be quite a fiddle – but can save money and saves you having to strip down a broken electric door mirror. You just stick the replacement over the broken original after first cleaning up the surface of the glass with a spirit cleaning agent.

Seat belts must be in good condition with no signs of damage. The lock on an inertia reel type must operate when the belt is tugged sharply. The belt must then reel out smoothly and retract normally. Some earlier types of inertia reel seat belt will only lock under braking. If your car is fitted with this type, test them for yourself before going to the testing station – brake; tug (should lock); continue or stop (should move freely again). If your car is fitted with this type, it might be prudent to take the car's handbook with you, just in case the tester is not aware of this type of belt!

The buckle must hold and release as intended and the mountings must be secure. If the bodywork is rusty around the seat belt mounting point, you may have a major bodywork repair job on your hands.

Nowadays seats are a part of the test, too. If the backrest or seat mountings are not securely held, it's failure time! Repairs to a seat frame are frequently more expensive than purchasing a scrap-yard replacement. If your car is relatively unusual, you may not have the luxury of being able to find one with the same colour and trim as your own. Take a careful look at the way in which the trim covers are held on. Chances are it will mainly be with clips and screws, allowing you to use a second-hand replacement frame with your existing trim. You may even be able to purchase a seat with faulty trim at quite low cost, but obviously you must check the mechanism carefully. Also, before rushing off to buy a replacement seat, make certain that the seat mountings aren't loose because of a rusty floorpan – bad news indeed!

A seat that has sagged so badly that the driver could not see properly would also result in failure under the 'serious impairment to vision' part of the test. So would a cracked and possibly a chipped windscreen if it appears in the critical zone ahead of the driver's vision. Although the wording of the information put out by the Vehicle Inspectorate refers to 'serious obstruction to the driver's field of vision', you may wish to ask the man who will be carrying out the test for his opinion before he starts.

Doors must open from the inside, and, along with boot lids and tailgates, should stay shut when closed. At the time of writing, the locks are not a part of the test.

The handbrake should stay on when pulled up. If not, the ratchet may be worn. Inspect it and check for some teeth worn down more than others. Consider a second-hand replacement if you can find one in good condition, but check that the release mechanism operated by the release knob hasn't seized – another fail point. If it feels loose and floppy, from side-to-side, check that it is securely bolted down, usually beneath a rubber gaiter or sometimes beneath the car.

Body structure

Pretty well anyone would agree that if a car is so rusty that it is dangerous, it should be hounded off the road. Here's what the examiner will be looking for:

– All areas near suspension and steering gear mounting points, subframe mountings and anti-roll bar mountings must be completely sound.

– All main frame members, running along the length or across the car.

– The sills, both above and beneath the car.

– Top suspension mountings, seen most easily from inside the bonnet, at the inner wing tops – MacPherson strut-type suspension.

– The floor, inner wings, transmission tunnel and boot floor.

You can check all of these for yourself by tapping with a light hammer. The tester can check quite vigorously, so you won't be able to get away with anything! The Department of Transport provides an excellent guideline to testers to help them decide whether corrosion is bad enough to fail a car: if he or she would feel unsafe when driving the car at speed, bearing in mind the possible need to make an emergency stop, the car is unsafe. Also, the general rigidity of the car and its reduced road-holding abilities if badly corroded should be borne in mind, as well as its reduced crash resistance. When a car becomes rusty underneath, you need to make a careful decision about its future. Is it time to say goodbye? You have to ask yourself. More on this later.

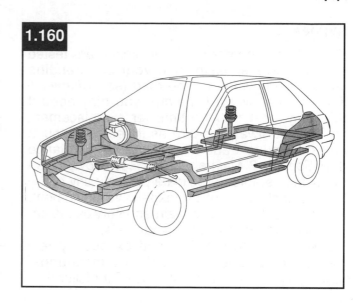

1.160 *The grey-shaded areas are typical of the top-side structural areas that can lead to failure.*

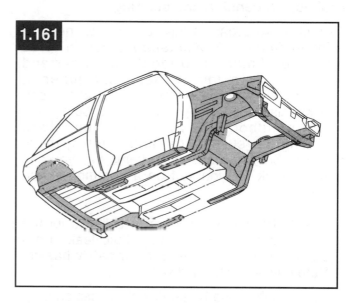

1.161 *These are the main underside structural areas. Note that inner wheel arches are included.* (Both these drawings courtesy Motor Industry Repair Research Centre.)

Outer body panels

Superficial rust is no problem! Even if a panel has begun to rust through you mighty get away with it, unless the tester decides that the car has become structurally weakened. What you won't get away with, in the words of the Vehicle Inspectorate once again, is 'sharp or jagged edges arising from excessive corrosion or damage which might cause injury to other road users'.

Number plates have to be 'standard issue' with no obscured characters, nor with characters moved around to personalize the number. 'Hi SARA' will have to revert to H15 ARA. Spoil-sports!

The fuel filler cap has to fit and its sealing ring has to be in good order. Beneath the car, the tank must be securely held and free of leaks.

Vehicles manufactured after 1980 must have a Vehicle Identification Number (VIN), once known as a chassis number. Obtaining a new one from your local Vehicle Licensing Centre will bring out the Kafka in your local bureaucrats. Some of them can be extremely officious and unhelpful – some are quite the reverse, of course – but don't risk it. Quite honestly, I would be a little bit concerned if my vehicle didn't have a VIN number on its bodywork but it had a VIN number shown on its Registration Document. Some people who find their vehicle to be without a VIN plate, get a local engineering workshop with a set of number punches to make up an aluminium plate with the VIN number from the Registration Document. They then fit it in place where it should be, as shown in the handbook. Without the VIN number your car will not be acceptable to the tester.

Engines

All engines, whether petrol or diesel, are tested for excessive emissions. If your car's engine smokes badly when on the road (see *Chapter 5 Buying a car worth keeping*), you may need it adjusting, or it may be time for a replacement engine, not always as dire as it seems although inevitably quite traumatic on the bank balance (*see Section 2 Maintenance, Recycled spares.*) You won't be able to replicate properly any of the Tester's tests without his expensive equipment, so you'll just have to maintain and service the car as well as you can and bite your nails.

Check that the manifold and exhaust system are secure and leak free. Faulty mountings, blowing pipes and joints: all mean F for failure!

Brakes, suspension and steering

To test these areas of the car, you will need to refer to *Section 2 Maintenance*, which gives advice on finding and identifying wear and weakness in many of these components, sometimes without even getting out of the car. You will also need a copy of a workshop manual and a handbook for your car if you intend checking the suspension and steering joints properly. But there are some items that you can easily check for yourself on a common sense basis:

– Check the wheel cylinders or callipers for the black stains that indicate a fluid leak and a surefire fail, as well as a major safety hazard. Stop driving while it is fixed.

– Bend each of the brake flexible hoses sharply, and have them replaced if any cracking is evident. Also check every inch of the metal brake pipes for pitting, and have the faulty ones replaced. If you see light surface rusting, save work in 12 months' time by cleaning to bright metal and painting on black Underbody Waxoyl.

– Brake pads must have plenty of life left in them and brake discs must not be too badly scored. Brake drums won't be removed by the tester, but common sense tells you to check the condition of the shoes yourself and also to check the condition of the drums. As with brake discs, scoring is not too bad a problem once new brake shoes have 'bedded in' – they then take on the shape of the scoring. But if the drums (or discs) have worn thin, they won't dissipate heat and therefore won't work so well. New replacements are then called for. Compare the thickness of a worn part of the drum or disc with an unworn part. If there is a noticeable difference, replace!

– Check steering rack gaiters and drive shafts gaiters. Splits mean failure and very rapid rack or drive shaft wear and replacement. Replace as soon as possible.

– Wear in drive shafts on front-wheel drive cars and independent suspension rear-wheel drive cars means failure, too.

– If your car is fitted with anti-lock brakes, the warning lights must work properly.

The best way to check steering is to have a friend turn the steering wheel from side to side with the front wheels on the ground while you check each joint in the steering system. Also check for movement between the steering rack or box and the body, and any steering idler or damper that may be fitted and the body. When power steering is fitted, the pump must be securely mounted and the pump, rack and hoses must be free from fluid leaks. Finally, raise the front of the car off the ground and move the steering from lock to lock. (Have the engine running if power steering is fitted.) You can thus check for any roughness in the steering and, *provided that you follow the safety rules for going beneath the car* (see *Appendices*), you may be able to check the condition of each steering rack gaiter in turn as it is placed at full stretch.

TIP 1: You may be able to emulate the MOT testers' 'wheel turntables' by driving each front wheel over a glossy magazine. The slipperiness of the paper may help you to spin the steering wheel easily.

TIP 2: You can then also check that brake hoses are not fouling when the steering is in each full lock position and that the tyres cannot rub on anything.

Wheel bearings

Jack each wheel off the ground and spin it. Listen for roughness or a grinding sound which indicates a failed bearing. Check also that there are no tight spots which could be badly adjusted brakes; could be badly adjusted bearings. Any of these faults can lead to major safety problems. *Have them dealt with immediately!*

Checking front suspension

The Vehicle Inspectorate, the people behind the MOT test, is naturally as keen as anyone that your car should be as safe as possible, and will give advice on checking your car's suspension. (All illustrations used are courtesy HMSO.) Note that your car's jack will almost certainly not be suitable, and instead you should use a trolley jack. Securely chock both rear wheels, in front and behind. Don't go beneath the car.

> SAFETY NOTE: Make absolutely certain that the car cannot slip off the jack!

1.162 *In the unlikely event that your car has a beam-type front axle (it would most likely be pre-war!) this is where you would jack it up.*

1.163 *This is where you would jack suspension with a lower wishbone and shock absorber acting as upper wishbone with coil spring.*

1.164 *Here's where to jack a Mini, for instance, with hydrolastic suspension.*

1.165 *One of the most common types of suspension and where to place the jack...*

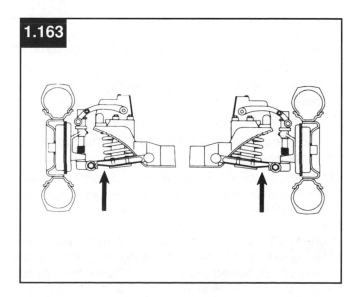

1.162

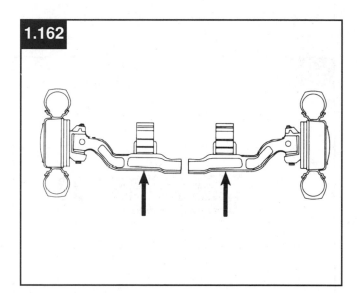

1.163

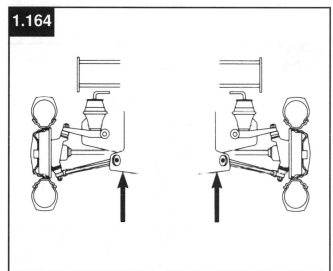

1.164

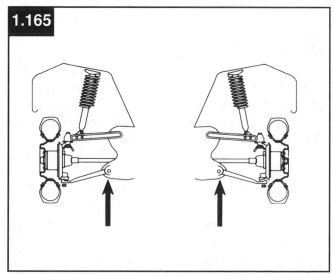

1.165

1.166

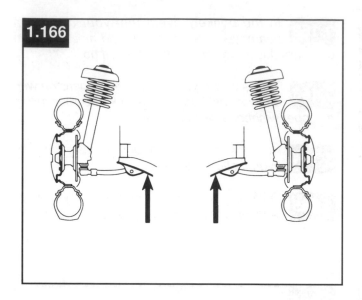

1.168

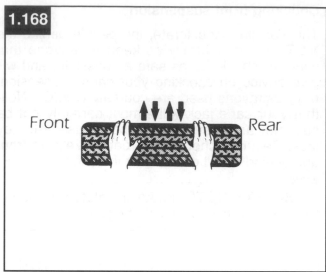

1.167

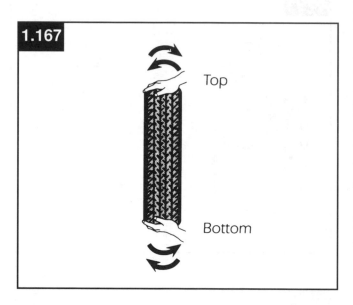

1.169

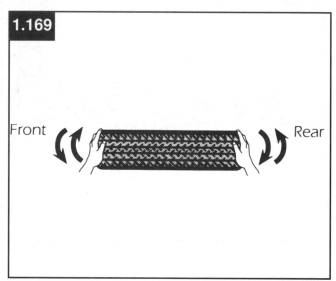

1.166 ... *and an alternative type.*

1.167 *DO NOT place hands immediately beneath the bottom of the tyre, just in case things go wrong and the car does slip off the jack. Have a friend rock the wheel with hands positioned at, say, the '12.30' and '6.30' position. You can check for movement:*

1. Between the kingpin and its bushes or in the axle boss.

2. Between the wishbone outer suspension ball joints and their housings.

3. In the upper inner wishbone bearings.

Then, with a bar under each front roadwheel, try to lift wheel and check for movement between:

1. Stub axle yoke and its housing at the thrust bearing.

2. Suspension ball joints and their housing.

Check beam axle, wishbones and stub axles for damage and distortion.

Examine the condition of the chassis frame and body shell structure around the suspension mounting points for fractures, corrosion and distortion.

1.168 *Place the front wheels on the ground and with each one on a slippery magazine so that they can be turned more easily. Place both hands near the top of the wheel and push and pull. Check:*

1. Wear in a shock absorber strut and/or bush.

2. Wear in rod.

3. Movement at upper support bearing.

4. Leak of fluid from gland.

5. Corrosion or damage to strut casing.

6. Condition of bonding between metal and flexible material in strut upper-support bearing.

1.169 *Hold the wheel at 3 o'clock and 9 o'clock. Swivel the wheel in short, sharp steering actions and check for movement of:*

1. Strut lower ball joint.

2. Track control arm inner bushes.

Also, repeating the hand positions for this and the previous illustration, shake the wheel vigorously. **Make sure the jack point is secure, don't go beneath the car, and keep your hand from beneath the bottom of the tyre. Check for:**

1. Play between ball and its housing in the suspension ball joint.

2. A seriously worn pin or bush in an inner wishbone bearing.

Shock absorbers

1.170 *Leaking fluid spells failure. Remember to check carefully coil-over-shock absorber arrangements where the shock absorber will be partly concealed behind a coil spring. Try bouncing each corner of the car in turn: there should be no more than one-and-a-half rebounds. Also check mounting bushes for wear.*

1.170

If your car has passed the checks outlined here, it's a pretty safe bet that it will pass the test. Do remember, however, that the examiner will probably be far more experienced than you and that he might spot something you have missed, in which case console yourself with the thought that a re-test fee will be cheaper than having an accident because of a failure on your car!

If you are convinced that the tester is wrong, you can appeal. Obtain form VT17 and submit it to your local Vehicle Inspectorate District Office. (MOT testing stations are obliged to give the address and copies of the form, on request.) You will have to pay a fee which you will get back if your appeal succeeds. This form must be received by the Inspectorate within 14 days of the test date. They don't recommend repairing or altering the components whose condition you are disputing!

Tyres

The rules at present give a minimum tread depth of 1.6 mm over the centre ¾ of the tyre. Also, the remaining ⅛ of the tyre on each side must have visible tread. These depths have to be present all around the tyre, needless to say. Common sense says that you should change your tyres before they become this badly worn. They will of course fail the test if there are any bulges in the tyre sidewalls or any splits or cuts.

Time to say goodbye?

When your car is worn out, you might have as much trouble as Ella Fitzgerald in making the final push. But if your car really does have to go, obtain quotes from a number of local breakers. Some may be full or offer derisory amounts; others may offer quite sensible money and come and collect, if necessary. But what sort of factors should make you wave the handkerchief?

Mechanical problems should rarely spell the end, if you take the advice given elsewhere in this book. If your car is worth so little that the cost of a second-hand gearbox will be more than the car's value you might consider it, but that is rarely the case. If you find a whole host of mechanical problems looming, total up the cost of replacement and look not at the value of the car, but the cost of a replacement. Remember that you will lose money on the 'new' car through depreciation, remember the cost of borrowing if you can't buy outright, and remember that things may go wrong with the replacement car. On the other hand, an elderly Audi in need of an automatic gearbox, power steering pump and a turbocharger could well be a candidate for the chop. But the final determinant may be the bodywork.

Bodywork is the big killer for old cars, although increasingly, breaker's yards are dumping grounds for cars whose bodywork is relatively sound. Manufacturers' rust-proofing has been much improved since around 1980, which makes many more cars savable than previously. If you are not competent to weld and repair bodywork yourself consider i) going to evening classes to learn (a bit long-term if your car has just comprehensively failed the MOT!), ii) having a garage quote to carry out the work, iii) having a 'mobile welder' come to you to work in your own garage. Try *Yellow Pages* or just ask around. It's surprising who knows whom when you start asking. You could buy an angle grinder and hire a MIG welder and still save a packet. Do ensure that bodywork repairs, especially if extensive, are properly carried out. The main point is that all rusty metal must be cut away and never just plated over with fresh steel. Many motor trade bodgers do just that and don't seem to understand that they are wasting everyone's time and money. Sure, the punter drives out thinking his/her car is sound, but the rust will come streaming through the new metal in no time – the rotten apples in the barrel syndrome.

Therefore, one of the biggest car killers is the discovery that a succession of bodywork bodge jobs have already been carried out. If you see layers of rusty steel, and rust extending up into seams and joints beneath the car, as well as panel joints above; if the door pillars are loose when you try to lift the doors up and down; if the main chassis rails have been welded up and rusted through again; or you find great blobs of filler hanging out of the floor or chassis rails where some truly evil person has pulled the wool over the eyes of the MOT tester with a dangerous 'repair'; if you find any of these things, it may be time to say enough is enough! To carry out weld repairs on a car, the old truism goes, you have to have something to weld to...

Electrical faults, in the author's humble opinion, lead to more cars being pointlessly scrapped, or at least sold on, than anything else. When things electrical go wrong, you become truly fed up of the car. The wipers fail; the heater gives out; the car conks out in a storm; or it won't start in the morning. These are some of the most aggravating things that can happen and are all

the worse because they can happen again and again. Don't get fed up! Read *Section 1 Making sure it starts* and *Section 2 Maintenance* – and keep that car!

Section 6 Emergency!

Breakdown safety for women

For many women, the thought of breaking down whilst on a journey is a terrifying prospect. While no one has the right to say that such fears are misplaced, it is important for the general health and well-being of the individual that they are not exaggerated. The dangers that arise from driving the car, or from moving traffic whilst the car is broken down and stationary are far in excess of any other risks to the woman – or man – driver in this situation. The UK's abominable and unsavoury tabloid press make matters worse by making it seem that dangers lurk around every corner. Sensational stories and people's fears sell newspapers and make profits, which is all they are concerned about, while in truth the overwhelming majority of ordinary people are just that: ordinary people like you and like me. This sense of fear often breeds suspicion where none is justified, so much so that the driver who has broken down is far more in danger of being ignored by her fellow citizens than being attacked by them!

Having said that, such fears do persist and it's no good denying them. If you feel afraid of flying, you can believe totally in the well-proven fact that flying is the safest form of transport but still feel terrified of the experience. In the case of a motoring breakdown, however, there are steps that you can take to reduce the risk and the sense of danger.

– Join one of the leading motoring organizations so that if the worst comes to the worst, you know that there will always be someone you can call on for assistance.

– If you feel particularly afraid, and especially if you break down at night, go to the nearest house with a telephone wire attached to it and ask if you can telephone for help.

– If your fear becomes a phobia and you have to drive a great deal by yourself, invest in one of the lower-cost mobile telephones that are less expensive to rent but more expensive to use, and save it for emergencies only.

– Tell someone at the other end of your journey what time you are setting out and when you expect to be there, as well as the route you will be taking, so that if you do get stranded they will know where to come and look for you.

– If you are unlucky enough to break down and you need to telephone for assistance, take careful note of street names, nearby shops or signposts when in the countryside, as well as the registration number, colour, make and model of your vehicle so that the breakdown services can find you easily.

– If you are a women travelling alone and you break down on the motorway tell the police staff at the other end of the emergency roadside telephone, and it may be possible for them to send a patrol car to keep an eye on you.

– When you return to the car, you would be well advised to wait well away from the road – as far as possible but still within sight of the vehicle for when the breakdown truck arrives. Police have the following advice for women travelling alone:

'Remember, the risk of being attacked is very, very small; 99.9 per cent of people who offer help are genuine. But the risk from traffic is very, very real. One: If a stranger stops and you are suspicious, have a story ready for them: say something like "my husband or boyfriend has just gone to phone and he'll be back in a minute". Two: When the breakdown services arrive, ask to see the driver's identification if he turns up in an unmarked car or van.'

One of the worst aspects of breaking down is the feeling that you are helpless and vulnerable. This is a passive feeling and it would be helpful for both practical and psychological reasons to do something about it!

Feel safer; be safer – learn how your car works!

If you follow the advice in this book and back it up by enroling for a course on car mechanics at your local evening school, you'll have a better grasp of how your car works. This will make it less likely that your car breaks down to start off with, it will help you to nurse your car along so that you can get somewhere where you feel safe, and it will give you an opportunity to do something about it if your car does break down.

Very many breakdowns are caused by small matters that could easily be put right – if only you knew how! If the distributor cap came off your car because a mechanic hadn't clipped it on properly, the car would stop dead in its tracks. To put it right would take 30 seconds – but only if you know how! If you have a puncture, you'll be sitting by the side of the road waiting for the emergency services to come. This could possibly take hours but if you know how to do it, you could change the wheel yourself in five to ten minutes. Furthermore, if you look busy and as though you know what you are doing, you are far less likely to be harassed, and you will feel far more positive and in control of the situation. This in itself will diminish the possibility of your being approached in an unwelcome way.

At all times observe the traffic safety points shown below: remember that you and your broken down vehicle are far more likely to be involved in an accident than you are to be attacked.

Dealing with punctures

There's only one way to be sure how to change the wheel on your car and that's to practise beforehand. This will have the double benefit that you will be learning how to do the job in an unhurried way and you will also be ensuring that everything works as it should.

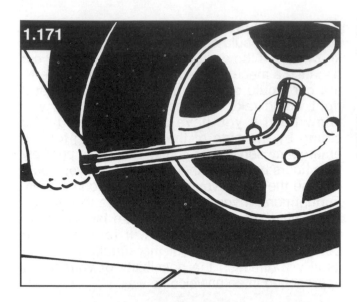

1.171

1.174

1.172

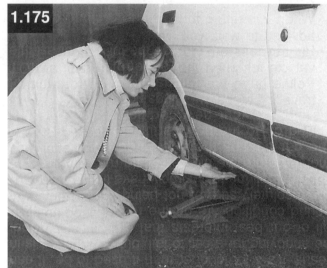

1.175

1.173

1.176

1.171 Get hold of one of these extendable spanners for removing stubborn wheel nuts. They're certainly not just for the so-called weaker sex; some mechanics mistakenly think that the tighter wheel nuts are the safer they are. They use their professional tools to put far too much pressure on the wheel nuts, and as a result the spanner that comes with the car is totally unable to cope. Ensure that the spanner you buy is the right size for the wheel nuts on your car. (This one has an interchangeable range of spanners as part of the kit.) If the wheels are non-original alloy types, the nuts could well be different again. (Courtesy Sykes-Pickavant)

1.172 Study your handbook and make sure that you understand how to take the wheel trims (if fitted) from the vehicle, and that you have the correct tools for pulling them off with you at all times.

1.173 Some wheels have these wheel nut covers fitted. They pull or lever off. Some are hexagonal and it is possible to confuse the covers with extra-long wheel nuts!

1.174 It might seem obvious, but if your car has got locking wheel nuts fitted to it, ensure that you carry the removal kit with you at all times.

1.175 Study your handbook once again and identify carefully the places where the lifting jack must be fitted to the bottom of the car. If you get it wrong, you could damage the car – or yourself if the jack collapses.

1.176 When you carry out your practice run the tyre on the car will be fully inflated, and it will be much easier to locate the jack beneath the car. Perhaps for added realism you should let the air out of the spare wheel after you have fitted it, and try it again. Obviously you will want to reinflate the spare wheel immediately afterwards!

1.177 Before raising the car off the ground, place it in gear, pull on the handbrake as far as it will go and slacken each of the wheel nuts. If you leave it until the wheel is in the air, you will have difficulty in stopping the wheel from turning.

1.178 The handbook says that a jack should always be operated when the vehicle is on firm ground. Drive the car – even on a flat tyre – to somewhere where the ground will support the weight of the jack. If necessary, look around you and even look at what you have lurking in your boot: you may be able to find a piece of wood or something else strong and flat that will help to support the jack on an even keel.

SAFETY NOTE: Wheel changing jacks are notoriously unsafe and unreliable, and you must never go beneath a car supported only by a jack. Also, try to keep your hands safely out of the way so that if the jack should collapse, you will not be trapped.

Place the wheel that is not on the car flat on the floor beneath the car so that if it should topple it won't fall right to the ground. If nothing else, this would enable you to get the jack back beneath the car so that you could lift it again.

If the car does topple, it will mean that you are trying to jack without having the vehicle on level ground; that the jack is digging into the floor and tipping; that the vehicle has not been secured properly with the handbrake and by leaving it in gear; that you have not located the jack properly at the correct jacking point; that you are not using the correct jack for the car; that the jacking point on the car is broken or is coming away from the car's bodywork. If there is any risk of causing an accident, abandon the exercise and call the emergency services.

Never work in a position that puts you at risk from oncoming traffic. If you have to sacrifice a tyre or a wheel by driving the car (at very low speed) with emergency lights flashing until you have found a place where you can safely change the wheel, that is much better than sacrificing a life!

1.179 *Place the spare wheel beneath the car before you start operating the jack. Then, if the jack becomes unstable after you have removed the road wheel, you can lower the car back onto the spare, pull out the jack and start again. You can now lift the car until the punctured tyre is clear of the ground.*

1.180 *Take the wheel nuts off, leaving the top one until last and pull the wheel clear of the studs. If the wheel is held on with bolts you will find it difficult to support the weight of the wheel while you take the last one out; there's no easy answer but see Author's Tip on page 81.*
Place the punctured tyre and wheel beneath the car and offer up the spare. When you carry out your dummy run, if you find the wheel and tyre difficult to lift – and heaven knows, many of them can be extremely heavy and awkward, especially in this position – carry with you a plank of wood which you can use as a lever to lift the wheel far more easily.

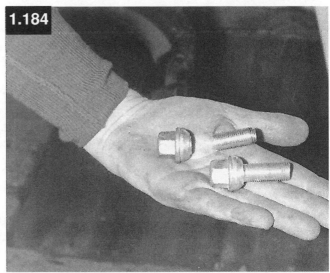

1.181 *You may find that you have to lift the jack some more before you can get the non-punctured, full-size tyre in place. Tighten the wheel nuts by hand; tighten them reasonably with the spanner...*

1.182 *... then tighten them fully when the car has been lowered to the ground. The wheel nuts are tight when you have been able to apply good arm pressure. You should not stand on the spanner or, unless you are a small person, apply your full body weight but check your handbook for advice on your particular car. Tighten the nuts all the way round, working in diagonally opposite corners one after the other several times to ensure that all are secure.*

1.183 *Author's tip: If your car has bolts rather than nuts holding the wheels in place, it can make life very awkward unless you make up your own special tools to make the job much simpler. Find out the thread size of the bolts used on your car and purchase two mild steel bolts the same size from your local engineering supplier. (You can't use scrap-yard wheel bolts for this because the metal is too hard – unless you grind it.)*

1.184 *Cut the heads off the bolts. Cut a slot in the end of each one...*

1.185 *... and if you screw these two dummy bolts into the wheel hub before offering up the* *replacement wheel, you will have something to slide the wheel on to. The proper mounting bolts can then be fitted and a screwdriver used in the slot you have sawn in the end of each special mounting bolt to enable you to get them out if they are a little stiff.*

Note: *Having successfully changed the wheel, don't forget to have the puncture repaired as soon as possible. It's very easy to keep putting it off until 'tomorrow' – the trouble is that 'tomorrow' can turn out to be the day you have another puncture.*

Motorway breakdown

If you are unlucky enough to breakdown on a motorway or other similar major road, note that the risks of being hit by other vehicles are quite significant. As soon as you feel your car starting to run into trouble – you might find it slowing down in spite of your putting your foot down on the throttle pedal, it might start missing and spluttering, or wipers and electrical equipment fail – look in your mirror, indicate left and pull in towards the hard shoulder, as soon as the traffic allows you to do so. **Look out for other stopped vehicles** and pull on to the hard shoulder whilst continuing to indicate. Switch on your hazard warning lights as soon as you can. You may be able to coast to the nearest telephone, but in any case pull over as far away from the road as you can. You and your passengers should get out of the car on the passenger (left-hand) side of the vehicle only, but leave any animals that you may have in the car. If the weather is hot, open each of the windows a couple of inches. In hot weather, they can die from heat exhaustion in a remarkably short length of time. Nevertheless, it would be extremely foolish and probably illegal to remove them from the car

On a motorway, walk to the nearest marker post where you will see a logo or drawing of a telephone and an arrow pointing in the direction of the nearest emergency phone. Since these are situated one mile apart, you can not be more than half a mile away from the nearest one. When you get to the phone, the police services who answer will be able to tell you where you are, but it will give them extra assistance if you note down the number shown on the marker post by which you have broken down. All the while, remember that if you have children with you they will be much safer out of the car than if left in it where, if it was struck by a passing truck, their chances of survival would be slim. For that reason, you should walk as far away from the

road as you can, even to the extent of clambering up a grass embankment if there is one and walking along there.

Be prepared for the shock of the sound and fury of other traffic on the motorway. It all seems relatively calm whilst you are driving along in the same direction as everyone else. But when you are standing by the road, a series of trucks going past at high speed create an enormous noise and a surprising amount of wind turbulence, as well as gallons of soaking spray in wet weather. Be prepared for it, and you will be more likely to take a deep breath and handle it calmly should the occasion arise. Whatever you do, **do not try to cross the motorway for any reason whatsoever**. To do so would be breaking the law and it has been made illegal for this reason: the road is wide and by the time you had reached the central reservation, a vehicle that would have been invisible to you when you set out could have appeared from nowhere at high speed with no chance of avoiding you. At such a speed, a car is impossible to manoeuvre and it will be equally impossible for you to get out of the way in time.

Avoid injury

If you break down on a road other than a motorway, get the car off the road and as far from the traffic as possible. If you have to stop on or very close to the road itself, switch on the hazard warning lights, and if you have a red warning triangle place it about 50 yd behind the car on the shoulder of the road, not in the road itself.

If you break down on an extremely busy main road which resembles a motorway, use your common sense and treat it like a motorway, taking the advice in the paragraphs above.

Whilst you're working on a car don't smoke or use a naked flame. Take care whilst looking into the engine bay not to touch any of the moving parts such as fan belt or fan, and bear in mind that an electric fan can start up without notice. Tuck away loose clothing and long hair, and remove jewellery, especially rings or necklaces, as it can get caught in moving parts or cause shocks or burns from electrical components. If you are wearing a tie, take it off.

If the engine has overheated and you think you might need to top up the coolant, be very careful when removing the radiator cap. Even several minutes after switching off, removal of the cap can cause the water in the radiator to boil and spurt upwards by several feet and you could suffer quite a nasty burn. If in spite of taking care you accidentally burn yourself, try to get to a nearby house or shop and run the burned part in cold running water for several minutes.

Don't touch any of the ignition parts whilst the engine is running because you could suffer an electric shock. Don't try going beneath the car supported only by a jack because it can topple without warning. Take very great care to stand or work well away from passing traffic – it's easy to forget! Take note that your car will be very vulnerable to being hit so leave the hazard warning lights on. Do, however, turn your headlamps off as they will dazzle oncoming traffic, they won't warn traffic on the side where the danger lies, and will rapidly flatten the battery.

Identify the problem

The following check points cover the main areas of breakdown that you're likely to encounter. After each problem, a probable solution is given. Refer back to *Section 1 Making sure it starts* and *Section 2 Maintenance* for information on how to deal with each of the problems shown here. Sometimes there's a temporary repair that can be carried out and if so you'll find it indicated below. If you do carry out the temporary 'fix', you should put matters permanently to rights as soon as you possibly can.

1.186 *Holts Tyreweld tyre sealant can effect a temporary puncture repair.*

Problem 1 Car begins to wallow on cornering,

1.186

pulls to one side or the other, or you hear a rhythmic clunking sound coming from the back of the car, rather like driving over cat's eyes.

Cause Puncture. See earlier sections for how to handle it. If you find that the spare tyre has not been checked and it is flat, you might be able to save the day if there is a garage or motorists' shop within walking distance where you can buy a tyre sealant. Screw it on to the tyre valve, squirt into the tyre and effect a temporary repair. Better still, carry some with you!

Problem 2 You hear a moaning or non-rhythmic banging sound from under the bonnet; steam comes from under the bonnet; temperature gauge or warning light indicates trouble; possibly the ignition light will come on.

Cause The coolant is boiling in the engine block. Open the bonnet carefully, ensuring that there is no gush of escaping steam. Look first to see if the fan belt has broken or frayed and become very loose, or if the alternator mountings have become loose, allowing the fan belt to come adrift. This is probably the most common cause of overheating. If so, leave the engine for as long as it takes to cool down properly (it could take quite a long time – leave the bonnet open). **Don't take off the radiator cap until the engine has cooled down fully!** If you try to remove the cap too soon, the reduction in pressure may cause the water suddenly to boil again. To be sure, cover the cap with a bundled rag and release very slowly and tentatively. If water or steam starts to be ejected as the cap is moved, **screw it down again and leave to cool further.**

The next most common cause is probably a small leak through a hose or a joint which has allowed water to trickle out unnoticed over a period of time, leaving you with insufficient water in the cooling system. Once again it is essential that you leave the engine to cool down before removing the radiator cap and topping up with fresh water. If you have any choice in the matter, use hot water; if not, trickle the water in slowly to reduce the thermal shock inside the engine. Water can also easily be lost through a blown head gasket, and if this is the case you might still be able to continue your journey by carrying extra water with you and topping up as you go. However, the engine will be prone to boiling, so keep your speed down and watch the temperature gauge or warning light. There are many other causes of an overheating engine, but usually only a severe leak such as through a cracked radiator tank or a completely split hose will stop you from travelling any further. To effect a temporary repair, wrap carpet tape or any other waterproof tape around the split hose, and you might be able to limp home. Garages often sell special tape for carrying out temporary hose repairs. If you can't carry out even a temporary cure, try turning the heater and fan on 'full'. This might at least enable you to limp home or off the motorway and turn the engine off (ignition and heater still on) when sitting in static traffic.

1.187 *If you can't get hold of the right type of replacement fan belt, you may be able to buy a temporary universal-sized fan belt which has to be cut to length. The old-time advice of using a lady's stocking has the problem that modern ladies usually wear tights! If you can cut off one 'leg' you might be able to jury-rig a repair, but you may have to take the new 'fan belt' around the drive pulley on the crank and the water pump pulley only, missing out the alternator which requires a good deal of tension to make it work. If your journey is on the open road, and the fan is of the mechanical type, you could cut down drag even further by taking the blades off the water pump pulley.*

Problem 3 Headlamps become dull at night; engine loses power and stops; battery is so low that engine cannot be restarted; ignition warning light comes on; engine temperature rises higher than normal.

Cause Either the generator (alternator or dynamo) has failed, the drive belt has broken or come adrift, or the generator mountings have come loose, allowing it to move out of tension. Remedies for a broken drive belt are as above, with added emphasis on the fact that you may find it difficult to drive an alternator sufficiently to charge the battery, especially if you need the lights on as well. You may try reducing the load on the battery during the daylight hours by turning off every piece of electrical equipment inside the car. That way, you might just get away with the use of a temporary drive belt.

If the generator itself has failed there is very little you can do about it in the short term except have your car's battery charged (which normally takes several hours) or borrow a battery in good condition to help you on your journey. If you are travelling in convoy with someone else, swap batteries with them. This will allow your battery to charge up in their car while their battery drives your car's engine for long enough to get you home.

Problem 4 You suffer a loss of power, there are knocking sounds from the engine, the oil pressure warning light, possibly accompanied by the temperature warning light.

Cause Loss of oil pressure in the engine is always a reason to slow right down and stop as soon as you possibly can. If you're very lucky, the oil level will have just become low and you'll need to top it up without delay. You may well still have damaged the engine, however. Proceed with very great care, and if knocking noises continue from the engine drive very slowly, putting no pressure upon the unit, and abandon your journey as soon as possible. If all appears well, stop at regular intervals and look beneath the car to see if there is an oil leak, and check that the oil level stays sufficiently high. The worst thing that can have happened is that the engine has become terminally worn and you will need to turn to an earlier section to find the most economical way of buying a replacement engine.

Problem 5 The engine loses power totally then fires up again before losing power once more. Probably occurs when driving up a hill.

Cause Classic symptoms of the car running out of fuel. You may have a faulty fuel gauge – or more likely you simply forgot to look! It happens to the best of us! However, the fuel pump may have stopped working. If it is of the electrical type, try giving it a sharp rap with the end of a spanner with the ignition turned on. If it clicks back into life you may be able to continue, but expect to have to carry out the treatment several more times. Alternatively, you may have a blocked filter because of contamination coming through from the petrol tank. You may be able to remove the filter and clean or bypass it in order to continue your journey. If the weather is very hot and the engine restarts and appears to run normally after a period of cooling down, you may be suffering from fuel vaporization. This might be because you're using a higher grade of petrol than that recommended for your car; or it might be that the switch, either automatic or manual, used to direct hot air from the exhaust manifold in the winter is set to the wrong position. Try pulling off the feed pipe that feeds hot air in to the air filter from the exhaust manifold if your car is fitted with one. (This won't enable you to restart a car that shows no signs of so doing; it may help prevent the car from stalling again whilst on your journey if you have managed to restart it.) Try releasing the fuel filler cap. If you hear a 'whoosh' as the cap is removed and the car restarts and runs normally until the problem happens again and is cured in the same way, you may have found the culprit – a blocked breather in the fuel cap. Buy a replacement.

Problem 6 The engine seems to lose power gradually until it eventually stops altogether.

Cause The heel on the contact breaker points has probably not been lubricated or is faulty and has worn itself down until the contact breaker points have closed up. Set the heel of the contact breaker points on the top of the cam and try setting the gap by eye or by using a piece of very thin card if you don't have a feeler gauge with you. This is very rough and ready, but should enable the car to start again if this is the problem.

Problem 7 Power cuts out instantaneously; you put your foot down on the throttle pedal but all you get is a hollow sound as mixture is sucked uselessly into the engine. The engine cannot be restarted and doesn't show any signs of firing when you try to start it up.

Cause 1 Sudden loss of ignition in these instances is usually due to something dropping off! Check the large HT lead from the coil to the distributor; check that the distributor cap hasn't come loose; check that nothing inside the distributor, such as the contact breaker points, has come loose; check the (small) low tension connections to distributor and coil. If after a period of cooling down, the engine starts up again, it is just about possible that the coil has failed, but as it cools down contact is re-made internally – not very likely but possible! It could be failed electronic ignition components, in which case you may need a tow home.

Cause 2 The petrol system has a vapour lock. Ensure fuel pipe(s) are not near hot components such as exhaust pipe, radiator, oil cooler.

Problem 8 Engine loses power, judders and fails, accompanied by mechanical clashing noises.

Cause This is not something that you want to experience! It could well mean that the timing gear has failed in some way, either because a sprocket has come loose or (far more likely) a timing belt has broken. Don't attempt to restart the engine as you may simply cause more damage. This may be another situation where you will be looking for a replacement engine at the lowest possible cost. Make a mental note to replace the timing belt on your car if it has done 40,000 miles or more, before this happens to you!

Tools to carry

There's no point equipping yourself like a service crew on the Safari Rally, but a selection of tools and equipment covering the most likely causes of breakdown could prevent you from being seriously delayed on your journey. Even if you don't feel competent to use some of the equipment shown below, you could save yourself a lengthy wait if the repair man who is called out doesn't have the correct specific parts for your car.

- Telephone number of your motoring organization and your membership card, or the phone number of a breakdown company.

- Car jack and jack handle plus special tools, as appropriate, for removing wheel trims.

- Easy-to-use wheel nut spanner.

- Set of good quality jump leads.

- Set of ring and open-ended combination ring

spanners of the correct type for your car (ie Imperial, AF or metric).

– Pliers and a self-grip wrench.

– Both cross-point and straight-point screwdrivers.

– Spark plug spanner.

– Tyre pressure gauge.

– Fan belt.

– Torch and batteries in good condition, or a car-battery powered torch.

– Warning triangle.

– First aid kit.

– Set of bulbs, including head lamp bulbs.

– Tow rope, preferably with hooks to enable you to connect up to towing eyes fitted to more modern cars.

– Travel rug or blanket for when travelling in the winter.

It's not normally necessary to carry spare fuel, but if you must do so, only use a proper fuel can, *not* an old oil can. If your car is a hatchback or an estate, *do not smoke* while carrying fuel in any sort of can. Open the windows and check the can for leaks *immediately* if fuel smells are noticed.

Using jump leads

1.188 *If you feel like being a good Samaritan when someone else can't start their car because of a flat battery, or you leave your interior light on and your battery goes flat, a pair of jump leads will prove invaluable. You will find accessory shops selling cheap sets of jump leads, but frankly many of them are not worth the paper some of them seem to be made of! Only buy heavy duty, good quality jump leads with powerful-looking jaws and thick cables. Otherwise, they will not transmit enough power to do the job and they may even melt the plastic insulation. These jump leads are excellent because of their well insulated jaws.*

When jump-starting a car using a booster battery, observe the following precautions.

(a) Before connecting the booster battery, make sure that the ignition is switched off.

(b) Ensure that all electrical equipment (lights, heater, wipers, etc.) is switched off.

(c) Make sure that the booster battery is the same voltage as the discharged one in the vehicle.

1.188

(d) If the battery is being jump-started from the battery in another vehicle, the two vehicles *MUST NOT TOUCH* each other.

(e) Make sure that the transmission is in neutral (manual gearbox) or Park (automatic transmission).

Connect one jump lead between the positive (+) terminals of the two batteries. Connect the other lead first to the negative (–) terminal of the booster battery, and then to a good earthing point on the vehicle to be started, such as a bolt or bracket on the engine block, *at least 45cm from* the battery if possible. Make sure that the jump leads will not come into contact with the fan, drivebelts or other moving parts of the engine.

Start the engine using the booster battery, then with the engine running at idle speed, disconnect the jump leads in the reverse order of connection.

Bump starting the car

If you have no access to jump leads you can bump start your car. Turn the ignition on, get the car rolling, press the clutch down and select second or third gear. Let the clutch out – whilst slightly depressing the accelerator pedal – when the car is rolling as fast as possible. (Use the choke if the engine is cold.) The engine will turn over and should start up. *Never bump start in reverse, as it could damage the gearbox.*

Towing a broken down vehicle

There might be nothing for it but to tow your car out of trouble. It goes without saying that you need a tow car that's powerful enough to do the job, and it helps if the drivers of both cars are equipped with extra sensory perception! There are some ground rules, however, that will make the job far, far simpler.

– The driver of the towing vehicle must always pull away from rest very slowly so as not to snatch the tow rope. Snatching the rope is the main cause of rope breakage and can be very embarrassing if you are halfway across the A5 trunk road with a 40 tonne truck bearing down on you. If the worst does happen, and the battery of the towed vehicle has some life in it, put the car into second gear or reverse, whichever seems most appropriate at the time,

take your foot off the clutch and crank the car out of harm's way with the starter motor.

– It is the main responsibility of the person being towed to keep the tow rope taut at all times. The tendency will be for the rope to be taut when you go uphill; for it to go slack when you go downhill. Then, when the towing car accelerates again the rope becomes snatched with the inevitable unfortunate results. If you are in the towed vehicle don't be afraid of using or even slightly abusing the brakes in order to keep the rope taught. If you are in the towing vehicle, try to keep your speed up on the downhill stretches – it might seem a little reckless and I'm not suggesting that you drive fast in this way, but don't slow right down either.

– When coming up to a junction, it is the job of the driver of the car being towed to slow both cars almost to a stop, thus keeping the rope taut for pulling away again. The driver of the towing vehicle can help here by slowing down gradually and in plenty of time for the junction.

– The driver of the towing vehicle must have limitless patience when pulling out from a junction and remember the enormous amount of time that will be taken for both vehicles to get into the traffic stream.

– According to the law, you should never use hazard warning lights when driving along the road. But if I were in a vehicle being towed and the circumstances seem in any way dangerous, I would happily turn on my hazard warning lights and let them flash away! If there is no battery power to the vehicle being towed, vigorous hand signals would be the next best thing.

– Both vehicles must be in a roadworthy condition, MOT tested, taxed and insured, and the driver must be properly licensed to drive the vehicle being towed.

– DON'T ATTEMPT TO TOW A VEHICLE OVER A LONG DISTANCE IF YOU ARE NOT EXPERIENCED.

– Do not fix a tow rope to the bumper on the car; all you will achieve is to pull it off! Either use the manufacturer's towing eye or a substantial part of the chassis or the sub-frame. You could use the leaf-spring shackles on the rear of some cars, but do not use any part of the

suspension or the steering gear. Ensure that the rope will not damage the bumper or the bodywork when the slack is taken up and that it will not rub on anything or be burnt through by the heat of the exhaust pipe.

ESSENTIAL: The towed vehicle must have the ignition switch turned so that the steering lock is not operative.

– The law says that you must cover up the number plate on the towed car and replace it with a sign displaying the number of the towing car. An 'On tow' sign is not compulsory but it could help in informing other drivers. The maximum tow-rope length allowed between the cars is 16 ft 5 in (5 m) and you should tie a piece of coloured cloth or plastic halfway along the rope to warn pedestrians. The maximum towing speed allowed is 40 mph (64 km/h) and the towing car must be at least the same size

and weight as the vehicle being towed. Towing on a motorway is allowed but only as far as the next exit slip road.

– If the towed car is fitted with power steering and servo-assisted brakes it might take a very great deal of effort to steer and brake the car. If this is the case, abandon the idea of towing it. In any case only tow at very low speeds.

1.189 *If you use just one knot to secure the rope, you will find that the knot pulls so tight that it will be all but impossible to undo later because of the inevitable 'snatching' that will take place. Tie one knot near the vehicle, then another pair of knots some way away from the first. Keep the rope taut as the tow vehicle takes up the strain so that the knots stay in place. You'll find that they stay loose enough to undo easily!*

Chapter 2

KEEPING YOUR CAR LOOKING GOOD

Keeping your car in top mechanical trim is essential if you want to save yourself the hassle of a car that won't start in the mornings. But keeping your car looking good has two more entirely different but valuable benefits. One is that a good-looking car is good for morale. There's nothing worse than driving round in an old nail of a car that looks as if it's just escaped from the clutches of the scrap-yard crusher. Even more important though, a car that is in poor bodily shape may be unsafe and will certainly 'die' younger than one that is in good condition. In fact, it might be said that all the emphasis that people place on maintaining their cars' engines is misplaced if at the same time they ignore the bodywork. Body maintenance saves you far more money than changing the oil!

This chapter is intended to help in the following ways:

- You may have seen a car you would like to buy that is basically sound but looks tatty, or you just want to prevent your car from looking a disgrace to the neighbourhood.

- It will help you to carry out rust repairs before they take too much of a hold.

- It shows how to preserve your car against the ravages of rust.

Face lift

Why is it that every car you see for sale in a showroom looks immaculate? It's not because the business concerned sells cars that are above average. On the contrary, cars for sale in some garages are often very average, at best! They all look immaculate because garage proprietors take a lot of time and trouble to clean and polish cars until they shine. There is no magic formula to this, but there is an approach to follow if you want to raise the appearance of your car to showroom standards.

Most people think of shiny paint when they think of a showroom car but there's a lot more to it than that:

- Next time you look at a car, note how much of its surface area is glass. Cleaning the glass makes a big difference to the car's appearance.

- Chrome trim is an obvious area for pouring on the old elbow grease. But don't neglect black or grey trim, whether paint or plastic. The latter goes off very gradually so that you don't notice it. Lift its appearance as shown below, and then you'll see the difference!

- Wheels and tyres have a life of automotive hell, if you think about it. Small wonder that they eventually take on the appearance of all the stuff they have been driving through. Improving wheels may take more than just hard polishing; tyres are easy meat!

- If you improve the appearance of the engine bay and the interior of the car, you'll feel a lot better about it. Not only does this make it more enjoyable to use, it also makes it more likely that you will treat it with more respect, and you'll find it easier to pick up on engine bay faults, such as oil leaks or cracked hoses, if the engine bay is clean.

Cleaning and protecting bodywork

2.1 *Gather together your tools; a brush kit for your hose pipe will make short work of the dirtiest and save on the fingernails into the bargain. On the left is the cleaning brush and on the right is the complete cleaning set, including lance, body brush and wheel brush.*

2.2 *Whichever you use, they can all be connected to your garden hosepipe by using this simple adaptor. You can then use the lance to turn a trickle into a stream.*

2.3 *Start the cleaning process by hosing down the entire car. This helps to remove loose dirt and prevent the possibility of harsh particles damaging the paintwork.*

2.4 *Now is the time to get some of that encrusted mud from under the wheel arches, where it does an excellent job of retaining rust-creating moisture and salt. Do it now rather than later – you don't want to cover your sparkling wheels with all that dirt!*

2.5 *A pressure washer will be much more efficient at removing thick layers of mud but be careful not to use it on its narrowest, fiercest setting because it will probably remove underseal as well. You will be able to hire one from your local tool hire shop if you don't want to 'splash out'!*

2.6 *Car shampoo with wax does a better job than washing-up liquid, but only because it puts a protective layer on as you wash. Most washing-up liquids are perfectly good for cars that are very grimy, although it will need a good rinsing off or the paintwork may discolour. Save the more expensive car wash and wax for the second wash.*

2.7 *Always take care not to get wax-based products onto the glass where it could smear, particularly on the windscreen where it could potentially be very dangerous. It is best to make glass the last job.*

2.8 *Rinse off the excess suds using a hose or by throwing clean water over the car. In order to prevent streaking, you should always wipe away excess water using a quality chamois.*

2.9 *Leave washing wheels and tyres until last. Wash the worst of the grime off with the last of your washing water but be sure to rinse the sponge before using it on the bodywork again.*

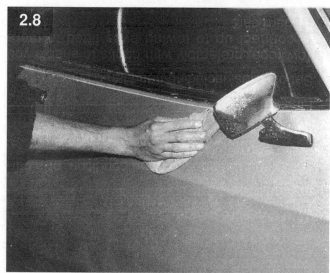

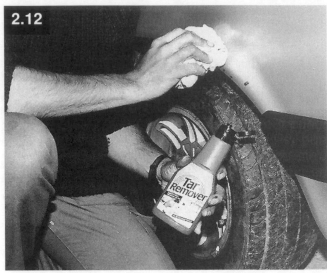

2.10 Alloy wheels can generally be hard to clean but front wheels can become especially heavily coated in brake dust. Squirt on a wheel cleaner: I do so before starting to wash the car so that it has had time to start working.

2.11 Heavy coatings are best removed by working the cleaner into the nooks and crannies with an old paint brush (much cheaper than a proper wheel brush), then squirting on a little more cleaner. Don't apply it to wheels that are wet.

2.12 Having washed away the layers of dirt and grime, look closely at your paintwork. You're bound to see those nasty black spots of tar. Remove them simply and quickly by using tar remover, applied

with a soft cloth and then wiped over with a clean one. White spirit also works but takes longer to dissolve the tar. DON'T use it if your car has been given a respray in cheap, oil-based paint. DON'T use cellulose thinners!

2.13 Only when the tar has been removed is it time to wax the paintwork. This will give a high gloss shine and protect against oxidization and the ever-increasing amounts of acid rain. However, do not polish your car in direct sunlight or if the heat from the engine has made the bonnet warm. Also, take care to avoid getting polish on to the glass area.

2.14 *Polish off with a clean, soft cloth. Any hard bits of grit or dirt in the cloth will cause scratches in the paintwork. Turn the cloth regularly, shake it often to get rid of the polish dust that builds up, and swap it for another clean cloth when the need arises.*

2.15 *It is easy to forget the large area of your car that isn't metal, namely the glass! Proprietary brands of glass cleaner can be used inside and out, and is especially useful for the windscreen where it removes traffic film and squashed insects. After spraying a thin film over the glass area...*

2.16 *... it can be wiped clean with a soft cloth. Again, it's best not to do this in direct sunlight.*

2.17 *Trim cleaner is available in black or grey, to match the colour of your plastic body trim. Some comes in the colour of the trim, which means that you get the same colour all over your hands if you don't wear gloves. Some is a clear silicone liquid which, nevertheless, brings back faded black trim – paint as well as plastic – like magic. You can also use it under the bonnet to restore the appearance of hoses and painted areas.*

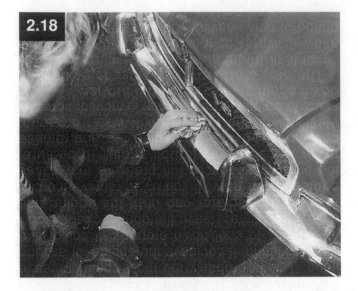

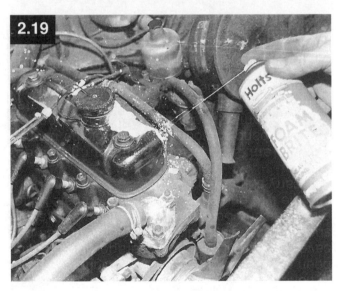

near the sump, then use a spray-on engine cleaner. Spray it on; give it plenty of time to dissolve the grime, (apply a second coat if things look well set); work into the deepest grime with an old paintbrush, then use the same brush with hot, soapy water to wash the emulsified crud away. Choose an engine-cleaner with a built-in corrosion inhibitor, otherwise newly cleaned bare metal will soon turn brown with rust!

Steel wheel appeal

2.20 The only way to make a lasting improvement to steel wheels is to paint them. Begin by cleaning off every speck of rust with abrasive paper, which is best done with wheels off the car. Use coarse paper first, then transfer to finer paper so that the scratches don't show through the paint.

2.21 It is extremely difficult to persuade masking tape to stick to tyre rubber. A quick though not perfect way of masking off is to use a piece of card. Hold it tight against the wheel rim and rub around the edge of the rim with your (preferable grubby!) thumb.

2.22 Carefully cut along the thumb print with scissors...

2.23 ... and use the card as a movable masking strip as you spray the wheel. Wear gloves so that you don't spray paint all over your fingers. You're bound to suffer from a little over-spray but tyre black applied later should take care of that.

2.24 You'll need masking tape if you hope to do the job properly, and you'll certainly need it if the wheels are of more than one colour.

2.25 Specially made wheel paint may prove to be tougher than ordinary paint – but don't bank on it! The results won't be as long-lasting as the original finish, but the alternative – taking the wheels to a specialist (see adverts in classic car magazines) – is far more expensive.

2.18 Chrome trim still demands the elbow grease treatment, coupled with a proprietary brand of chrome cleaner. If chromework has deteriorated to the point where rust blisters have started to burst through, the ideal solution is to have the part replated or replaced (perhaps with a scrap-yard part). Most often, old cars are just not worth it. You can get rid of the worst of the rust by rubbing with a scouring pad, then wipe an oily rag over the improved chromework to delay the return of the rust. The solution is only temporary, but you might be able to keep on top of the problem with regular polish and waxing.

2.19 Don't neglect the appearance under the bonnet. Years of oil mist coagulated with road dust will form an almost impenetrable grime. Scrape thick deposits away, usually found low down,

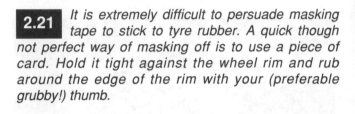

2.26 Don't neglect wheel trim or hub caps.

2.27 Tyre black won't last for very long, but it gives the appearance of the whole car a subtle lift whenever you apply it. It's especially useful if you inadvertently end up with paint overspray on the tyre.

Aerosol paint

Aerosol spray paint is ideal for refinishing small areas of car bodywork.

2.28 Use wet-or-dry paper with water to feather out any filler that may have been applied, leaving no trace of a hard edge.

2.29 Before starting to spray using primer, take the can outside, shake it vigorously, and clear the nozzle.

2.30 Hold the can about 6 in (10 cm) away, and spray the primer on to the bare metal. When choosing your primer colour, go for red for dark shades of top coat, grey for lighter coats, and grey or preferably white for white top coats and metallics.

2.31 Spray high-build putty on to the whole area and then, extending a little wider than the area of the original primer, apply a second coat of spray putty after the first has dried.

2.32 Provided that the filler work is carried out properly, the use of high-build spray putty will allow you to remove every last blemish when you sand it out with fine 'wet-or-dry' supported on a flat rubbing block.

2.33 For the car shown here, we chose to spray on grey primer paint as a barrier colour between the yellow and the white top coat to follow. Red and yellow have a nasty habit of 'grinning through' white surface coats above them. Plenty of water, a few spots of washing-up liquid and the finest grade of 'wet-or-dry' and the final primer coat can be prepared for finish painting.

Safety note: Aerosol paint has many of the safety hazards associated with conventional paint spraying. Read the safety instructions on the can carefully. In particular, use only in a well-ventilated area; keep sparks and flames away from spray vapour. Do not puncture the can or apply heat to it. Wear gloves and keep wet paint and mist away from skin and eyes.

2.28

2.31

2.29

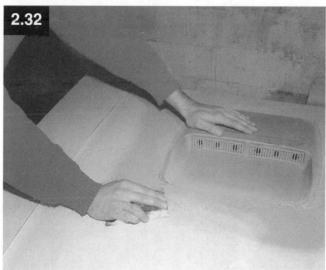

2.32

2.30

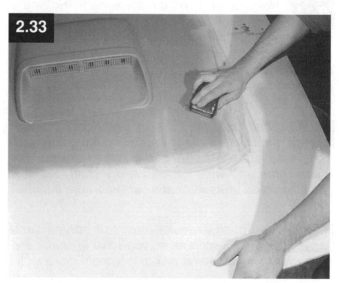

2.33

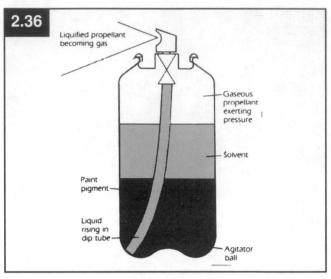

2.34 Now here's a tip from the experts. Holding a tin of black spray paint about 12 in (30 cm) or more away from the job, dust a light coat on to the work surface. The idea is not to change the colour of the panel, but just to put an even sprinkling of paint over the whole area.

2.35 Sand the entire panel all over once more with the finest grade of paper and the guide coat, as it is called, will be rubbed off in all but the low areas. After you wipe off with a dry cloth, any low spots and blemishes will stand out like a sore thumb!

2.36 Inside an aerosol can, the solvent and pigment separate, so you have to shake and shake for that little metal ball to mix them thoroughly!

This diagram also explains why paint stops coming out when you invert the can.

2.37 If you do what comes naturally, the part of your finger sticking forwards catches the edge of the spray which builds up into a drip which is then shot forward as a blob on to your lovely handiwork. Most annoying! Hold the nozzle down with the top of your finger, or better still buy an accessory trigger sold with some brands of aerosol paint.

2.38 It is best to practise your spraying on a spare scrap of sheet metal. Hold the can too close and the paint will run; too far away and you'll have a 'dry-look' finish.

2.39 *The first coat should be applied in regular strips up and down the bonnet, concentrating on obtaining an even cover without trying to blanket out the colour underneath. That's the way to achieve runs! You must leave a few minutes for the solvent in the first coat to 'flash off'.*

2.40 *The second coat should follow in a pattern which criss-crosses the first, and the colour underneath will disappear from view. Ideally, you may want to give another one or two coats. If any little bits of dust land in the paint surface, you may be able to polish them out with fine cutting compound, but be most careful not to go right through the paint and don't try it until the paint has had several days to dry really hard.*

Cosmetic surgery

This section shows a host of techniques and tricks for putting a shine on a car for which the spotlight has long gone out. Make no mistake: the following tips won't make the car last a lot longer; they won't make it go faster or stop better; most important of all, they won't make it any safer. It is only worthwhile carrying out any of the cosmetic repairs that follow if the car's structure and running gear are safe. That is something that you must determine for yourself, if necessary with the aid of a professional tester. But it is surprising how even a basically sound car can be so badly knocked about and neglected that it looks far worse than it really is. So, if you are tired of punk-rockers wanting to take your car home as a souvenir, or of police patrol men pulling you up to count the rust bubbles, this section could be just what you have been waiting for. Read on! The author – with a little help from his father and friends – shows how it's done.

Important: Read each of the safety notes throughout this section, those in the Appendices and those on the product packaging before commencing work.

2.41

2.44

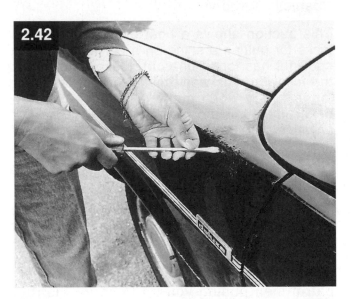

2.42

2.45

2.43

2.46

2.41 Well, this is it! I picked this one up with no MOT road-worthiness certificate, no Road Fund Licence, and a clutch that had rust-welded itself on to the flywheel. The owner was just about to chop off the rear axle and turn it into a trailer when I spotted the chariot's startling potential(!) and for around the cost of a dozen pints of best bitter, the deal was struck, leaving the ex-owner alcoholically ecstatic and the new owner stone cold sober at the realization of what was to come. The car's underframe was sound, everything shone, tooted and flashed as it should and, by dramatic and distinctly unorthodox means, the clutch was freed in a trice.

2.42 There were several places where rust was disturbing the surface of the paint and I knew that many of these would reveal gaping holes when they were prodded. At the rear of the same wing, the bubbling was even worse, and pushing a screwdriver into the corroded metal was as easy as breaking thin ice. Quite a big patch was going to be needed here.

2.43 This body scratch is typical of the sort of calling card that some morons leave behind to greet you on your return to the car park. It was even worse than it looks in this picture and you could feel and see a shallow dent right along the line of the scratch.

2.44 The wheel arch was of the back-to-nature variety; it was rapidly returning to its original metallurgical state! Michelle, a friend and neighbour, called around and said, 'Oh, look how this comes apart when you touch it!' Who needs enemies... But seriously, it just shows how weak rust is, and how filler

applied some time ago will pop straight off again under the force of expanding rust beneath it.

2.45 Michelle tried the same trick with the front wing, but this time the paint just flaked off to reveal sound metal beneath. You never can tell just by looking.

2.46 This was not staged! It just goes to show how you can disregard an already battered-looking car. I normally pride myself on being able to judge a car's dimensions, but this time I got it slightly wrong! However, just to make things equal, my wife clobbered the other side of the car the very next day. Now believe it or not, denting cars is not something we make a habit of. It's just that there's a real psychological difference in the way you treat a car when it looks respectable.

2.47 Michelle seems to be saying, 'How on earth d'you think you are going to repair this?' I didn't even try but simply visited the local breaker's yard and bought a more presentable seat, along with the hub cap to replace the one missing from the rear right-hand wheel.

2.48 I started off by nibbling away at a bubbling area with an old woodworking chisel. The paint scraped and flaked away quite easily and revealed metal that was pitted but which hadn't yet gone right through. The paint was scraped back beyond the obvious area of rust, out to shiny metal. That way, you make sure that you don't miss any rust that might have started to creep under the paint without anything showing on the surface.

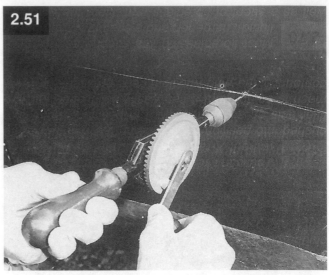

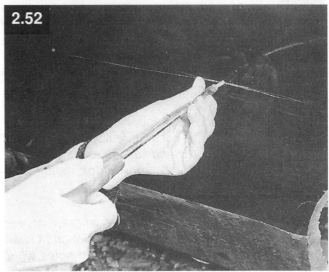

2.49 Next, rust-proofer was applied according to the instructions and with the brush supplied. I've always had reservations about how well any of these rust killers actually work, but they might help to hold it back a little and they surely can't do any harm.

2.50 I've missed out all the filling and masking pictures (see the other sections for details), but note that once the filler was flatted it was sprayed with primer then straight away with a light coat of finish paint. Filler is absorbent and I didn't want it soaking up any moisture whilst the rest of the car was attended to. Incidentally, after using the rust-proofer but before applying the filler, the metal was sprayed with several coats of zinc spray. Now, I know that zinc helps to hold back rust.

2.51 If you recall, the deep scratch down the left-and side panel was accompanied by a valley in the panel itself. There was no ready access to the rear of the panel without time-consuming stripping out of the trim panels. First, a hole was drilled in the centre of the dent, using a ⅛ in drill.

2.52 Than a self-tapping screw with a flat head was screwed into the panel, making sure that it didn't go so far in that it damaged anything behind the panel, but taking it in far enough to get a strong grip.

2.53 The art of improvisation! A woodworker's claw hammer was used to grip the screw head while a strip of wood was used both as a fulcrum

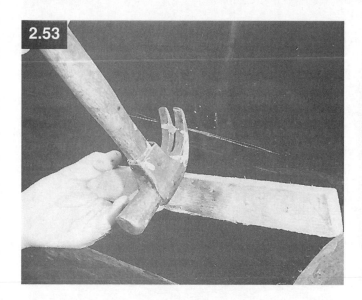

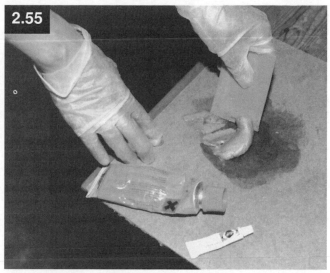

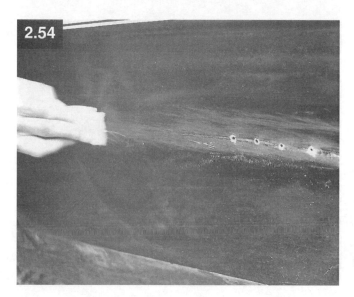

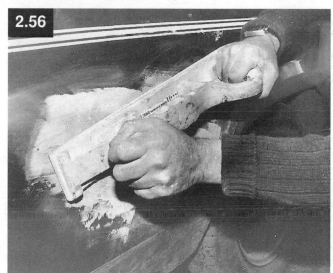

point and as a cushion to prevent the hammer marking the panel. The dent will come out really easily; the trick lies in not overdoing it.

2.54 When the dent had been pulled out all the way along its length (and actually, it was left just a little low, which is greatly preferable to creating a raised ridge), the paint was prepared for the application of filler by roughening the surface with medium-grade production paper. If filler is applied over shiny paint, its adhesion is poor, it becomes prone to cracking out, and it won't feather edge properly so its edges always show.

2.55 Try not to use the same surface twice for mixing your filler, otherwise you will pick up hard pieces of filler from the previous mixing which will then drag across the surface as you attempt to spread the filler, leaving furrows which are infuriatingly difficult to get rid of.

2.56 Here a professional sanding block is being used. It accepts ready-made strips of self-adhesive backed production paper strips (any paint factor will stock them) and helps to create a true, flat surface. Attaining a flat surface is easier if you sand in more than one direction. Coarse production paper can be used at this stage.

2.57 My father lends a hand here, using his power sander which really shifts the dust! That's why he is wearing a particle mask, and a hat to keep the dust out of his hair. While the power sander is quicker, it is not so easy to produce a flat surface over a large flat area.

2.58 Leaping ahead now to the time when filling is almost finished, a tin of spray paint was used to spray a very thin 'guide coat' of paint over the surface of the filler. The can was held further away than normal so that the paint landed as an almost dry, dusting coat. When flatted off with a rubbing block and a fine grade production paper, the paint was removed from the high spots leaving the low areas standing out in stark relief. Depending on how deep these areas are, they can be brought out with filler or stopper, as

already described. When using a guide coat, choose a colour that contrasts with the surrounding colours.

2.59 The dent on the front wing was in a very awkward place, just where the wing formed a fairly complex wheel arch extension. The DIY tools used here were an ordinary woodworker's G-cramp and the ubiquitous piece of wood again!

2.60 The G-cramp was used right behind the worst part of the dent and then again each side of the first 'pull' to force the dented metal back to the line of the wood, which was the same as the rest of the wheel arch. If the head of the G-cramp had not fitted so snugly inside the wheel arch, I would have used another, smaller piece of wood, shaped if necessary, to pull the metal to the correct shape.

2.61 A small kink was left inside the wheel arch and this was easily knocked back into line using a panel-beater's hammer.

2.62 Well, all right, the G-cramp did leave a small mark. Unfortunately it had pushed a little of the concave curve out of line, but it was easily restored to the correct position with the cross-pein end of the panel-beater's hammer.

2.63 The repaired area was flatted with medium-rade production paper, as were the scratches to the rear of the wing and the front of the door. The surfaces were filled, as shown and described earlier, and the concave curve was flatted, this time using a slightly different technique. The production paper was rolled into a tube, the shape of which followed that of the concave part of the wing.

2.64 Finally the filler was sprayed with primer to protect it from the elements.

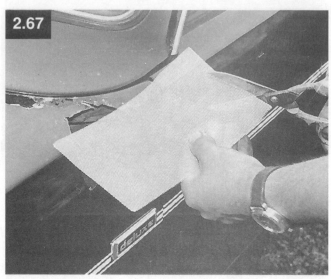

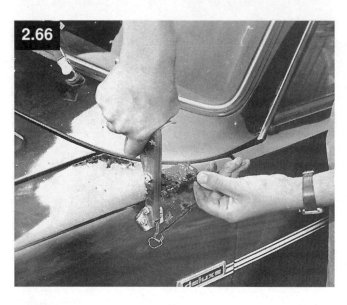

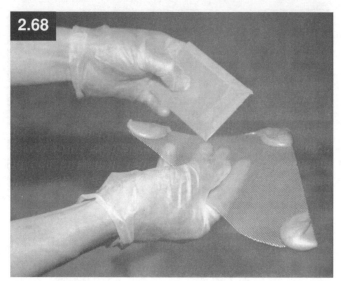

2.65 *Rust frequently takes its strongest hold in the places where mud becomes lodged, and this area at the top of the wing is one of those places. When the surface was lightly tapped with the old wood chisel, the metal just fell into holes.*

2.66 *I started by cutting away all the rusty steel using a Monodex cutter (available from specialist tool suppliers: See display ads. in Practical Classics magazine or Hemmings News in the USA) leaving only sound metal in place. A couple of fiddly bits wouldn't come out using the Monodex, and they were finished off with a hammer and the trusty old wood chisel.*

2.67 *Included in the body repair kit was a sheet of aluminium mesh. This can be bent and folded very easily and can even be cut with scissors. It isn't intended to impart any strength to the job but just acts as a bridge for fibreglass and filler while it goes off. You can't fill a gaping hole without putting in a support first, and aluminium is ideal because it doesn't encourage the steel to start rusting again.*

2.68 *The aluminium mesh was cut so that it covered the area of the holes, and then a dollop of filler was placed on each corner of the mesh. You are strongly advised to wear gloves: plastic filler and resin (see below) contain a skin irritant. When the mesh is actually applied, the job is done out of sight, beneath the wing. Gloves are worn because of the way in which filler will inevitably become coated over the fingers!*

2.69 - 2.71

2.69 *You can't really see what is going on here without X-ray vision, but the mesh is being pushed into position from beneath the wing while the filler acts as a glue to hold it in position. Aluminium mesh is so soft that it can easily be pushed into the contours of the wing with light hand pressure.*

2.70 *Most fibreglassing kits supply resin (a thick liquid), hardener, and a spatula for stirring, as well as a sheet of fibreglass mat. Here the hardener was mixed with resin to the prescribed proportions, and then spread over the mesh and the edges of the steel. Then pieces of fibreglass mat were cut to size, placed over the mesh, and stippled down with resin until the mat became almost transparent.*

2.71 *The resin was left to go hard, then a scrape of filler was taken from the tin and mixed with the appropriate amount of hardener. This was spread over the depressed surface of the repair in the knowledge that there was a fairly sound foundation beneath. Note that the edges of surplus fibreglass are treated as irrelevant at this stage.*

Safety: It is especially important that you wear an efficient particle mask when carrying out this job because as well as particles of solidified polyester filler, there are also particles of glass fibre floating around, and this can be extremely dangerous to health if inhaled. Keep filler, resin and especially hardener off skin and well away from eyes. Read carefully the safety instructions on the packaging.

Always wear gloves – or even a large plastic bag pulled over each hand and tied at the wrist, providing no-cost disposable gloves – when mixing and spreading filler and resin.

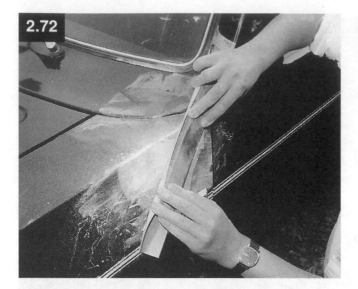

2.72 *Once the filler had been applied and gone hard it had to be levelled out. As an alternative to using a professional sanding block, I used a sheet of P80 grade self-adhesive backed production paper and mounted it on to a piece of wood. Remember to sand first in one direction and then the other, turning and turning about every six to ten strokes, to avoid the very real risk of rippling the surface.*

2.73 *There is no way with a job of this sort that you're going to want to remove the badges and sidestripes, so simply mask them. Take care in doing so because poor masking and overspray can look almost as bad as the rust you have spent so much time cutting out. Fortunately there is not so much power in an aerosol can that overspray is a real problem, so masking off to within a couple of feet of where you are spraying should be adequate. On the other hand, if you are working out of doors the ultra-light spray can carry on the wind. If it's windy, either transfer indoors, find a really sheltered spot, or wait for a calmer day. Here, a coat of primer is being sprayed, working a strip at a time across the repair.*

2.74 *After priming the panel and allowing the paint to harden off thoroughly, rub the edges of the primer and the surrounding area with an abrasive paint polishing compound. This serves two purposes: it gives a very fine feather edge to the edge of the primer, so blending its thickness into that of its surrounds; and it polishes the oxides and traffic film off the surrounding colour, which brings it back to its original colour and increases the chances of a good colour match with the paint you are spraying.*

2.75 *Spray on a light first coat. Don't even try to cover the colours beneath completely, but spray on a coat which is light enough to let them show through. The paint should dry within a couple of minutes, after which the second and later a third coat can be applied. Each coat should be sprayed as a series of horizontal or vertical strips, each half covering the one that went before. If you get runs, you're passing too slowly or you're too close. If you get a dull, dry finish, you're passing too quickly or you're holding the can too far away. Only trial and error can determine what will be exactly right for you and the conditions in which you are working. Remember that a gust of wind will 'bend' the spray and spoil your aim, and that damp air will cause blooming, ie the surface of the paint will go a milky colour. (Blooming can sometimes be polished out if it hasn't gone too deep.)*

2.75

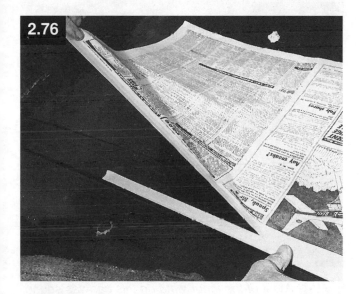

2.76

2.76 *Finally, here's a tip to remember when putting masking paper in place. Put a line of tape down the edge you want to protect, taking care to place it accurately, then put a strip of tape half over the edge of a piece of newspaper before sticking that down to the first piece of masking tape. If you try to position the tape plus paper you will find it too cumbersome to handle easily.*

Safety: When spraying aerosol paint, always wear an efficient face mask purchased from your local paint factor or DIY store. Check on the labelling to ensure that you have purchased the correct type of mask for spraying paint, ie not one that is only suitable for filtering out dust and solid particles.

Heavy metal – Part I: Bolt-on wings

Sometimes, panels have corroded beyond the point of no return. In this case it is better to cut your losses and set about replacing the rusty panels. The easiest to replace are bolt-on panels, although don't be lulled into thinking that there won't be more work than first meets the eye! Even so, it is well within the bounds of possibility for the home enthusiast to set about replacing rusty bolt-on panels. The main problem might be that you will find corrosion in the inner wing panels which are not, of course, bolt-on, but which are almost certainly structural members. In fact, inner wing corrosion is often a cause of MOT roadworthiness test failure. If you do find heavy corrosion when you remove the bolt-on wing, you will not be able to drive the car to a garage to have repair work carried out, because the car will be illegal to drive on the road. You may be able to get round it by temporarily bolting the wing back in place, ensuring that lights work in accordance with the requirements of the law. It will be far, far easier to pop on and off again the second time around! As the following section shows, it's the first time a bolted-on wing is removed that presents the biggest challenge

2.77 *Bolt-on wings are undoubtedly the easiest of body panels to change, and for this reason many manufacturers use them. Their reasoning is quite simple: lower repair costs. For the home repairer, bolt-on wings come easily within the realms of the possible but with one proviso: if the wings have corroded badly enough to require replacement, it is highly likely that the surfaces beneath the wing will*

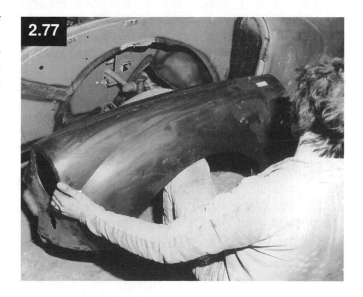

2.77

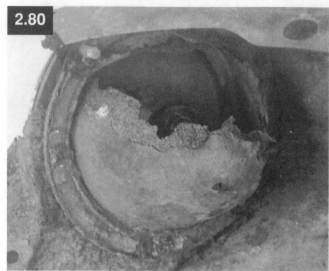

have corroded and require welding. Still, if you live close to a body repairer or you can find someone who will do the work on your premises, even if you can't do it yourself replacing a bolt-on wing will still be straightforward in most cases.

2.78 First step in removing a rotten bolt-on wing when the bolts are underneath is to chisel away the wing. Your instinct is to grovel beneath the wing and try to find the securing bolts, but if it's to be scrapped anyway, why bother? Incidentally, bolts in this position are usually corroded solidly into place.

> Safety: Wear industrial-type leather gloves to protect your hands against jagged edges and wear goggles when chiselling.

2.79 Most of the inner wing on this car was sound, but door pillars are always prone to corrosion because of their exposed position. Typically, the Morris Minor pillar rots out at its base. This one would have to be replaced before the new wing was fitted.

2.80 Behind this old wing, a very badly corroded headlamp bowl shows just how grim things can get! Replacement bowls come in plastic and steel varieties and cheaper ones are usually supplied without their fixtures and fittings, so either be prepared to save all your old clips and screws or to pay a little more when buying.

2.81 Having had to pay the cost of wing corrosion once, it would be the height of folly not to attempt to do something about making the new wings last a little longer. Here the wing flange is being sprayed with an aerosol of rust inhibiting fluid, the

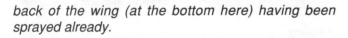
back of the wing (at the bottom here) having been sprayed already.

2.82 As a general rule, the areas most prone to rusting should be given the most thorough treatment. Look out for welded seams which trap moisture, and mud traps such as this one behind the headlamp bowls. Here, and in areas subject to 'machine-gunning' by road grit and water from the tyres, a heavier undersealant has been used. Don't expect underseal or rust inhibitor of any sort to last forever. Be prepared to clean the underside of the car and re-treat at least annually if you want to stand a chance of keeping rust at bay.

2.83 As well as new front wings, new rear wings were also fitted to this car, and they too are of the bolt-on variety. Here a bead of seam sealer is being applied . Another has to go on the wing flange

itself, and the wing beading will be sandwiched between the two, like the filling in a sandwich. Incidentally, do remember to insert and line-up the beading before fitting the bolts; it can be very frustrating to have to take the wing off again because you have forgotten it.

2.84 Before attempting the actual fitting, offer up the wing and see how it looks. Motor factor's wings (ie non-original equipment) can sometimes be a poor fit and might need some modification. Even the manufacturer's wings are not always perfect and might need bolt holes enlarging or moving a little. This is especially true of cars with long production runs where shapes may alter subtly as the factory's tooling wears.

2.85 Don't fit any ancillaries until the wing is in place: the freer the access to those hidden nuts the better! Always clean out and lubricate captive

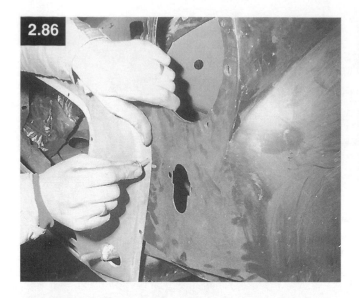

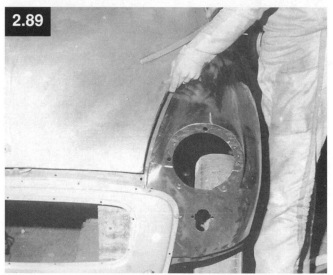

nut threads before fitting the wing – the bolts go in so much more easily that way. Whatever you do, don't tighten up any of the bolts until all are in place, so that there remains room for manoeuvring of the panel right up until the end.

2.86 This area is actually held by bolts that pass through the chrome trim on the Minor. For the purposes of alignment and location a couple of standard bolts are preferable.

2.87 Fitting the wing so that the wing-door gap is consistent is essential, but it is equally important that the door opens and closes without fouling and with sufficient clearance to ensure that the build-up of paint on the panels will not cause rubbing or chipping later on.

2.88 Where there is some degree of door hinge adjustment, the doors themselves can be brought into the game...

2.89 ... while the bonnet itself completes the triangle of adjustments, and compromises between the fit of the various panels and their gaps. At this stage, slightly uneven gaps always look far worse than when the panels have all been painted the same colour. Once the best compromise possible has been achieved, all the bolts can be finally 'nipped' tight and the ancillaries fitted into place.

Heavy metal – Part II: Weld-on wings

Weld-on wings are not all that difficult to replace, although you will obviously need to be able to weld. In practice that is not as difficult as it may at first seem. Many thousands of people have purchased simple welding equipment and either taught themselves to weld or (a far better option) enrolled for a course at their local evening institute, where they have been taught how to do the job and – even more important – how to do it safely.

Safety: Beware sparks from the grinder, and razor-sharp edges when removing the old wing. Wear goggles and thick industrial-type leather gloves. When welding, take all the precautions described in the *Appendix* to this book. Obtain, read and note the safety instructions produced by the manufacturers or sellers of all the equipment you use.

This section shows how to replace a weld-on wing by describing the replacement of a Mini front wing. As you will see, the level of welding skills required is not all that high, but you must ensure that you are able to weld a strong joint by practising first on pieces of scrap steel. It is *most* important that every scrap of rust, paint, grease and other contamination is removed from all of the surfaces to be welded together. Otherwise, the weld will look untidy and, worst of all, will not be sound or strong.

There are several different types of welding that can be used for this sort of work, but when it comes down to it, there are only two that are at all suitable for car bodywork repair:

– Gas welding: It's versatile, expensive to obtain, and takes more practice to develop the necessary skills. It can also be used for braze welding which is easier to carry out and useful where some surface rust may be present, but is not considered to be strong enough for structural repairs. The author has produced, in association with BOC, a teach-yourself video showing how to Gas Weld. See Appendices.

– MIG welding. Sets are available at affordable prices but you *do* need a separate supply of argon-mix gas. This is obtainable in small, disposable canisters, but they are horribly expensive if any more than the minimum amount of work is to be carried out. For instance, you might be able to get away with just using two of them when carrying out the work described here; you might need more! More expensive to start off with but cheaper in

the long run are larger cylinders which are connected to the set with a regulator. They are available from BOC cylinder centres nationwide. MIG is the easiest technique to learn but *demands* the use of clean metal.

2.90 *In the unlikely event that the wing is sound but the headlamp fixing area is corroded, it is sometimes possible to purchase headlamp rings to replace the corroded area. Since other areas are certain to be corroded too, this can only be considered a temporary measure.*

2.91 *One way of removing the front wing from the inner wing panel is to drill out the spot welds (it might be necessary to paint-strip the area first, so that you can actually see the spot welds)...*

2.92

2.95

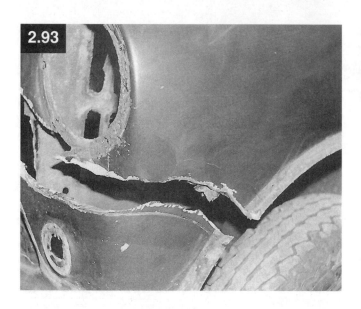

2.93

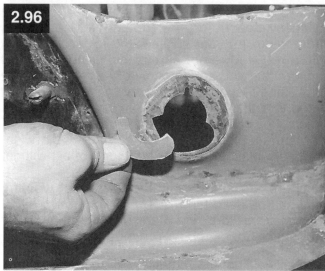

2.96

2.94

2.97

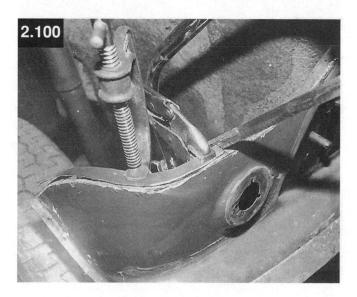

2.92 ... while another is to cut away the wing with a sharp bolster chisel just a little way in from the front panel, the top scuttle panel and the A-panel.

2.93 If you decide to do it this way, make certain that you do not cut into the surrounding panels. Surplus metal can easily be cut or ground away later.

2.94 After removing the wing like this, it is still necessary to drill out the spot welds in order to clean up the seam, but access is now much easier, especially for prizing open any spot welds that still 'hold' even after being drilled.

2.95 A front panel such as this one might be sound enough to save, but it will still require some remedial work. A favourite rust spot is the moisture trap behind the indicator lamp.

2.96 After filing away the rust until sound metal is reached, a suitable repair patch can be accurately cut out and filed to shape – actually easier than it looks! Start by cutting a square of metal, hold it behind the repair, scribe round the opening and cut out to the scribe line. It doesn't matter if there are small gaps because the welding or brazing will sort them out.

2.97 A Sykes-Pickavant welder's clamp is shown here holding the repair in place so that it can be tacked in several places holding it firmly in position.

2.98 Then the repair can be seam welded into place before being sanded smooth with a power sander. Wear goggles!

2.99 This Mini was suffering from corrosion in the front panel flanges too, but these were easily replaced. First a piece of steel was held along the top of the front panel after the old flange had been cleaned off. From beneath, a pencil line was drawn following the shape of the panel. A car strip template was cut out, transferred to steel, and the steel strip – matching the shape of the front panel when viewed from above – was easily bent to the shape of the panel viewed from straight ahead.

2.100 The repair was clamped into place and used as a guide to cut the edge of the flange with a hacksaw. This way is even better than marking out and cutting because it guarantees a perfect fit!

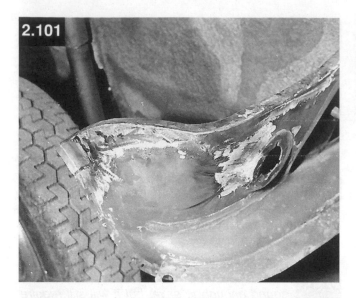

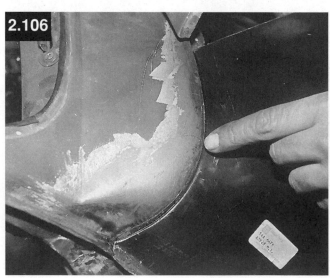

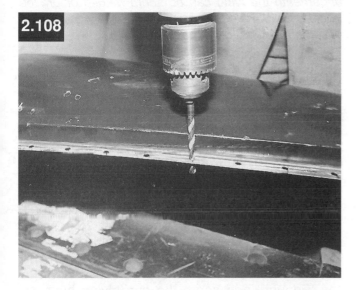

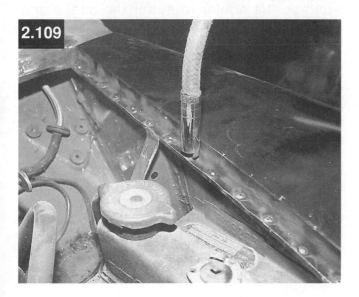

2.101 The new flange was then welded into place with the MIG welder, before the weld was cleaned off with the power sander.

2.102 At the rear corner it was necessary to make a simple but fussy little repair to replace corroded metal. Again, a card template-cum-model of the repair was carefully created first to ensure accuracy.

2.103 The moment of truth for those repairs comes when the wing is offered up. In fact, it would be a foolish worker who failed to offer up the wing to the car after tacking each repair into place to ensure accuracy of fit before permanently welding them.

2.104 The new wing is held in place with a number of clamps, or, if the welding is being done elsewhere, it could even be held in place with self-tapping screws while you take the car to have the work done. Don't be lulled into thinking that they will provide a safe, permanent fixing, however; they won't, and the safety of your car depends on having all the bodyshell panels properly welded into place.

2.105 Before carrying out any final fixing, check that the wing is fitted properly all the way round. (It will take a little pulling and pushing into place if necessary.) Pay special attention to the front panel fit...

2.106 ... and to the scuttle-top fit. You will be able to bend wing flanges carefully with pliers or a suitable hammer and dolly which might help gaps to close.

2.107 The wing will move fairly freely here to line it up accurately with the flange on the front panel. Don't forget also to sit the bonnet in place to check that all is well with levels and gaps.

2.108 When you are satisfied that everything fits nicely, drill a series of small holes along the rain channel at the top of the wing. It may be possible to spot-weld it if the car has been stripped right out giving clearance in the engine bay, but most people will spot-weld using MIG, gas welding or brazing: the holes allow the weld or braze to 'spot' the panels together. Best of all, drill through just the wing flange, not the inner wing flange as well.

2.109 This car was 'spot' welded using the MIG welder with the spot welding nozzle attached.

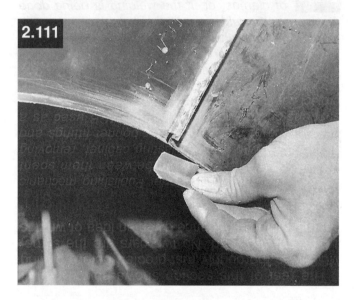

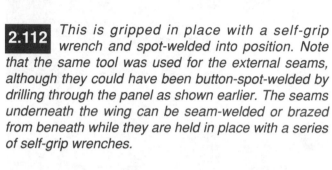

2.110 *The raised 'buttons' of weld were ground flush using an angle grinder fitted with a grinding wheel.*

2.111 *Many people forget the small, simple, angle plate (made out of thin steel) which fits at the base of the wing to-A-panel joint on the Mini and strengthens it by helping to stop flexing and cracking open. Look out for any additional strengtheners on your car and always replace them: they are there for a purpose!*

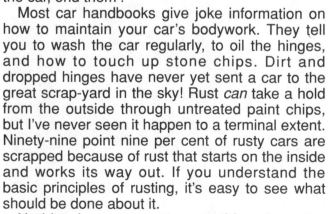

2.112 *This is gripped in place with a self-grip wrench and spot-welded into position. Note that the same tool was used for the external seams, although they could have been button-spot-welded by drilling through the panel as shown earlier. The seams underneath the wing can be seam-welded or brazed from beneath while they are held in place with a series of self-grip wrenches.*

Body maintenance

Unless it has a very low value, mechanical problems rarely finish off a car, and even if a car has become worth very little, second-hand spares can keep it going. On the other hand, once the bodywork and underframe have gone, that's it; the car is finished, because the cost of repairs can be many times the value of the car.

If you really want to keep your car alive, you'll take body maintenance seriously. If your car is rusty and you're not sure whether the rust is terminal, see *Chapter 1 Section 5 Getting through the MOT test*, where I discuss when to say 'Enough' and scrap the car, giving hints on whether "tis nobler to suffer the slings and arrows of outrageous bodywork or, by scrapping the car, end them'!

Most car handbooks give joke information on how to maintain your car's bodywork. They tell you to wash the car regularly, to oil the hinges, and how to touch up stone chips. Dirt and dropped hinges have never yet sent a car to the great scrap-yard in the sky! Rust *can* take a hold from the outside through untreated paint chips, but I've never seen it happen to a terminal extent. Ninety-nine point nine per cent of rusty cars are scrapped because of rust that starts on the inside and works its way out. If you understand the basic principles of rusting, it's easy to see what should be done about it.

Nothing is permanent; everything, from the

moment it is first formed, is in a process of deterioration. You can't stop corrosion but you can slow it down, so that instead of your car rusting away in a few years, it will give you 10, 15 or more. Some cars are fitted with zinc-plated panels and they slow down the rusting process quite dramatically, but even they will eventually turn into little piles of brown dust if left unchecked. Here's what happens and what to do about it:

– Steel starts off as brown-coloured iron ore; it would dearly like to return to something that looks similar!

– Minute electric currents pass between areas of steel panels. This is known as electrolytic action – or rusting to you and me.

– Electrolytic action works best between dissimilar pieces of steel held close together. Separate sections held together with spot welds fit the bill admirably.

– Electrolytic action needs close physical contact, the presence of both air and moisture, and loves a temperature just a little higher than freezing point. Salt helps the process along wonderfully well.

– A perfect rust bath consists of mud from the road thrown up against joints in steel work, such as under wheel arches and in chassis sections, where salt water can soak in to form a damp poultice, which works away when the temperature rises above freezing.

– It also loves to have a film of moisture trapped against the surface of the steel. Underseal (of the old-fashioned, paint-on variety) creates the perfect spot, as it dries out and becomes brittle, trapping water underneath, where it lifts from the steel it is meant to protect.

– Electrolytic action dislikes having water and air excluded, and salt water closed off.

So, the basic principles of rust proofing are extremely simple: shut out air and water and you shut out rust.

On the outside of the bodywork, paint does the job of shutting out air and water, while underneath, paint is also fine – but only for a short while. Beneath the car, there is a constant shot-blasting factory at work. In addition, the salt and mud poultices work their way beneath the

paint in a very short while; that's why manufacturers use underseal – it works for longer. But as I said before, when it goes wrong by drying out, it adds to the problem that it was put there to solve.

When it comes to older cars, where rust will invariably have made a start, the process of rust prevention is simple, but it requires you to be thorough. It also requires you to repeat the treatment on a regular basis. Although it never appears in any workshop or service manuals, if you really want to keep your car alive, you must regard body maintenance as an essential part of servicing. First of all, here's how to keep the car's outer panels in shape:

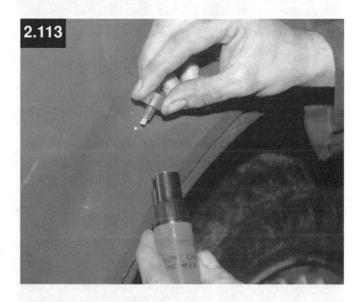

2.113

2.113 *Paintwork will chip just about anywhere it can, not just on the leading edge of the bonnet, though that is obviously a major area. If you can't stop the paint coming off, at least you can stop the rust spreading from the chips by using Corroless Stone Chip Primer. In the top of the can is a handy brush made specifically for dealing with small areas. It unscrews and you can treat the affected areas in seconds.*

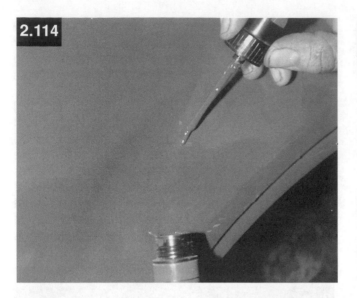

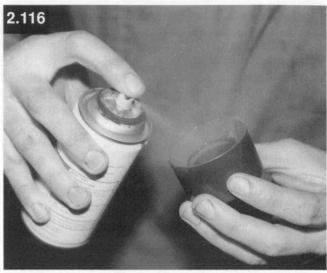

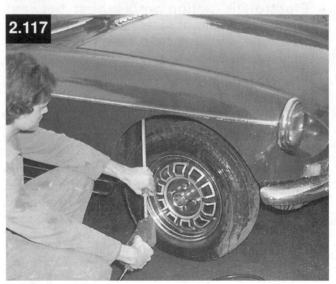

2.114 *A skirmish with an unknown enemy in a car park has left this patch without paint. Application of primer will stop the rust spreading, though it is in your own interest to get some paint on the damaged area as soon as possible, because primer is more porous than finish paint.*

2.115 *Another use is where holes have been drilled in the bodywork. You should always make a point of tidying up any burrs or rough edges from new holes and rust-proofing them, otherwise, rust will get a hold and make the hole considerably larger. Always cover primer paint with touch-up paint applied with a small brush.*

2.116 *Here some finish paint in an aerosol can is being sprayed into the cap, from where it could be brushed on with a fine paint brush. Paint for spraying is too thin for brushing, so leave the cap to stand for a while to let the paint thicken. Alternatively, you can buy touch-up paint in a small tube with an applicator, similar to those shown above.*

Beneath the car, the process is a lot more 'earthy' and it becomes even more essential that you carry it out properly. None of the work is what you might call pleasant, but the first time is the worst. The majority of cars never receive this treatment; the majority of cars rot away before they should. The choice is yours! A word of warning, however. Some manufacturers of rust-proofing products make it sound as though, by using their process, you can effectively rust-proof your car with very little effort. I'm sure it helps them to sell their product but I'm equally sure that it doesn't work that way.

Don't waste your time by rust-proofing your car in winter. The underside will be wet, it will be unpleasant to work on and, worse still, the rust-proofer is unlikely to work properly. However, one essential part of body maintenance should be carried out twice a year, once at the start of winter and once at the end:

2.117 *Remove the mud from beneath your car that traps the salt water and you've removed a potent source of corrosion. You can scrape it off by hand, use a pressure washer such as the one shown here or even take a piece of copper tubing, hammer one end to make a thin, flat nozzle and insert the other end into the end of a hose pipe, holding it in place with a jubilee clip.*

Injecting rust-proofing fluid

– Rust prevention should be regarded as a regular maintenance job, by which means you can extend the life of your car by many years – and that will save you real money!

– You'll have to inject rust-proofing fluid into all the enclosed box sections and chassis sections on your car. In many cases, you'll find holes already in place; in others, you'll be able to take off a cover, a piece or trim or a door lock in order to gain access. But in quite a few cases, you'll need to drill holes to gain an entry.

– Decide on your drill size with reference to the size of the injector nozzle and the size of grommets that you can obtain for blanking the holes off again afterwards. (You only need bother if the hole faces forwards or up, in which case you will want to keep water out, or if it is visible, such as inside door openings.)

– The hand pump injectors that you can buy from DIY shops are often worse than useless. They don't usually make a proper spray, but simply squirt a jet of fluid that does nothing to give the all-over cover required. Make a dummy box section out of a cardboard box – cut it and fold to make it about 4 or 6 in (10 or 15 cm) square – and make a trial run. Open up and see if it has worked. If you haven't obtained full misting of the fluid, you could be making the problem

worse. Remember, rust strikes even harder in those areas that aren't covered!

– Consider investing in a full professional rust-proofing gun. They are expensive but the cost is minute compared with the cost of replacing or repairing your car. You could buy jointly with friends; persuade your car club to buy one and hire it out; attempt to hire from a local body shop; or hire a compressor from a tool hire shop to keep the cost down.

– Consider taking your car to a garage with suitable equipment and having them do the work for you. It may not be quite as thoroughly carried out as if you do the work yourself – unless you are allowed to lend a hand and point out the areas where you would like fluid to be injected – but full, professional injection equipment as shown in the following picture sequences will make the fluid reach much further and deeper than amateur equipment.

– If you carry out the work at home, place newspaper beneath the car to catch the inevitable drips that will flow out of bodywork drain holes.

– Make absolutely certain that you don't clog drain holes by injecting far too much fluid, especially in door bottoms where water could gather and form a veritable indoor(!) pond.

Safety: Before using rust-proofer, read the manufacturer's safety notes. Keep it off the exhaust or any other components where it could ignite. Keep it off and out of brake components – cover them with plastic bags before starting work. Wear an efficient face mask so that you don't inhale vapour. Wear goggles to keep material out of your eyes. Follow the safety notes in the *Appendix* with regard to safe working beneath a car raised off the ground.

2.118 *Waxoyl underbody seal is much better than most underseal. It remains flexible, unlike the conventional type that hardens, becomes brittle and traps moisture beneath it. The aerosol type is easy to apply, but some masking-off may be required – and see the safety note above.*

2.119 *Waxoyl is probably the best known make of rust inhibitor on the UK market and it certainly seems to do the trick! Hand-operated applicators are available but they are very inefficient at injecting fluid in the right way. The applicator shown here pumps up pressure rather like a garden sprayer. It is better but is still not ideal.*

2.120 *Best of all by a long way is the professional rust-proofing gun, such as the SATA shown here. It is quite expensive to buy, but much less expensive than corrosion in your car. You will need a compressor to run it, but you may be able to hire one from your local tool hire shop.*

Note that the following areas on a car should *not* be treated with rust inhibiting fluid: engine; gearbox; back axle; prop-shaft and drive shafts; wheel hubs; brake drums and discs (*most important!*); brake cables; door-mounted speakers. Mask them off with paper or plastic sheet and masking tape to protect from fluid. A plastic bag will be fine for brake drums or discs. Also, if retractable seat belts are housed within box sections, pull them out and hold them fully

have to drill fresh ones, try to do so beneath trim or carpet so that they can't be seen. Otherwise, plug visible holes with rubber blanking grommets available from your accessory shop.

Important footnote: The author has restored a number of vehicles over the years and at one time ran a small restoration business. The 'insides' of quite a number of vehicles have therefore been inspected from time to time. On a number of occasions, rusty vehicles that have been treated with wax rust inhibitors have been given an autopsy and their insides inspected. If fluids such as Waxoyl are sprayed on in cold weather, the rust inhibitor may simply sit on top of the rust instead of soaking into it, and it also seems to fail to creep around spot welded joints where there is dirt or more rust present.

The first priority when treating a car that already has rust present is to use a fluid that will soak right into the rust and creep into every crack and crevice. One way to help rust-inhibiting fluids to do their job is to stand the tin in a bowl of warm water for some time before commencing work so that the fluid becomes thinner. (Don't *ever* do so with pressurized or aerosol containers, only screw-top cans of Waxoyl.) Better still, mix the fluid 50/50 with new engine oil. This thins it down considerably and the oil will creep into all of the places where you need to exclude air and water. Hopefully, it will take some of the rust inhibiting fluid with it; at least it won't leave it sitting on the surface. You can use the cheapest engine oil that you can lay your hands on for this, of course, but don't be tempted to re-use old engine oil as this contains contaminants that can cause more harm than good.

The rest of this section shows how a rebuilt MGB was thoroughly rust-proofed before putting it back on the road. No two cars are the same, but this picture sequence gives an idea of what is involved...

extended before spraying. When you have finished, make sure that you have cleared out all bodywork drain holes to allow trapped water to disperse. Also ensure that door windows are wound fully up to avoid spraying rust inhibitor on to the glass.

2.121 *Another type of rust inhibiting fluid is sold as Corroless and comes in aerosol cans. It is fairly expensive to buy, but it is certainly less expensive than having to buy injection equipment. On the other hand, when it comes to re-treatment or time to treat another car, it will cost you a lot less money to have the proper equipment to hand.*

2.122 *There are many places where fluid can be injected through pre-existing holes but if you*

2.123 *The author and Porter Publishing mechanic Graham Macdonald between them spent many hours with a sand-blasting cabinet, removing every trace of rust from under bonnet fittings and suspension components from an MGB used as a project car in another Haynes book.*

2.124 *All of these components were first of all painted with Würth zinc-rich primer (ring around your local professional paint factors to find a stockist), which is said to have the highest concentration of zinc in any paint primer available. This provides an excellent disincentive for rust to take further hold, especially when the components to be finished in black have been painted in Hammerite Smooth Finish Paint which gives an exceptionally hard and long-lasting finish. It also provides just the right shade of black for those under-bonnet components that should be painted in black. Of course, it's not exactly an option unless you are repainting said component, in which case it's worth bearing in mind.*

2.125 *Before applying rust prevention to the project car, Graham applied Würth seam sealer to*

every single joint where water could find a way in. This involved some time crawling beneath the car and sealing off every access point. All of the enclosed box sections and the bottoms of the doors, as well as the insides of the framing in the bonnet and boot, were injected with conventional Waxoyl rust-proofing fluid – available in a yellowy wax colour or in black – and all of the exposed underbody areas were sprayed with Waxoyl underbody seal.

2.126 *Graham used the spray lance to introduce ordinary Waxoyl into the insides of the crossmember prior to having it fitted. Nicol Transmissions, who rebuilt the car's gearbox and rear axle, had arranged for both the rear axle tubing and the crossmember to be plastic-coated, which gives an exceptionally durable and attractive finish.*

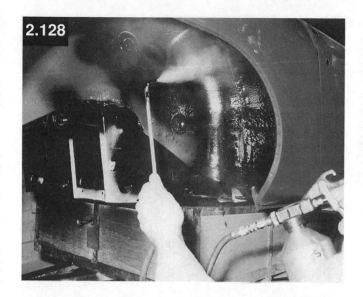

2.127 *The inside of the front valence was also sprayed with Waxoyl prior to fitting it to the body.*

2.128 *Beneath the wheel arches, Waxoyl underbody seal was applied. This never goes completely hard and is almost impervious to damage from stone chips. The sprayed-on appearance is quite attractive. Spend quite some time cleaning off mud, rust and loose paint from areas to be treated. Ignore any claims that it's acceptable to apply preservatives over damp or dirty metal. It's best to clean surfaces with nothing more penetrating than a garden hose. If you use a power washer, leave the car for a week or two in dry, summery weather for the innards to dry out before rust-proofing commences.*

2.129 *The rear of the underbody was sprayed with the same underbody seal...*

2.130 *... and the bottoms of the floor panels sprayed right up to the edge of the sills. Overspray was cleaned off later with plenty of rags and white spirit.*

2.131 *Access to the double-skinned front bulkhead is easily found through various apertures cut beneath the scuttle top.*

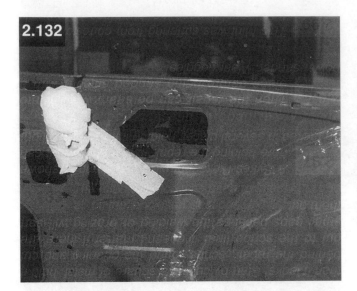

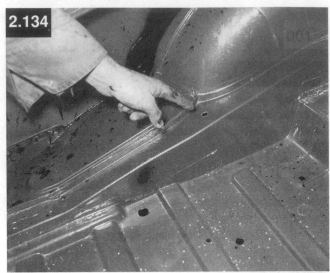

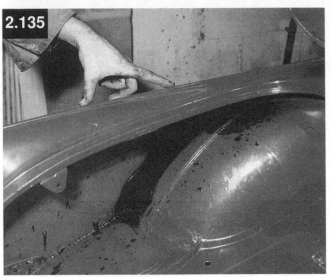

2.132 *Parts of the insides of the rear wings could also be accessed through ready made apertures – but beware! Waxoyl does tend to slide uselessly off shiny metal if you put too much on.*

2.133 *The injector lance was used to inject fluid into all of the enclosed sections. Whilst many of them could be accessed through existing holes, some new holes had to be drilled, such as this one at the end of the toe boards – an easy spot to miss!*

2.134 *All of the chassis rails and crossmembers will have to be injected, of course. Access to the rear rails can only be obtained by drilling a hole at around the mid point inside the boot. This enables the lance to reach full distance in both directions. The*

lance is inserted through the hole and when it reaches the end of the chassis member the trigger is pressed on the gun. As the lance is withdrawn, the inside of the box section is fully coated with Waxoyl which 'creeps' into all the seams.

2.135 *The tops of the wing beadings are prone to corrosion, but if they are sealed from above with paint and covered from beneath with fresh Waxoyl the problem should be deferred almost indefinitely.*

Chapter 3

KEEPING YOUR CAR COMFORTABLE

So, you've made your car reliable, you've made it sound, it looks presentable, and it starts first time every morning. Isn't that enough? Well, when your car won't get you to work, or your neighbours fill it full of old mattresses, mistaking it for a skip, it certainly feels as though this would be enough. But in practice, in the day-to-day business of using your car, all of those things can become taken for granted. At least, that's what you as on old-car owner are *aiming* for, for heaven's sake! When that degree of satisfaction sets in, it's the little things that irritate most. Let me give you an illustration:

If you own a Mini, you become used to the fact that there are a good few mechanical noises going on around you. The gearbox may be noisier than that on most cars, the little wheels can be heard to be in intimate contact with the road, and the whizzer of an engine does just that – it whizzes! For all you know – or care! – the seat belt buckles might rattle a touch, or the spare wheel gives the occasional lurch in the boot, if it's not properly fastened down. But none of that matters; you're too busy Mini-ing to notice. But put minor – or even Mini – rattles into a Bentley or a Mercedes, for instance, and they would stand out like an aural sore thumb! Same sounds; different irritation levels. And it's the same with an older car and its more basic qualities. If you drive a car that looks like something that has 'gone off', and starts only when there's an R in the month, you won't be too worried about a door window that is stiff to turn or a ripped seat cover; you're too grateful to the great god Spark for having permitted your car to start at all! Make your car boringly reliable ('Oh, please!') and that drip of water that lands on your right knee – always the right knee; the one you can't move out of the way – when it rains, the heater that doesn't try hard enough; all these

little things will club together to annoy you. In fact, as we all know, it can be a combination of annoyances that can kill off the high regard in which you may once have held your car. Here's how to keep alive your enthusiasm for your car, without necessarily breaking the piggy bank.

Dealing with sagging seats

The springing inside very many types of car seat depends on rubber for its supportive qualities. Rubber hardens with age, breaks with predictability, and leaves you, the driver, with your bottom getting closer and closer to the floor of the car. It's quite a common problem: so much so that the next person you see with head tilted back, hands clasping top of steering wheel, peering desperately along their nose and over the dashboard top may not, in fact be amazingly short; it's more likely that their car seat has collapsed.

Before setting about repairing the seat's suspension, check that the seat frame itself is sound. If that has collapsed, scrap the seat and buy a replacement from a scrap-yard. If you can't find one of the right colour and you don't want to use seat covers, you could always transfer the manufacturer's trim cover from your old seat to the new one, as outlined later in this chapter.

Some seats have purpose-made seat suspension. There may be a sheet of rubber – a membrane – held at the edges with special clips. You may need to purchase a replacement from your main dealer, if the part is still in production. Alternatively, you might find one in a scrap-yard from a passenger seat – driver's side seats are all likely to be suffering from the same complaint. Many car seats use one of the most traditional of all types of seat supports, a technique that was used by upholsterers in the days before cars

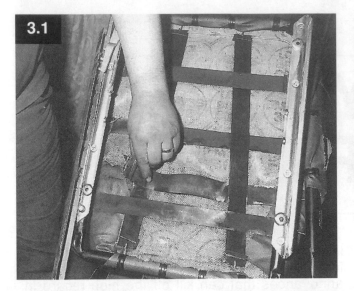

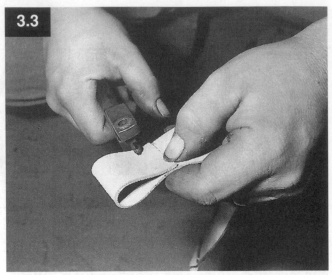

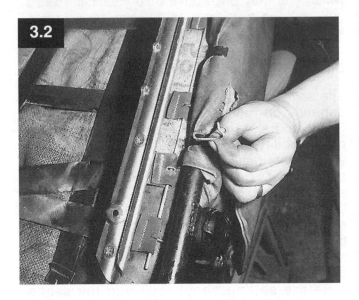

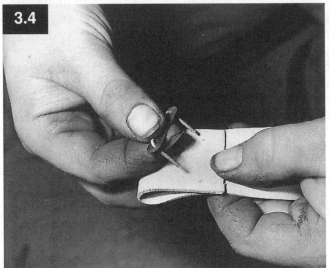

were thought of, namely webbing – albeit Pirelli rubber webbing these days, criss-crossed beneath the seat base and attached at the outer edges of the frame. If all else fails, it might be possible to convert your seat into this type, by getting hold of a set of suitable clips from your local upholsterer – or even that scrap-yard again!

3.1 *This is a typical case of seat webbing disintegration, just at the point where the posterior is most likely to come into contact with the floor beneath! New Pirelli webbing is available from most trim shops.*

3.2 *Each piece of webbing passes round a rod which is in turn hooked on to the edge of the seat frame with a clip such as this one.*

3.3 *We borrowed a fabric hole punch to make the necessary holes in the rubber webbing...*

3.4 *... before passing through new webbing clips that were also available from the trim supplier.*

3.5 *The legs of the clips were passed through a fixing plate and then bent over with a hammer.*

3.6 *A slight modification to the original: instead of cutting a slot, we simply punched another hole just inboard of where the wire would pass through the loop.*

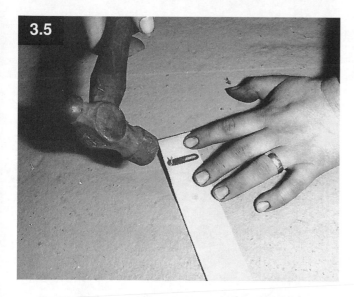

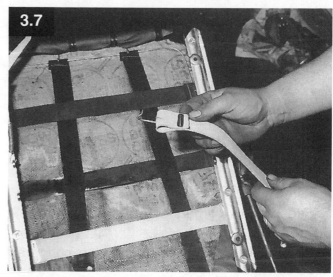

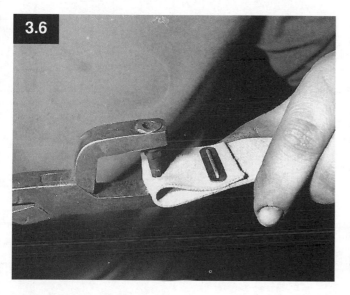

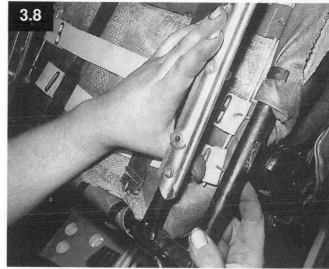

3.7 *Following the same pattern as the original webbing, the new sections were looped under and over as before.*

3.8 *Some care had to be taken in ensuring that the loops came in exactly the right place, but then it was just plain sailing.*

Recycled trim

Do you remember the truly shocking parts of Hitchcock's *Psycho*; the bits that give the back of your neck electric shocks? Here's how you can recreate that delicious fear for free, without incurring the price of a video hire: go to your local main dealer and ask for the price of a complete, replacement seat for your car. Ziiiing! Ziiiing!

'How much?!' You grab the counter, reeling, then walk out thanking goodness it isn't real.

Alternatively if, like me, you prefer a quieter life, you repair the trim you have got or purchase replacements from the scrap-yard. Recycled trim can be among the best bargains in most scrap-yards. There isn't much call for it and most is just thrown away. There are a few basic rules to follow:

- Take a sample of your old trim with you to make sure that you get the right colour.

- Bring back all the small trim parts that go with the bit you have chosen, such as trim finishers, as well as all fixings, especially steel clips that rust out and plastic ones that tend to break.

– If you're not sure how something comes apart, see if you can find another similar one in the yard that is damaged and has no value; practise on that.

– Don't be put off by grime; it almost always cleans off remarkably well.

– **Do** be put off by rips and tears, scuffing or heavy stains from spills of one sort or another, or by worn out materials. If you can't do better, try another scrap-yard, or even make a replacement part yourself.

– Faded black carpets can be resurrected with fabric dye.

– Door seals and driver's side carpets can rarely be salvaged.

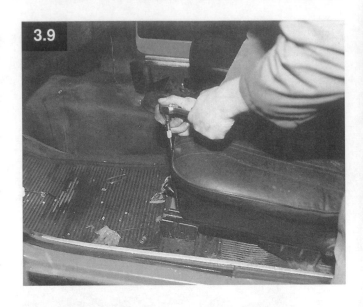

Removing trim

3.9 *Most seats are easy to remove. Slide right back, as far as possible, to give access to front mounting bolts...*

3.10 *... then push the seat right forwards to get at the rear ones. You might have to use a soft-faced mallet on the frame if the runners have gone stiff and if the bolts are well hidden.*

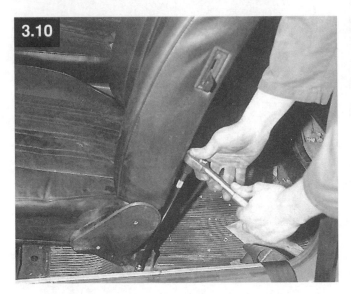

3.11 *If you can't find a usable driver's side seat, check mountings, runners and release mechanisms on a passenger seat. It's just possible that you might be able to do a swap.*

3.12 *Don't think of a seat as a single unit; think of it as the parts it has been made from. You may be able to swap just a backrest, just a slide release mechanism, or even the trim cover. Trim covers come off usually in a simple and logical manner, once you start work on them. Start taking them apart at the bottom, at the back, where on most cars, the fixings for seat backrest cover and seat base may be found. Other seat base covers may simply be held from beneath.*

3.13 *Door trims require you to remove winder and door handles first. Some winder handles are held on with a screw or nut: some have a finisher cap that has to be levered off first.*

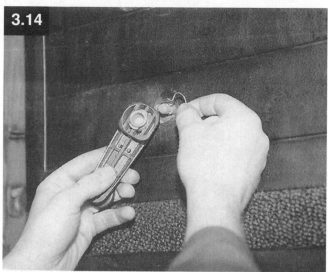

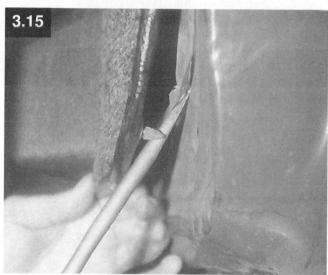

3.14 Others are held on with a concealed spring or a pin through the shank of the handle. Push the trim hard around the handle and such concealed fixings will become visible.

If you can't work out how to remove a concealed fixing just consult your Haynes workshop manual. If you've forgotten to take it with you or the car in question is rare, remember what was said earlier about experimenting on a scrap part elsewhere in the yard – destroying it if necessary, with the agreement of the yard owner – in order to work out how the part is assembled.

3.15 Trim panels are invariably held on with concealed steel spring clips or plastic clips pushed through holes in the door frame. Find them one by one; ease a screwdriver – or better still, the correct trim removal tool – as near as possible to the clip, and lever carefully. Trim board at the bottom of the door can often have become wet and it will then become rather weak.

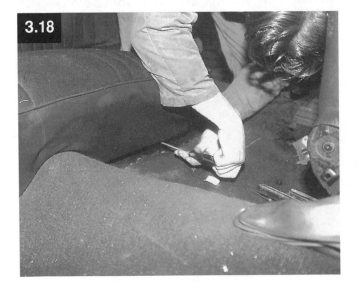

3.16 You may or may not be able to find a better hatchback parcel shelf than the one on your car...

3.17 ... but rear seats are commonly in good condition, good news for those whose cats have used the car as a litter tray. Seat bases are fixed to the hinges on hatchbacks...

3.18 ... and are often only held at the front, with two screws or clips on saloons. After taking them out, lift the front, pull forwards and the base is out.

3.19 Some seat bases – and some backrests too – are held down with clips. This one just pushes down and back on to a hook built in to the floor of the car, beneath the seat base.

3.20 The backrest usually pushes down on to retainers, and lifts up and out. The backrest top also just lifts up and out, but there may be more hooks. Occasionally, there is a tab of metal bent over holding the hook in place.

Rescuing damaged trim

Repair or refurbishment might be all that your car's trim requires. Even split vinyl trim can be rescued, although the repair may never be totally invisible. However, if the alternative is the total replacement of a dashboard assembly, with all the complications that involves, you may prefer to settle for the lesser of two evils!

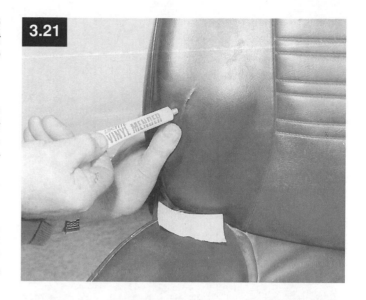

3.21 The common vinyl type of seat covering is also prone to splitting as the material hardens with age, but splits can be repaired. First roughen the edges of the split with fine sand paper, then apply vinyl adhesive, available from motoring and DIY shops.

3.22 Really bad splits need support from behind, especially if they are unsupported by padding. The base of this seat was held on with claws which were bent open with a screwdriver, allowing the cover to be pulled loose.

3.23 A piece of vinyl was slid up behind the tear, using a piece of card as a slipway. It would otherwise have dragged on the padding inside the seat.

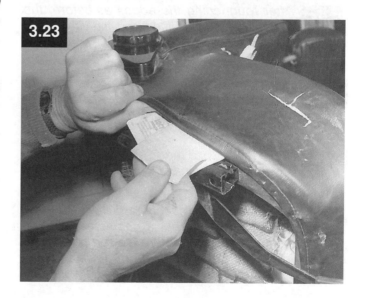

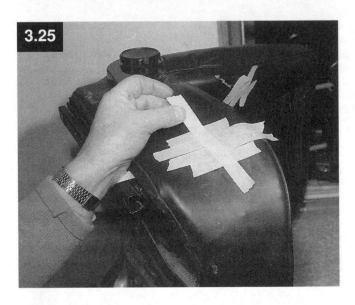

3.24 After roughening the edges as before, the flaps of vinyl were lifted and the vinyl glued down to the vinyl backing piece behind...

3.25 ... and the edges were pulled close together with masking tape, which was left in place until the repair was completely dry.

3.26 While the finished repair was far from invisible, it was vastly preferable to a gaping tear.

3.27 Vinyl seating can become dull without your really noticing it, but a good clean-up can make a dramatic difference. Here the sort of silicone-based vinyl restorer available from any motorist's store has been rubbed on to the right-hand half of the seat. The extra shine it gave did not disappear even when the polish was completely dry – as indeed it was in this picture -and the vinyl actually felt more supple.

3.28 Cloth upholstery can be a little more difficult to clean, if only because it absorbs more dirt. Start by using a blunt table knife to scrape off any clods of chocolate or dirt that might have embedded themselves into the fabric. Then spray on an aerosol upholstery cleaner, taking care not to soak the fabric as this could cause shrinking.

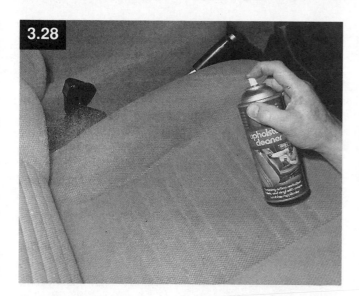

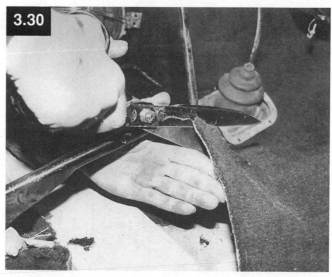

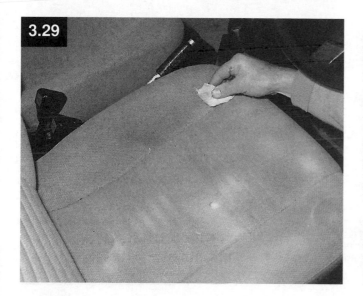

3.29 Then rub off the cleaner with a clean cloth. You can fetch off a surprising amount of dirt in this way, but be prepared to have several goes at a really dirty seat, allowing the cloth to dry out between each cleaning. A wet-and-dry vacuum cleaner works particularly well.

3.30 It seems that with replacement carpets almost more than anything else, you get what you pay for – and no more! Top-quality carpets sold by a main agent or a specialist in your car should fit straight into place, but even only slightly down-market carpets may need a considerable amount of trimming to get them to fit properly.

3.31 Unless carpets are clipped down they will slip about, look untidy, and make a thorough nuisance of themselves. They may also present a safety hazard if they slip beneath your foot pedals whilst you are driving. When you receive your new carpets and, if necessary, after you have trimmed them to shape, start by placing them in the car, feeling for the position of the floor clip and marking it with chalk. Press the clawed ring down on to the top of the carpet...

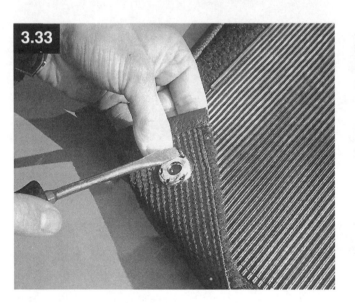

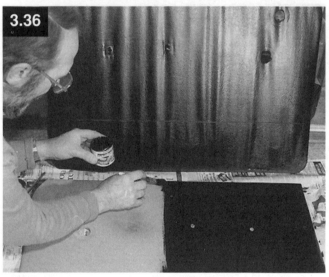

3.32 ... so that the claws protrude through the carpet.

3.33 Place the clip over the claws and fold the claws inwards with a screwdriver.

3.34 It may be that the floor clips are missing for some reason, in which case it is a simple matter to fix new ones in place using self-tapping screws or pop-rivets. If you fit sound-deadening materials beneath the carpets it will be necessary to raise the position of the studs, using pieces of plywood placed beneath the stud and longer screws.

Different makers may use different types of fixings but most should be available from your main agent.

3.35 *It is then simplicity itself to clip the carpets into place, with the added bonus of being able to unclip them in a moment for cleaning.*

3.36 *Plasticized seat covers and door trim materials can be given a new lease of life by painting them with upholstery paint. Fumes from the paint could be dangerous if used in a confined area, by the way, so ventilate the work area thoroughly. The wrinkling you can see in the painted door panel at the rear disappeared after a day or two, presumably as all the solvent dried out. Strangely, this type of paint always seems to have covered properly when it is still wet only to look patchy when dry, so buy enough for two coats. Paint only in straight lines so that the brush marks don't show.*

Make the heater work – and the rear screen heater, too

You're driving home from work in heavy traffic, in the dark and it starts to sleet. You're tired, you're cold, and as fast as you wipe the windows with the back of your hand, they steam up again. Do you (a) set fire to the passenger seat in an effort to warm yourself through and revive your flagging spirits; (b) drive into the nearest lamp post so that you can scrap the car and claim from the insurance money; (c) think happy thoughts; or (d) resolve to fix the heater when you get home? Here's how to score maximum points...

First of all, you must work out why it is that the heater doesn't heat. It is a simple piece of kit and a little logic will soon enable the finger to be placed decisively on the spot. All that happens is that hot water from the engine's cooling system is circulated through a radiator somewhere beneath the dashboard, once the engine has warmed up. Air is blown over the radiator, into the footwells and on to the screen. The air comes from outside the car, either via the car's forward motion which forces air to be blown in or via the action of a fan. There are one or two slight variations on the theme, but in essence that is it! Some cars, particularly those made in Japan, have the option of being able to recirculate the air inside the car once the fan is turned on. Others have speed-adjustable fans. But all are similar, apart from those with air-conditioning and some with the added complication of 'climate control', where a set temperature is maintained inside the car – but you're into specialist country here! So, what's bugging your car's central heating system?

Problem 1 If the blower fan doesn't work, you will know about it because when it's on you should be able to hear it clearly. You should also be able to feel with your hand the air coming out of vents. Check that all wires are in place. Check fuses. If necessary, have an auto electrician (see *Yellow Pages*) run a tester over the viability of the blower unit.

Problem 2 If the air passages are blocked, you will hear the fan trying hard (unless it has burned itself out in a vain effort to push air against an immovable object), but you won't feel any air coming through the vents or footwells, even though the car is driven at open road speeds. You may be able to feel some heat inside or beneath the dash, but, annoyingly, it doesn't get to where it is wanted! Double-check by finding the heater radiator (see your workshop manual) and feel the hoses running through the engine bay, to and from the heater radiator. If they feel hot when the engine is hot but no heat comes through, your heater outlets are blocked.

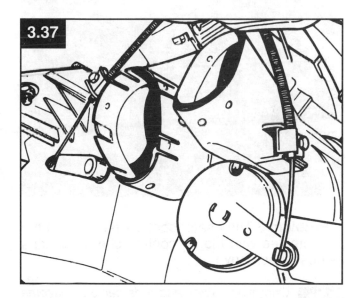

3.37

3.37 *As this diagram shows, in the base of the heater unit are flaps controlled by cables. If the flaps have all become jammed shut, the flow of air from the unit could be nil. You will also have to check the air intake into the heater unit – it could have become blocked with a plastic bag or other debris sucked inside. The air intake chamber will have a drain hole at the base; ensure that it is unblocked so that water can drain out. Incidentally, air-cooled cars have their own specific problems in this area. Check your Haynes manual.*

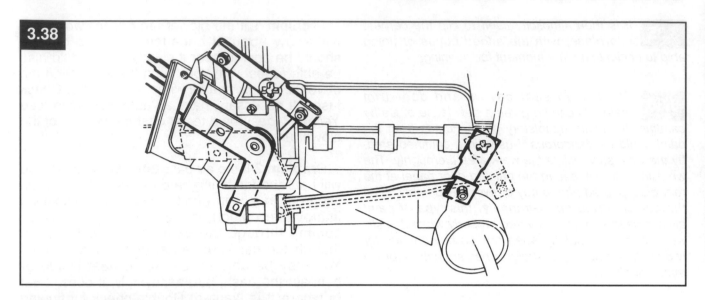

3.38

3.39

Problem 3 The heater controls feel solid. If the problem lies with the air control, check the flaps as described above.

3.38 *Operating cables and rods can also become seized solid with rust, especially if they haven't been used for a time. Disconnect one end, feed releasing fluid into the outer cable, and work the cable until it becomes free. Then dribble lubricating oil inside the outer cable.*

Problem 4 The problem will be similar to Problem 3, except that the hot-cold controls will be seized. You will find plenty of *cold* air blowing into the car, but none of the lovely hot variety! Once again, the cable could be seized, in which

case the remedy will be the same, or it could be a seized tap.

3.39 *Somewhere on or near the engine – or alternatively at the other end of a pipe leading from the engine (try beneath the dashboard) – may be a tap for directing the flow of hot water from the cooling system into the heating system. The tap can seize solid during the summer months, the fittings between cable and tap can come adrift, and the inside of the tap can become solidly filled with residue. You might be able to remove, clean out and/or free the tap; or you might have to look for a scrap-yard or new replacement (the cost should not be too high, but check before buying), and you must replace the gasket between tap and engine block with a new one. Gasket 'goo' simply won't do! Fail to do so and you could be building in a cooling system breakdown in weeks to come, as the coolant slowly dribbles away, leaving you suddenly with a boiling engine when you least expect it.*

Problem 5 The controls all work and the heater tap can be seen to work. You have removed it and found it to be clear. Air comes out of the vents but it's still cold – not even cool; cold!

3.40 *It is possible for the internal walls of heater hoses to collapse to the extent that they close themselves off. They will look externally pretty ratty for certain by the time they get to this stage! The only solution will be to replace them. Don't try pulling the old hose off the unions at its ends. You may damage the connections, especially at the fragile*

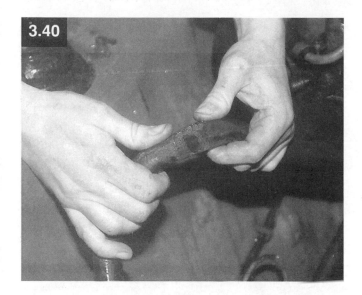

heater radiator beneath the dash, and you will probably damage your temper and your hands as the pipes refuse to let go. After removing the clips, use a redundant hacksaw blade and carefully saw through the rubber hose at an angle, until you can peel it free.

Problem 6 You have the same symptoms as Problem 5, except that air comes through, and after quite a while warms up a little, but not enough for really cold weather.

3.41 *The solution might lie in the steps shown above, but it is quite likely that your car's engine is failing to warm up properly. Use your workshop manual to see how to replace the thermostat, which might be stuck opon, or you may even find that a former owner has taken it out because it failed shut. Once again, be certain to use a brand new gasket when refitting. Incidentally, the thermostat housing can be a swine to remove. Try removing the nuts and soaking the threads in releasing fluid for a couple of days beforehand; try pouring boiling water over it before attempting to remove (with engine cold); be prepared to tap with a soft-faced mallet, push and pull like mad on the hose stub and swear a lot. Don't lever between the housing and cylinder head in case you create leak-inducing damage. In extremis, you may have to hit the housing to destruction in order to remove it. Have a replacement ready before doing so that you don't lose the use of your car.*

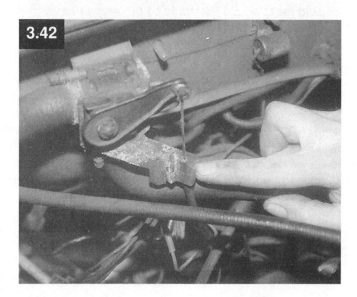

3.42 *Check to see if the heater controls on the tap and on the heater flaps are adjustable. It may be that they have slipped – it certainly has been known – so that 'full on' on your dashboard controls means 'let them have a dribble of heat' in practice. Free off cable adjustments at tap or flap, giving a jolly good squirt of releasing fluid first, and use – usually – a combination of spanner and pliers or self-grip wrench to slacken the adjuster on the cable. Set the control to fully 'on' inside the car; turn the tap or flap manually to the same position and tighten the adjuster.*

3.43 *Problems 5 and 6 could also both be caused by an air block in the heater pipework. Some heater pipes can be extremely difficult to purge of air, some have bleed valves built into them like the one shown here. Follow the instructions in your manual to the very letter – there is often an essential procedure to follow. If you still have problems, try driving the front of the car on to ramps while you follow the instructions*

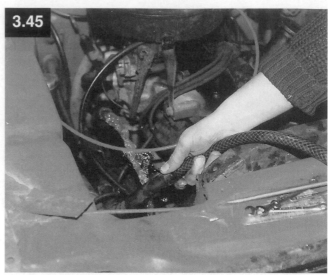

in the manual. Alternatively, try raising the rear of the car in the same way. I have even heard of an Audi specialist raising the front of the car high off the ground on a workshop trolley jack to persuade the air out!

3.44 Over a period of years the heater system can become blocked, especially if a poor-quality anti-freeze has been used. (Good quality anti-freeze contains effective corrosion inhibitors which prevent sludging.) Pour radiator flushing agent into the radiator before you carry out the work described next, so that you loosen any build up of sludge from the system. Ensure that the heater tap is turned full on while the flushing agent works. Disconnect the radiator hoses, insert a garden hose into the bottom hose, plugging it with a rag and 'reverse flush' the

cooling radiator. Do the same to the engine block and the heater system, inserting the garden hose into each bottom hose stub in turn.

3.45 The operation described above is unlikely to help the heating system directly, but you will have ensured that the cooling system stays alive for longer. Carry out the same process on the heater hoses, blasting water from the garden hose into the lower of the two heater hoses. You may be surprised by the amount of muck that comes out! If the heater radiator has been blocked with sediment, you have found the solution to your heater problem! Do make certain that all hoses are in sound condition and that they are connected up properly.

3.46 *If the cooling system radiator or the heater radiator weeps slightly as a result of cleaning them out – not unheard of, by any means – you could carry out a temporary repair with a rad weld type of product. Pour the liquid into the radiator as shown on the instructions and any small leaks will self-seal. The repair may not be permanent and certainly won't work well on larger leaks, so if either of your rads do start to leak, start looking out for a replacement.*

Problem 7 Quite commonly, air will come out of some outlets but not others. If the outlet that isn't working is the one that keeps the driver's side of the screen clear of mist and ice, you could be in for some frustrating, not to say unsafe, journeys.

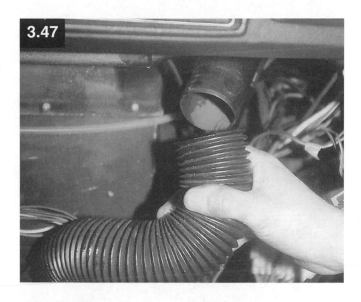

3.47 *If a whole set of vents fails to work, suspect the flaps (see earlier) on the heater unit. In the case of a single vent failing to function, you will usually find that an air hose has simply dropped off the relevant stub. You can usually make a permanent repair just by pushing the offending trunking back on, but if it's too badly damaged, look for a scrap-yard replacement, or see below.*

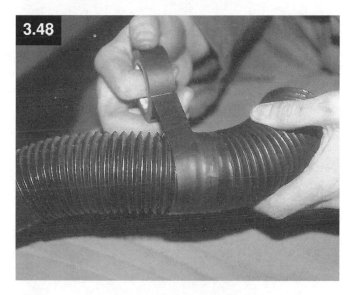

3.48 *Sometimes a vent works but is less powerful than the others. With the blower turned on, feel along the trunking for splits – you'll feel air coming out where it's not wanted. If the trunking has age hardened and split look for a replacement, but small areas of damage can easily be repaired with ordinary plastic electrical insulation tape.*

Problem 8 When the car's rear screen heater fails, it becomes a chore to have to clear the screen of mist and ice, and reversing at journey's end becomes a pain. The screen heater consists of thin wires fixed to the inner surface of the screen. They are easily damaged, so *never* use an ice scraper over the inside of the rear screen, and *always* ensure that luggage in a hatchback is arranged so that it can't scrape across the heater elements, because they break easily.

3.49 *Check whether the supply is good by holding a test lamp across the terminals, and...*

3.50

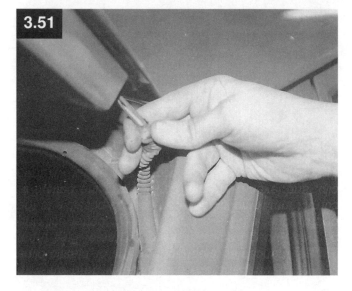

3.51

3.52

3.50 *...check whether the heater elements are continuous by pulling off both of the screen contacts and putting a bulb or circuit tester in the line. Supply a feed from a 12 volt battery to the other contact and to the free end of the circuit tester. If the bulb lights up, the heater element is sound. If not, start searching for the break!*

3.51 *A common place for wire breakage is where wiring passes from the bodywork into the tailgate. Expose the wiring, and pull! If wires are broken off inside, you'll see the plastic insulation stretch.*

3.52 *Fortunately, small breaks in the heater element can be repaired with paint-on repairer which bridges the gap with electrically conductive material. Follow the instructions on the pack. Faults could also lie in the fuse, relay, switch or wiring circuit to the rear of the car, while connectors on the screen can break if not handled with care. If your heated screen is beyond redemption, check for a potential scrap-yard replacement as described above before removing it from the car – you'll need to borrow a battery from the yard owner, of course.*

Screen removal

Removing a screen held in by screen rubbers is easy! Use a sharp craft knife and have water with washing up liquid in it near to hand. (See *Chapter 1, Section 3 Recycled spares – scrap-yard.*) Dip the knife blade in the soapy water and it will slice cleanly through the rubber which cannot be reused, of course. (Try doing this dry and you'll have a mighty struggle!) When you've finished, have an assistant help to lift the screen out and consider taking it to a windscreen specialist for refitting. Purchase new rubbers to avoid messy and damaging water leaks when the replacement is fitted to your car.

> Safety: Wear thick industrial-type gloves when handling glass by its edges.

Keep water out

As rubber dries out, it becomes brittle and loses its elasticity. Since most windscreens are held in place with rubber, older cars are rather prone to letting in the rain through porous screen

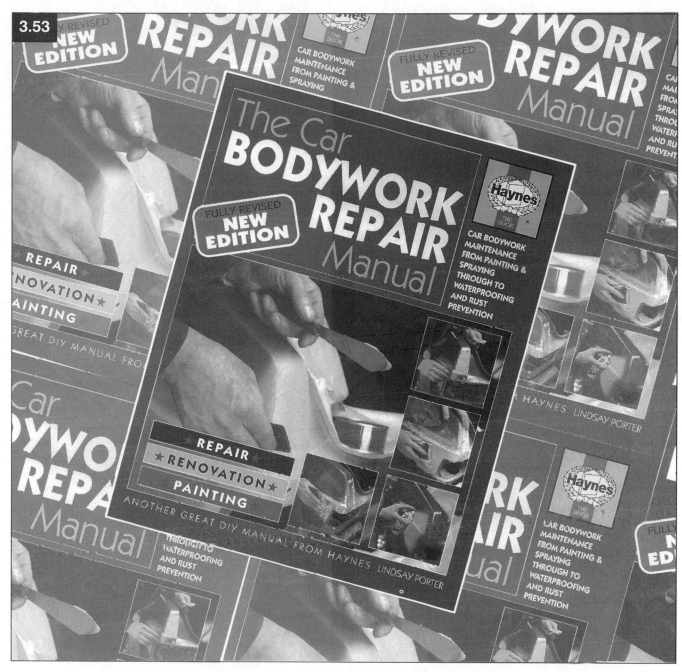

surrounds. There is only one permanent solution and that is to have the screen removed, the surround cleaned up, and a new one fitted. In order to save money, you might consider cutting out the old screen yourself (as described above), and then you can take as long as you like to clean the inevitable rust from the screen surround, prime and paint it, and then arrange for professional windscreen fitters to come and fit the screen, along with a new rubber.

Unfortunately, a leaking screen fairly quickly makes its own, worse problems if left unattended for long. Water gathers and becomes trapped beneath a rubber that fails to seal properly. As a result, the steelwork behind the rubber can rapidly rust away, which means that a leaking screen surround just might need some welded repairs carried out to it.

3.53 *Work of this nature is beyond the scope of this book, but the author has written a book called* The Car Bodywork Repair Manual, *also published by Haynes, which shows how to carry out all the work you will require, and specifically shows how to let in a windscreen frame repair section cut from a sound vehicle in the scrap-yard.*

3.54 *Windscreen sealer makes an excellent temporary repair. Open the rubber, ensure that the insides are perfectly dry, then insert the nozzle. Inject the sealant, and a good, watertight bond will be formed. Concentrate on the top and bottom corners of the screen where most leaks are found.*

With your car warm, dry and comfortable, with visibility crystal clear and a cooling system on top form, driving your car in winter will become routine instead of a major chore.

Chapter 4

KEEPING YOUR CAR

Car-related crime is the commonest form of crime in the UK and the figures make for alarming reading, if you'll excuse the pun. If you include commercial vehicles in the figures, well over four million acts of car related theft take place each year. *Four million!* In one recent year, the rate of increase was a staggering 25 per cent, but at least that year's figures have shocked people into doing something about the problem, and at the time of writing, a small drop in car crime figures has at last been recorded.

4.1 *'CAR CRIME. TOGETHER WE'LL CRACK IT.' At last, the government, insurance companies and car makers have woken up to the problem – and first results are promising.*

Make no mistake about it; the problem has not gone away! The recent drop has come about because at last steps are being taken to stop the criminal. The great majority of thieves are opportunists. If the opportunity presents itself, if the risk is small enough, the criminal will help himself. While you will never be able to guarantee totally that your car or its contents won't be stolen, it does not take a great deal of effort to cut down the risk to a very low level. It's all a bit like the advice I gave earlier in this book about reducing the risk of your car breaking down. Life being what it is, there will always be a possibility that things will go wrong. But if you don't take steps to reduce the risk, you are asking for trouble.

Car crime is not something to be taken lightly. Quite often, personal belongings are snatched from inside a car after one of the windows has been smashed. Just imagine the mess and inconvenience! Just imagine losing your favourite case, coat or purse! And if your car is stolen, your problems could be intense. About one in four cars reported missing each year is never recovered. Many of those that are have been vandalized, sometimes in a disgusting way; many are damaged and need repairs, and you can hardly imagine that they will have been driven with care or respect can you!

It can take a month or more before insurance companies agree to pay out – you can't blame them for waiting to see if the car turns up – but they often take a disgracefully long time to come up with the money, even after they have agreed to do so. If repairs are needed, more delays will be built in, and what will you do for a car in the meantime?

Having painted a black picture of what will happen if your car is stolen or broken into, it comes as something of a relief to find that you can take quite simple steps to reduce dramatically the risk of it happening to you. Helping to keep the criminals away from your car need not be difficult, and there's no need to be fooled into thinking that car security is too expensive for you; it isn't. In fact, some of the best car security comes cheap – or even free!

Security – Stage One

Think of car crime prevention as something you can carry out in layers. The top layer costs little or nothing and cuts out the largest number of potential thieves. The next layer involves a little more time and expense, but takes out most of the rest of the self-help brigade. The bottom layers will make life tough for all but the hardened minority of skilled criminals, and unless you're driving a highly valuable car, you just don't have to worry about them. It is said that the Ford Sierra Cosworth is the most oft-stolen car on British roads. What is little realized is that valuable classic cars are also high on the shopping list for those who don't believe in using checkouts. The attractions of the Cosworth are easy to see: the car is easy to sell to one of the lads at a knockdown price, and they're highly coveted by joy-riders. They are also worth a lot of money when taken apart and sold for spares. Classic cars also come into the latter category, and they have the added virtue of being easy to steal. The moral is that you don't have to worry about the fanatical determination of a Cossie-stealer unless you actually own one, in which case a visit to an alarm specialist should be top of your list. You do have to work at making your car less inviting to drive away than a '60s classic with help-yourself door locks, windows and ignition systems, however.

(The following drawings are courtesy HMSO.)

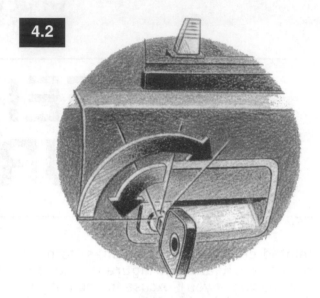

4.2 *Lock your car every time you leave it, otherwise, you might as we put a sign on the roof that says 'Steal me!' Police have observed young try-it-on criminals walk down a line of parked cars, casually pulling on each door handle as they go. If you leave your door open they're as good as driving off down the road or ripping the stereo from the dash.*

4.3 *Put your aerial down every time you park. (It helps to keep the action smooth if you keep it clean – wipe over with a rag after spraying it with releasing fluid.) Replacements are not particularly expensive, but they do cost good money and they can be a darned nuisance to fit. When you replace a vandalized aerial, consider going electric and having it wired into the stereo controls so that it retracts whenever you turn off.*

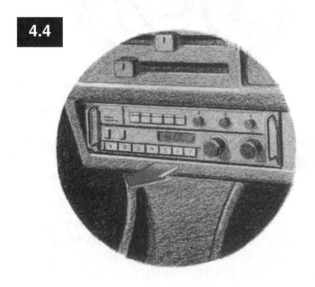

4.4 *When buying a replacement car stereo consider the sort that you can unplug from the dashboard and take with you. Insist on the sort that is security coded – it won't work again if somebody disconnects it from the battery without your 'pin' number being keyed in. If you have an expensive unit fitted, consider a cheap push-on plain covering plate from your accessory shop. It will only cost a couple of pounds and while the philosophical criminal may contemplate the fact that you have fitted the cover for a reason, there will be an element of doubt in his mind. And why should he take unnecessary chances when there will always be another sucker round the corner whose car will make an easier picking?*

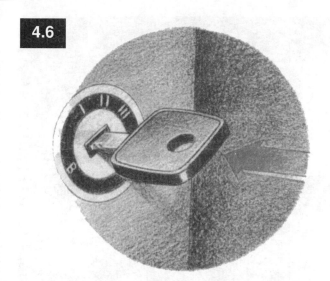

4.5 *In London, the risk of your car receiving attention from the thieves is huge. The first step in fighting the criminals is to watch where you park. If you live in a house with a garage, put the car away every time. Car crime committed outside people's houses while they sit watching the TV inside is not uncommon. Generally though, criminals don't want to risk being seen. When parking in a town, try to park in a prominent place, one that is well lit at night. (If it's daylight and you will be leaving your car until after dark, remember to look for a lamp to park under.)*

4.6 *Always take out your ignition key, even when your car is 'safely' locked in a garage. It's true that most thieves could bypass the ignition system, but it comes back to the fact that if you make life tougher and riskier for the thief, he will be more likely to go elsewhere.*

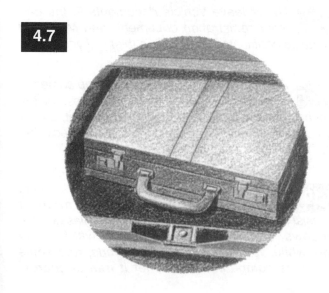

4.7 *Even the most sophisticated alarm in the world won't prevent a determined and cheeky thief from smashing a window (time taken – 2 seconds), reaching in (time taken – 1 second), and grabbing the brief case or handbag that you have left on the seat (time taken – 2 seconds), and in five seconds he will be running off down the road with your alarm bleating uselessly behind him. Always lock valuables in the boot, or, if that is impossible, either take them with you or throw a jacket or blanket casually over the top. Breaking in to a car always presents some risk to a thief and it is not likely that he will take the risk just to rummage through your old travelling rug!*

4.8

4.9

4.10

4.11

4.12

4.8 *Never leave vehicle documents in the car. Your registration document, and MOT and insurance certificates could help a thief sell your car.*

4.9 *A lockable fuel cap isn't just to stop someone pinching the petrol. It also means that the thief has to abandon your car when it runs out, unless he wants the hassle of dismantling the filler neck. Yet another low-cost snag for the thief to trip over.*

4.10 *If your car has any resale value as a 'runner', the cost of having your registration or chassis/VIN number etched on to all the glassware – windows, sunroof and headlamps – will be very worthwhile. It only costs a few pounds, and some insurance companies even offer it free of charge.*

And have you seen the price of replacement headlamp units? Another persuasive reason for the thief to leave your car alone!

4.11 *Probably the cheapest car immobilizer for older, non-electronic ignition cars is the old trick of taking the rotor arm out of the distributor. This is an excellent idea if you have to leave your car in an exposed spot for any length of time – not exactly suitable if you have stopped to fill up with petrol, of course!*

4.12 *Equally cheap – free, in other words – is the trick of swapping over two of your plug leads. If it doesn't prevent the car starting all together, it will make it run like a bag of nails – not exactly what the thief will want for a quick get away!*

Another form of deterrent is the Car Watch Scheme. Most people in Britain have heard of Neighbourhood Watch Schemes, where groups of people in a neighbourhood get together and pledge to keep an eye on each other's property in a general sort of way. Signs are then erected in the area to let Those Who Need To Know that they may be watched, and if any funny business is spotted by any of the participants in the scheme, a car with a blue flashing light will be called immediately. The idea has worked so well over a period of years that police forces have launched the Car Watch Scheme. The idea is very different, but offers an equal level of disincentive to the crook. At the time of writing, police in Britain are, in theory at least, not permitted simply to stop a motorist just because they feel like doing so. The Car Watch Scheme consists of a sticker that the owner puts up in his/her car which says to the police in effect 'You may stop this car any time you like.' In other words, the thief knows that the car is liable to being pulled over and spot checked. He, the thief, then has the option of trying another car – or pulling the sticker off. Ah well... If you still think that the idea is worthwhile, your local cop shop will be able to advise.

The top layer of your defence against theft – the steps mentioned so far – costs nothing or next to nothing. Even the advice on the type of car stereo to buy need only be taken when it is time to change the set. Of course, another way of ensuring that your set does not become stolen – quite apart from doing without one at all (unthinkable to many of us!) – is to use a set that

no one would want to bother stealing. Just think about it: you make a trip down to your local breaker's yard, you buy an old fashioned looking set, lots of chrome, manual pre-set buttons on the radio, and fit that into your dashboard. You've saved a fortune on the cost of buying a set, you've fitted something that no streetwise thief would waste his time on – and you might even start a trend! Just a thought....

Security – Stage Two

The next layer of deterrents can cost a little more or take a little more time and trouble to fit, but places your car in the realms of one that only the most determined thief will waste time upon.

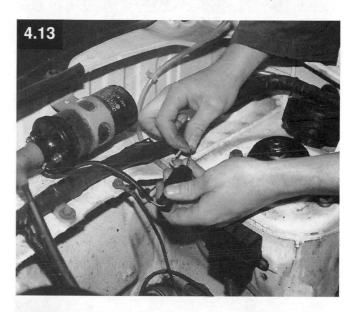

4.13

4.13 *Look in your workshop manual and you will see that a 'positive' wire runs from the coil to the ignition switch. Somewhere, either beneath the bonnet or beneath the dash, or right at one of the ends (at coil or switch), you will be able to break into the wire. It is a simple matter to add a switch, cunningly tucked out of sight where the thief won't see it. Switch it off; the car won't start. Come back to your car, reach beneath dash, switch on and away you go. The total cost will be in the pint of beer category. David Bowler who wrote the Foreword to this book also makes the following point: "You can also run the contact breaker side to earth via a hidden switch. This requires the thief to find and remove a wire, as opposed to a switch in the ignition switch cable which can be bridged by the thief. You may also wish to consider putting an 'open circuit' switch into the starter motor solenoid supply wire as yet another hurdle for our thief."*

4.14

4.17

4.15

4.18

4.16

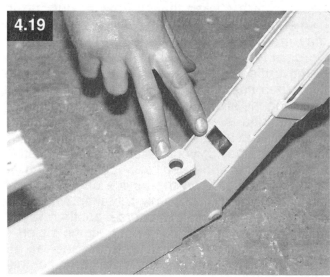

4.19

4.20

4.17 The Metro Stoplock clamps on to and through the steering wheel. This is claimed to be the top-selling steering immobilizer in the UK at the time of writing, and it certainly looks as though it would be pretty well impregnable to the casual thief.

4.18 A wheel clamp can easily be removed – by anyone with a portable angle grinder, an oxy-acetylene cutting set and several minutes to spare! The use of such gear would create so many sparks and such a stir that no thief would be prepared to take the risk for anything less than a Lamborghini. The Rimlok looks smart, and with practice can be fitted and removed by the owner in three seconds. It's brilliantly simple in use.

4.19 The idea is equally suitable for protecting a caravan parked in a driveway or on site. The Rimlok locks itself into position by means of this internal key-released steel bolt.

4.20 The Radio-Cassette Lock has a braided steel cable – resistant to both hacksaw and bolt cutter – which locks around the steering wheel. Removal is not possible without destroying the player.

4.14 If your car has an easily accessible electric fuel pump, the same trick can be carried out by adding a switch to the electric cable supplying current to the pump. You could do so where the wiring to the pump goes into the fuse box. Consult your manual to identify the correct wire.

4.15 The Dis-Car-Nect battery switch wouldn't delay the determined thief for long, but turning the power off at the battery would deter the great majority of joy-riders – exactly the sorts of people who are attracted to older cars. If the car won't start, they won't stop to carry out a methodical check; they'll be off! The Dis-Car-Nect has an optional fused by-pass that powers clocks and radio memories while it is in use, but which blows if anyone tries to start the car.

4.16 Steering wheel clamps such as the Minder are a popular deterrent, although it must be understood that some types can be removed quite simply by the thief who doesn't care if he bends the steering wheel to destruction. In other words, if it hooks on to the wheel, it must be possible for the wheel to be distorted so that it can be hooked off again. That's not to discount this type of clamp: the thief who wrestles with the steering wheel like Tarzan with an alligator is just as prone to drawing attention to himself. And so is a car being driven with a steering wheel with a highly modified shape. And to get the Minder steering wheel lock off, the wheel would have to be dramatically modified; destroyed, even!

This is by no means an exhaustive list of anti-theft devices. For instance, there was at one time a locking valve available to be fitted into the brake hydraulic line. You apply the brakes, turn the key, lock the brakes in the 'on' position, and the car is then rooted to the spot. Security fixtures and fittings come and go all the time as one good idea is superseded by another. Take time to contact the companies whose advertisements you see, look around the motorists' shops, and try the smaller independents as well as the ones belonging to a chain, because in that way you'll see a wider range of products.

Security – Stage Three: Fitting a car alarm

An experiment was recently carried out to see how long a competent thief would take to break into a properly locked car. A whole lot of modern cars were pitched against a poacher-turned-gamekeeper, a car thief who has turned to helping the police crack car crime. From the starting pistol, our friendly thief broke into a locked Vauxhall Nova in three seconds. *Three!* He took the same length of time to get into a properly locked Citroen ZX, and a Mercedes

190E was opened up in ten. He strolled through the whole assembly of 'properly secured' cars in little more time than it took to shout, 'Stop Thief!', and it wouldn't have been surprising if he had stolen a car transporter and driven them all away before a policeman could have found his bicycle clips. This is not to say that there is no point in locking your car; there clearly is because most opportunist thieves won't get as far or as fast as our (fortunately!) friendly expert. But you can't expect the key on your key fob to provide more than minimal protection.

As I said earlier, some of the most effective anti-theft steps are some of the simplest. Indeed, there's nothing to stop you using one or more of these ideas in association with something more sophisticated. You might even say that a back-up would be ideal, because there is not one of the alarms mentioned below that can't be cracked. An illustration of this fact was a sad, sad news story widely reported towards the end of 1992. Get your hankies out now. A police force constructed an 'unstealable' car using state-of-the-art anti-theft devices. Much thought went into this highly commendable attempt to show the public the ultimate in what could be done to deter the thief. The car appeared on television, and guess what happened. Yes, you're right – off it went the very next day, and it has never been seen again. It just goes to show that you can't guarantee that your car won't be stolen. You can make the game not worth the candle for the thief, and in the overwhelming majority of cases, our sorts of cars won't be of interest to the thief if they're fitted with a sensible deterrent or two. In the case of the 'unstealable' car, it was simply that the lawless couldn't resist the challenge, while the law didn't see it coming.

The third stage in keeping your car all to yourself is to fit some sort of alarm system. There are several types available and some have features that make them preferable to others in specific situations. You could have one professionally fitted for you, but another option would be to fit one of the simple-to-install units.

It is quite possible for a car thief to bypass any type of alarm known to man. But the effectiveness of an alarm system lies in its deterrent value. If your car is basically similar to a whole lot of other cars on the road, no thief is going to take the risk of getting caught when he can walk on and find another car that has not been fitted with an alarm. Your alarm will achieve its effect, therefore, only if the thief knows that it's

been fitted! The manufacturers of alarms supply suitable stickers to fix to the windows, and it certainly helps to have a well-known name such as Sparkrite, Philips, Bosch and so on, because otherwise what's to stop you buying stickers and not bothering to fit an alarm at all? It also helps to have a flashing LED light fitted to the car so that the thief is in no doubt that the car is alarmed. If he is still so stupid as to try to break in, you need the proof of the pudding: lots of noise and flashing lights to scare away the intruder. The alarms shown being fitted here are easily affordable by most people and therefore don't include such sophisticated extras as built-in battery packs. You therefore have to take care that the connections to the alarm cannot easily be reached by the thief from underneath the car.

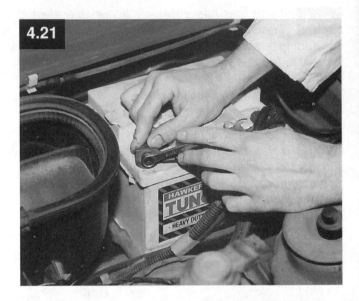

4.21

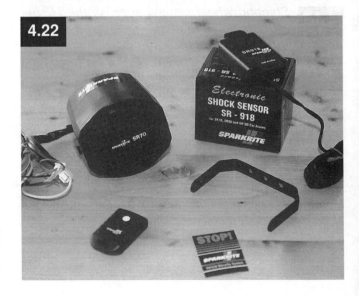

4.22

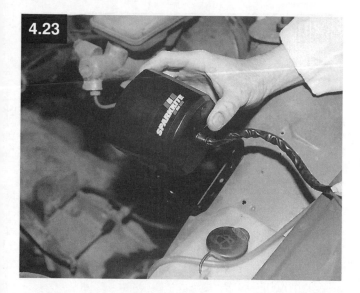

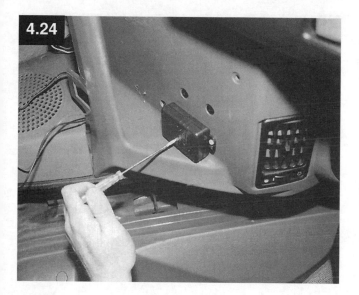

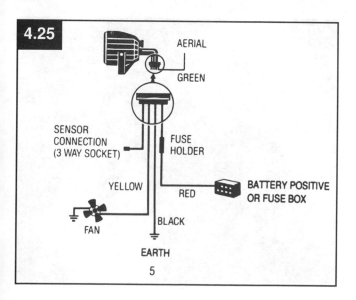

4.21 Safety note: Before starting work on the electrical system disconnect both terminals of the battery.

4.22 The Sparkrite SR70 is one of the most affordable alarm systems on the market. It comes complete with window stickers and one remote control transmitter. Also shown here is the SR918 shock sensor unit, which Sparkrite's senior engineer Neil Smith fitted as an optional extra on this particular installation. This picks up the vibrations if anyone smashes a window and sets off the alarm. The basic unit itself instantly detects any current drop caused by a door being opened (and the interior light coming on), or by anyone turning the ignition key, and in both cases the alarm sounds noisily.

4.23 The alarm unit itself should be situated in the engine compartment close to the front of the vehicle and away from areas of extreme heat, and at least 12 in (30 cm) away from the ignition system. After drilling the bodywork, Neil bolted the bracket to the car using the nuts and bolts provided, and then fitted the alarm unit on to the bracket.

4.24 The shock sensor unit has to be placed on a hard surface – a soft-mounted surface would absorb the vibrations that it needs to pick up – and the wires are led through the bulkhead using an existing wiring grommet, and fitted to the main alarm unit using the plugs and sockets fitted by the manufacturers to the respective components. Couldn't be easier!

4.25 The SR70 only has four wire connections coming from it. One is fitted with a socket into which you can plug the optional extras available with the SR70; two more go respectively to the feed wire and the earth, while the fourth, the yellow cable, is for fitting to the fan on those vehicles where the electric fan can come on after you've turned the engine off. If you didn't use this connection on those vehicles, the cooling fan turning itself on would of course trigger the alarm. (Courtesy Sparkrite)

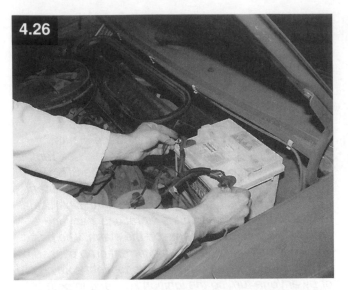

4.26

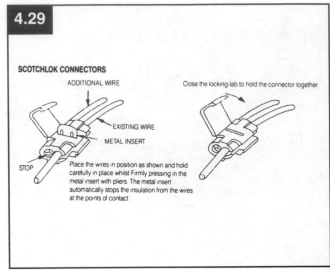

4.29

SCOTCHLOK CONNECTORS

ADDITIONAL WIRE

Close the locking-tab to hold the connector together.

EXISTING WIRE

METAL INSERT

STOP

Place the wires in position as shown and hold carefully in place whilst firmly pressing in the metal insert with pliers. The metal insert automatically stops the insulation from the wires at the points of contact.

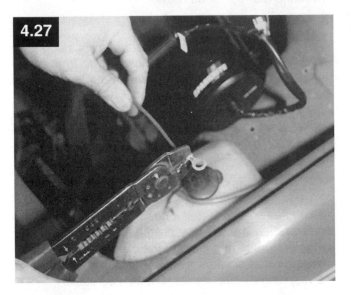

4.27

4.30

4.28

4.31

4.32

4.26 Neil holds the red and black terminals on to the positive and negative terminals on the battery (battery connections re-made), asks someone else to arm the alarm by pressing the remote sensor and then after allowing 30 seconds for the alarm to set itself, one of the car doors is opened. This is just to check that the alarm is working correctly. He then carries out a further test by re-arming the alarm and then banging the car doors outer panel with the flat of the hand just to check that the shock sensor is working and not too sensitive. The sensitivity can be adjusted by turning a screw mounted on the unit.

4.27 On this Ford Escort, the alarm was found to work perfectly when connected directly to the battery rather than through the fusebox, and so Neil fitted crimped-on terminals which allowed the wires to be bolted on to the battery terminals. You could easily purchase the right type of terminals from your local accessory shop and crimp them in place with a pair of pliers. If the alarm had not worked satisfactorily when connected to the battery, it would have been necessary to connect the positive wire to the fuse box, following the instructions supplied with the SR70 kit.

4.28 The Sparkrite SR100 is a slightly more advanced unit, and should only be fitted by those who feel they have a basic competence in identifying the correct wires from a wiring diagram in the workshop manual, and in making simple wiring connections. Otherwise, it could be quickly and inexpensively fitted by an auto-electrician. Top right of this picture is the SR915 ultra-sonic sensor unit which is a plug-in optional. The SR100 comes with two remote control transmitters and a facility for automatic

arming. It can easily be set so that the alarm automatically comes into operation 30 seconds after closing the last door on the car. It also has a built-in impact sensor and it immobilizes the starter motor circuit when the alarm is sounding. As the alarm sets it not only gives the 'chirp' sound of the SR70, but it also flashes the indicators. It is also possible to wire the SR100 into a central locking system, so that the same remote sensor operates both the alarm and the central locking at the same time.

4.29 Sparkrite supply sufficient Scotchlok connectors to enable you to wire in to your existing wiring circuit without the need for any wire stripping. It is essential that you ensure that all such wiring connections are carried out inside the passenger compartment of the car and away from any damp, which could cause corrosion to be set up in the connections. (Courtesy Sparkrite)

4.30 The alarm unit itself is fitted inside the engine compartment, following the same guide lines as for the SR70. The sensitivity control for the shock sensor is built into the alarm unit and is tweaked with a screwdriver, as shown. You are also provided with a key which enables you to turn off the unit via a connector on the back.

4.31 Neil mounted the LED flashing light near the ignition key, but you can fit it anywhere that would be easily visible to the would-be thief. If you purchase one of the more simple units, such as the SR70, you can also buy a separate flashing LED to operate in conjunction with the alarm supplied under the Sparkrite number SR123. It is easily connected into the ignition circuit.

4.32 The movement detectors are clipped behind the door trim and the wire run down the back of the door trim. They couldn't be easier to fit...

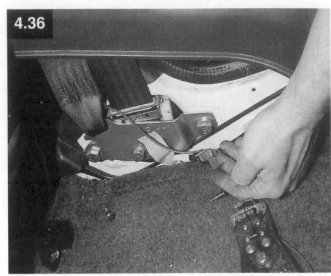

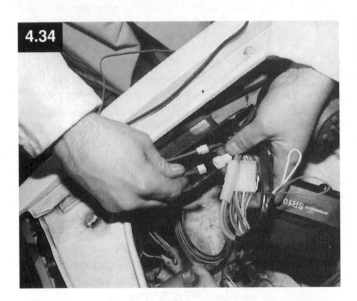

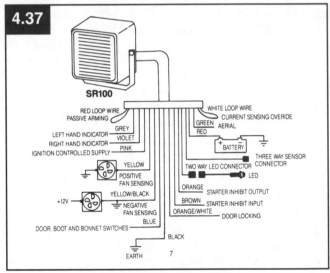

SR100

RED LOOP WIRE
PASSIVE ARMING   GREY

LEFT HAND INDICATOR   VIOLET
RIGHT HAND INDICATOR   PINK
IGNITION CONTROLLED SUPPLY

                                        YELLOW
                                        POSITIVE
                                        FAN SENSING
                                        YELLOW/BLACK
+12V   NEGATIVE
                                        FAN SENSING
                                        BLUE
DOOR, BOOT AND BONNET SWITCHES

                                        BLACK
                     EARTH   7

WHITE LOOP WIRE
CURRENT SENSING OVERIDE
GREEN   AERIAL
RED
        BATTERY
                        THREE WAY SENSOR
TWO WAY LED CONNECTOR   CONNECTOR
                LED
ORANGE   STARTER INHIBIT OUTPUT
BROWN   STARTER INHIBIT INPUT
ORANGE/WHITE   DOOR LOCKING

4.33 *... and the connection is simply plugged in to the 'black box' which you will later mount under the dashboard. Here Neil adjusts the sensitivity control so that it picks up any potential movement inside the car, without being triggered by air coming through any vents that you may inadvertently have left open.*

4.34 *The majority of the connections on the SR100 and its accessories are fed into the wiring harness through simple plugs and sockets.*

4.35 *Neil is shown here snipping through the wire that connects the unit to the cooling fan, in the case of those cars where the fan can run on after the ignition is switched off. If it's not wanted, it should be cut and insulated. The two loops of wire shown by Neil's left thumb are also for cutting or keeping as required. If you cut the red loop, passive alarming works, ie 15 seconds after shutting the car's door the alarm is automatically set. If you cut the white loop, the current sensing facility is done away with. Neil left both loops in place...*

4.36 *... but still connected the alarm into each of the door and the tailgate interior light switch wires. That way, the belt and braces approach of current sensing and wire connections was followed.*

4.37 *The SR100 certainly has a lot more connections than the SR70 but everything is clearly described in the instructions supplied with the kit. (Courtesy Sparkrite)*

4.38 *Finally Neil tries out the alarm unit, checking that everything works properly. Sparkrite can supply extra switches for tailgates, rear doors or bonnet, ready to be wired in to the main unit.*

Personal safety

An excellent feature on both of these Sparkrite units is the remote control panic feature. If you're followed back to your car by someone who seems to be threatening, you can point the sensor at the car, and by holding it down for three seconds the alarm will sound, drawing great attention to your plight and almost certainly frightening away the potential attacker. This is an excellent feature for people who have to go back to their cars in unsafe car parks late at night.

Chapter 5

BUYING A CAR WORTH KEEPING ALIVE

Buying a second-hand car is fraught with dangers. Get it wrong, and you could waste a lot of hard-earned cash. Here's how to get it right!

There are several sources of second-hand cars, but only one ideal way of buying one: with knowledge, energy and time. You, the reader, must supply the time and energy; the knowledge comes next!

First of all, you must identify for yourself which type of car is ideal for you. It's not so much a matter of whether you want a sports car or an estate. Only you can make that kind of decision, and it would be incredibly patronizing of this author to tell you what only you can find out for yourself. But there is one key phrase that you must remember time and again when looking for your ideal car: *don't let emotion make your choice*!

It very often happens that people start off by wanting one type of car, but then fall for another and buy it on a whim. Do remember that you're not talking pop-up toasters here; you're planning to buy what for most people is their second most expensive item, after housing. Write a list of your needs and carry it with you when you go car hunting. If you encounter something unsuitable but tempting, the modern day equivalent of a mermaid trying to lure you on to the rocks, take a look at your list... Cars are such seductive things, and emotion plays such a large part in their choice that otherwise you could – you almost certainly will:

– Buy the wrong type of car, in spite of what you intended.

– Buy because a car looks glossy and shiny instead of something in the right condition, and that you really need.

– Buy because you feel you can trust the person selling it.

– Live to regret your purchase!

Before venturing out into the used car market, you must ensure that you are mentally prepared. The next few paragraphs might seem a bit negative – they *are* a bit negative! – but they reflect reality. The good, positive stuff comes later.

Buying a used car is a bit like entering the world of a computer game. You will be encouraged to think that bad condition is good, that black is white, and that you should do what the majority of other buyers do. Wrong, wrong and wrong again! *This* is what you need to do:

Understand the rules of the game

Buying a used car is a game where, quite often, only one side understands the rules. Car dealers, whether on a back street site or in a glossy showroom, usually believe that customers ('punters' they call us) are there to be misled. Worse still, many people posing as private sellers are in fact back-street dealers, and can be quite difficult to spot – until you know the tell-tale signs, when they stand out like a bare bum on a beach.

Understand for yourself that when it comes to selling cars money and fear stand in the way of truth. Private sellers are often quite afraid of not receiving the money they need; sales staff who are paid mainly on commission are afraid of not earning a high enough salary.

Rule Number 1. is to believe *nothing* you are told. Rule Number 2 is to find out everything you need for yourself. Remember that you don't need to know a thing about cars in order to protect yourself. Follow the check points shown later in this chapter, or use a specialist to do it for you, and all should be well. Mind you, there can be no guarantees that you will *never* be duped! Things can always go wrong – this is life you're living in, after all! – but you can cut the risk of being ripped off.

Buying from a dealer

I said a while ago that sales staff can't be trusted. (They might make wonderful husbands, wives, friends and neighbours, but remember that the car-selling game is separate from the rest of life.) But salesmen and women don't come wearing the devil's horns; they're not that stupid! They smile, they are polite (at first!), they give you coffee, and they might even suggest that a particular car is not ideal for you – but only, of course, to show what honest, decent folk they are. But then they'll say, 'This car may be *exactly* what you are looking for. Don't you think?' (They love to get you to agree with them. Most people hate to argue, and once you've agreed with the salesperson you are done for!)

The solution, for most people, is to avoid sales staff as much as possible. When you are looking at a car, ask them to go away and leave you to look at it by yourself. Remember, it doesn't matter what the sales person may think of you; that is what they may play on. Assess the car, ask the factual questions you may need to know about, establish the price (see *Making an offer*), and keep it at that. If the seller won't tell you the price ('We need to see your car first'), won't tell you (or say they can't tell you) about former owners, warranty small print or any other facts, remember that you must do one thing only: *turn*

around -walk away, even though the sales person may try to keep the conversation going. (They are taught techniques for talking you round, but if you're walking in the opposite direction you are immune.) Remember that cars are made in their millions. It is *always* a buyer's market – they've still got the car; you've still got the money! And always ignore lies such as 'This is the best example I've seen in a long time/Three other people are interested/A member of my family wants to buy it if I don't sell it today' and so on.

The author once bought a three-year-old Jaguar – genuine low mileage, excellent condition, the right price (after a little negotiating). The salesman said, 'This is one of the few cars that I could recommend to one of my neighbours, if I was asked.' He also said, 'Our extended warranty is the best you can buy – which is why we sell it.' The car was found to have splits in three of its tyres – not pointed out by the garage – and the warranty failed to cover a faulty differential oil seal when it broke down three months later. The dealer was a main dealer (although Jaguar have now dropped them), and the warranty was provided by the most reputable of breakdown organizations. As I said before, you must *never* believe what you are told. Always check for yourself, and always read the small print, best of all by taking it away with you before signing on the dotted line, however embarrassing it may seem at the time. Most sales staff hate you to go away without making a decision (they are taught to 'close the deal', as if they are hunters and you the quarry). But remember, you don't have to care what they think.

Footnote: Later – just after writing the first draft of this book, the situation regarding my Jaguar was found to be even worse! The car was found to have been fitted with a new bodyshell but not given a chassis number. I had trusted a main dealer not to sell such a car – big mistake! *Always* have an AA or RAC inspection carried out.

Finding a main dealer bargain

My Jaguar was a bargain and is still a beautiful and well-engineered car, in spite of the salesman's elasticated truth bands. And in spite of the tricks I missed, you can find a bargain at a main dealership. Remembering what I said before about changing the odds in your favour, you will also stand a better chance of finding a 'genuine' car at a main dealers, because they know what to look for and are unlikely to have bought in a thoroughly poor car to start off with. When main dealers take in cars that they don't know much about or which might be disreputable in any way, they ensure that they have paid very little for them and then they sell them off to one of the string of down-market traders who feed off them, or the car goes to auction. However, this means that you will find it more difficult to find a bargain in the main dealer's showroom, unless circumstances are right for you.

Sometimes there is a glut of the sort of cars you are looking for, and even the main dealer will be keen to shift stock at a lower profit margin. For newish cars, look out for the months following peak times for selling new cars, when dealers will have taken more trade-ins than they know what to do with. With older cars, try waiting until the weeks before Christmas: the quietest time of year in the motor trade. However, most main dealers don't have too much to do with older cars – and you might be able to use that to advantage, even though you might want to buy a car up to, say, six or eight years old. If you know exactly the years and model types that you would be prepared to consider, try ringing round all the main dealers within travelling distance and ask them to let you know if the right car comes in. It's a bit of a long shot, but you just might then come across one of those one-owner, lower mileage cars that a proud owner is trading in after several years of service. But set yourself – and the sales person – a mileage and price limit, and make it clear (to yourself, as well!) that you won't accept mutton dressed up as lamb.

You'll want to check over the car with a fine toothcomb before buying it, no matter how expensive the sales person's suit, so use the checklist shown later in this chapter. And remember, above all, that no matter how prestigious the car-maker's name, the main dealership is entirely separately owned. You might be able to trust the manufacturers but it's safe and wise to assume that you can't trust car sales staff. There are certainly exceptions to this rule and there are no doubt some highly reputable people in the motor trade. But it's to your advantage to assume the worst.

One of the principal reasons usually given for buying from a main dealer is that you will receive a warranty. They will invariably fix faults discovered within the first few days, but then you're usually in the hands of the warranty purchased, either by the dealer or by yourself, through a third party – really a form of insurance. In fact, you can take these out yourself usually at a lower cost than buying one through a dealer.

General dealers

Here the advice is even simpler: steer clear! There simply must be honest, reliable, decent general car dealers, but it's not your job to go looking for one. Many general dealers seem to know little about cars; only about what *sells* cars. They know how to make cars shine, how to stick a label over a milometer which says 'We do not guarantee that this mileage is correct' (while knowing that you will still be impressed if it is low), and how to reassure the 'punters' superficially. They're often also pretty good at deflecting complaints and at selling expensive hire purchase deals. As you can see, I love 'em! I have never bought a car from a general dealer – although I have looked, sometimes in horror, at many – and I don't believe that I ever will.

Many general motor traders are among the people to whom main dealers sell the cars they don't want ('dogs', they call them). If you want to reduce by a large margin the risk of buying a 'dog' or even a 'pup', go elsewhere.

Making an offer

No car dealer will accept an absurdly low figure for a car, so there's little point in trying. Moreover, if you're trading in your car whilst buying another, you'll be in the weakest position of all. You'll be in a position to strike the best possible deal only if you sell your car privately. Remember that it's usually difficult if not impossible to sell your car for the book value shown in price guide magazines. Do your sums by calculating the very worst you might be able to sell your car for, find out what a dealer will offer as a trade-in, then try making an outright purchase offer for the car you want. (But *still* compare it with the asking price of cars sold privately.)

Do remember the golden rule when making an offer to a motor trader: your first offer should be rejected by the dealer. If it's not, you've offered too much! Normally, the dealer will say, in effect, politely or otherwise, 'You must be joking.' Build this into your plans. Offer to leave your telephone number, so that the dealer can call you if he or she can 'do anything' on the price. The minute they call you (probably with an offer you don't want to accept without further haggling), you've turned the tables; you're the hunter and they're the quarry because now it's out in the open, now they've admitted that they need you to buy their car. Go for it! But remember that you won't ever get away with daylight robbery. Even motor traders need to eat!

When you make an offer to a private seller, results are less predictable. Owners *might* be prepared to accept a realistic offer (and again, there's little point in offering a crazily low figure), but some can be stubborn. Owners who are desperate for the cash and anxious to hold out for the original asking price have been known to ask a high price for a car and to turn down sensible offers for months on end. You can't always wait but remember the old, true adage about there always being another car on offer, somewhere else...

Private sellers

Bigger bargains – better choice, if you live near a city – bigger risks: that sums up buying privately. However, if you really want to buy a bargain and you have enough stamina to do the job properly, this is one way of buying the right car at the right price. There are two main reasons for this. Firstly, you are not having to pay the profit that pays the overheads, such as wages, premises and so on. And secondly, the car will appear to be worth less because the private seller is rarely able to clean, valet and otherwise prepare the car to make it look better than it really is. This latter is very much to your advantage if you are looking for quality rather than simply appearance. Not only will you be able to see the car in its true light and be less likely to be blinded by a shine, you are also saving the cost of something that is very transitory. After all, the gleaming interior and engine bay won't look like that for long, if you are like most owners!

Of course, there may be snags. A main dealer should have checked the car over and will invariable put right any faults found within the first few days after selling the car. With a private seller you're on your own, and you may have to spend your own money on putting right unexpected faults found soon after purchase. But there are ways around this, such as having an independent examination of the car by the RAC or AA prior to purchase, or by taking out a warranty of your own. Warranties such as these only apply to cars with relatively low mileage and with a full *dealer-supplied* service record, so they

won't apply to cars at the most affordable end of the budget range. However, get this right and you won't need to worry too much about it! Later in this chapter, I will describe how to go about buying privately with more confidence.

Where to look

Try local newspapers, *Auto Trader* newspapers, *Exchange & Mart*, or one of the specialist magazines if you want something special. For instance, *Practical Classics, Your Classic, Popular Classics, Classic Cars, Classic and Sportscar* and a couple of weekly classic car magazines carry large numbers of advertisements for classic cars. Some older, cheaper cars are sometimes regarded as 'classics' while only being 10 or 12 years old. If they are sound, low mileage and well-maintained, a car considered by its owner as a classic could make a good buy. However, you must make sure that spares are readily available (some are excellent; some very poor – browse through the classic car magazines' ad. pages to see what is what), and you will have to be prepared to put up without some modern cars mod. cons.

Spot the rogue trader

One of the biggest dangers with buying privately is that you might encounter a real cheat: a trader masquerading as a private seller. Such people often 'do up' cars in their spare time, buying wherever they can find a car on the cheap and expending the minimum amount of money and the maximum amount of silicone polish. Cars offered in this way are likely to be among the worst on offer, they may have had their mileometers tampered with, and deep-seated faults may have been cleverly concealed. It is most important to try to avoid such 'dealers' and their cars. Here's how:

1 Take note of the way traders often word their advertisements. Private sellers don't usually use the same form of words, although of course some might – but it's a clue, all the same. Key phrases include 'a very clean car', 'very straight', 'a beautiful motorcar' and other similar, glib phrases.

2 When you telephone in response to an advertisement, *always* say, 'I'm telephoning about the car.' If the person on the other end takes cars in for repair or deals in cars, he/she will have to ask, 'Which car?', at which point

put the phone down or say that you are not interested in buying from a trader before the spiel starts. The car you are ringing about will invariably be one bought for the missus but it's too fast for her, or some such!

3 If you get past the telephone stage, take careful note of the attitude of the seller. Private sellers are almost always a touch anxious and keen to present the car in the best light. This is only natural, but if you were a part-time 'black economy' dealer, it would also be natural to be a little blasé, even bored by the whole thing.

4 Insist on looking at the Registration Document. This will tell you if the person who owns the car has owned it for long. Some part-timers do register the car in their own name, especially if it has been severely crash-damaged and is being repaired (if that's not too strong a word) part-time. An engineer's report will flush these out, however.

5 Are there lots of cars around, all of a similar type? Quite a few of us own more cars than common sense would suggest. However, enthusiasts often have a range of cars around them, whilst home-based 'private dealers' will tend only to sell cars that they 'move' easily. So, if you see three medium-sized Fords, all around the same age, ask yourself why they are there.

Spot the rogue car

A warning comes from HPI Autodata to members of the public hoping to purchase a bargain in the used car market: 'Beware - used cars have a history, and you cannot tell this just by looking! Is that personalised number plate a status symbol or a disguise? Is the car's condition reflected in the asking price or, could it be worth a lot less? Or worse, is it safe to drive? And, does the person selling the car have the right to do so or will the transaction leave the buyer out of pocket and without a car?'

Does the consumer really need to worry about all this? Well, in 1993, over 10,000 concerned members of the public called the company to find out if the car they were about to purchase had a 'record'. The results were shocking!

1 in 4 of the vehicles checked was recorded with HPI Autodata indicating that there may be cause for concern. The vehicle wasn't all it appeared: it had been reported stolen or at risk from theft; it was the subject of an accident write-off; or it was recorded as having outstanding finance against it.

With the national launch of HPI Autodata, The Used Car Information Line, consumers can take advantage of the good deals available in the used car market whilst reducing the risk of falling foul of the pitfalls which lie in wait.

HPI Autodata provides the following information

– Vehicle Identity. Confirmation of the vehicle's identity: its make, model, colour, engine size, transmission and fuel type for all vehicles registered after August 1986.

– Outstanding Finance. Whether the vehicle is recorded as being subject to an outstanding finance agreement.

– Condition Alert. Indicating if the vehicle has been subject of a major damage-related insurance claim.

– Stolen Vehicles and Security Watch. Whether the vehicle has been reported stolen or at high risk from fraud or theft.

– Plate Transfer. Identifying if the vehicle has been subject to a registration plate change. You might want to ask why!

In an area where consumers lack both knowledge and confidence, HPI Autodata is able to help reduce the risks they face. For a reasonable fee, callers will be given instant information, simply explained, followed by written confirmation, enabling them to check many of the things they cannot see about a car, before proceeding with their purchase. It's a small price to pay compared with around £5,000 - the average price of a used car for which HPI is asked for information.

The implications of the information available from HPI Autodata need to be fully understood:

– If a car still has an outstanding finance agreement recorded against it, the finance company may own the vehicle and whether the buyer can keep it or not depends on the nature of the finance agreement. If a car has been subject to a major damage-related insurance claim, it should be carefully inspected to ensure it is properly repaired and safe to drive.

– If a vehicle has undergone a registration plate change, although in many cases the reasons may be innocent, it could 'hide' the vehicle's history from the buyer.

A stolen vehicle always remains the property of the person or organisation from whom it was taken - irrespective of how innocently it was subsequently purchased.

– Being able to confirm the vehicle identity is also vital to the used car buyer. The HPI Autodata 'Vehicle Identity Check' confirms that the make, model, colour and engine type matches that on the vehicle Registration Document for all vehicles registered after August 1986. If the physical specifications do not tally, and the red four door saloon is recorded as a blue two door, the buyer is immediately alerted to the possibility of a fraud. A different colour or engine could also indicate that the car has been in an accident. Or, worse, that it could be two different vehicles welded together, known in the trade as a 'cut-and-shut', a potentially lethal combination.

During the first few months of 1993, HPI's Autodata checks showed that:

– 1 in 5 cars enquired upon was recorded as having had an outstanding finance agreement.

– 1 in 4 cars enquired upon was recorded as having had a major damage-related insurance claim.

– 1 in 94 cars enquired upon was recorded as stolen or at risk from theft and fraud.

It is important to remember that it is *always* a buyer's market with plenty of choice for the discriminating car purchaser - if he or she avoids being pressurised into buying a car until a check has been carried out.

The HPI Autodata hotline is open from 8.00 am - 8.00 pm, Monday to Saturday. During the summer months, the service will also be available from 10.00 am to 5.00 pm on Sundays. Credit card payment (Access, Visa or Mastercard) will be accepted for telephone enquiries on 0722 422422. Cheque or postal order payment will be accepted for enquiries made by post. (See Appendix for address.)

Telephoning around

There are two best times to buy from classified ads. One is when the ink is still wet on the newspaper – but only if you have found a real bargain! The other is a couple of weeks after the advertisement has appeared, by which time the seller is more likely to be amenable to accepting a lower price.

I have already mentioned the need to ask about 'the car' rather than saying which one. Also, have a notepad and pen alongside the phone before you make the call. You will want to know:

– The year and model.

– The colour.

– The price. It is not unknown for owners to place different adverts with different prices in them, especially if the one you have seen is not the first and the car is unsold.

– How much tax and MOT test is still current.

– The condition. Ask specific questions such as 'What condition is the engine/interior/bodywork in?' and 'Is there any rust?' or 'How much oil does the engine use?' That way, you'll obtain much more useful information.

– How long the seller has owned the car.

– Why he or she is selling it (sometimes very revealing; most often not).

– Does it have a full service history (but note that a 'yes' often becomes changed when you ask the necessary follow-up questions, such as, 'Does the record go right back to when the car was new?' and 'Is it a complete record/have any of the services been missed out?'.

The telephone survey should be carried out on all the likely candidates that you have put together – and there is no point carrying it out until the day, or at most the day before you are ready to spend time looking. Otherwise you are wasting your time and that of the seller's. And if you don't like the sound of what you hear, *please* don't go ahead and make an appointment to view in any case. So many people do so with no intention of fulfilling the appointment. If you can't stand the idea of being forthright on the telephone, just say something like, 'I'll call you back.' Everyone knows what that *really* means, anyway! Our survey will narrow your first short list down to the cars that you really want to see. But before you set out, remember that:

Half the cars you see will be much worse than described. This applies to both written and verbal descriptions. Let's be charitable and say that people often view their own cars through rose-tinted glasses. In any case, don't waste time on a car that obviously isn't worthy of consideration.

How much to pay

There are a number of good price guide magazines on the market. Occasionally they are a fair way off beam, but usually they will give you a good guide to the going rate. Compare them with actual advertisement asking prices and make an allowance for the fact that *asking* prices aren't necessarily *selling* prices.

But there is a better way to judge what cars are really selling for, if you've got the nerve. If you ring up about a car only to find that it has been sold, ask the vendor if he/she would mind giving you an idea how much these cars tend actually to sell for because it will help you to judge, etc, etc. You can't use dealers' prices as a guide because they are including their overheads – as indeed they should and must – in the asking price. On the other hand, if you find an optimistic private seller asking the same as would a local dealer, you'll know that there's something wrong! This could be an ideal candidate for that phone call two weeks later...

How to inspect a used vehicle

Even if you know nothing at all about cars, use this section, or the bits of it that you feel you can cope with, to root out the obvious no-hopers from your list. Then, if you're really keen, arrange for a local main agent to carry out an inspection for you, or ask the RAC or AA to do so. Alternatively, take someone with you who genuinely knows what he is talking about. It is sometimes said that there are just two things that every man will claim to be a total expert in: one of them is cars... If you doubt the expertise of any of your acquaintances, and you don't want to pay the cost of a full inspection, see if a mechanic from a local garage will look over a few cars for you. His (or, increasingly, her) expertise will probably just cost a few pounds an hour and will be money well spent.

Stage 1: Before you get heavily involved, a few quick checks will tell you whether the car is even worth considering. No matter how new or old the car, you would be best avoiding one that has suffered heavy crash damage, and you certainly want to avoid a car that has been daubed full of filler. So:
– Catch the light down the sides, roof and bonnet of the car. Can you see any ripples in

panels? (Panels that have been crash repaired usually remain rippled after the event. But not always!)

– Has the car been resprayed in a totally different colour? Check inside the door openings. (Ripples and other crash damage are easier to conceal on cars with light colours, especially white. Black, maroon and other dark cars are more difficult to repair without blemishes and ripples showing.)

– Stand back from the car. Does the colour and finish of the paintwork look the same all over? Check especially that front wings and bonnet, or tailgate/boot and rear wings are the same as the doors and roof. Metallic paints are especially difficult to match properly. You must find out why any respray work has been carried out.

– Check the following for overspray, sprayed paint that has clung to other bits of the car by mistake when a cheap respray is carried out; edges of windscreen rubbers, especially the corners where it is particularly difficult to persuade masking tape to stick; mud flaps and tyres; door-seal rubbers and chrome work; inside the engine bay, inside the front wings or even over the engine itself; inside grille apertures; on the edges of door mirrors. (Bad overspray indicates that a cheap 'n' quick respray has been carried out. It might soon fail – frost may cause it to blister, rust might soon break through – and you may wonder (1) why it was done at all, and (2) why a poor quality job has been carried out, and what that tells you about the way the car has been looked after.)

– Look **very carefully** inside the engine bay and inside the boot for evidence of rippling in the metal. You will usually have to look quite low down, mainly in the vicinity of structural box-section members designed to carry the strength of the car from the ends towards the centre. They are also designed to crumple under impact. This area may still look shiny and folds or ripples may look at first as though they should be there – check the other side of the car! Crash damage repairers often leave tell-tale signs such as these in the knowledge that most people will just look at the condition of the outer panels. You want to know more! The car may not be structurally true, there might be collateral suspension damage and the car could be unsafe to drive. Walk away from these cars.

– Look at the gaps between panels. Doors with tight or wide, open gaps are a strong indication that something may be amiss. Also, check bumper alignment, comparing one side of the body with the other.

Stage 2: If your car gets past these early stages you should start looking a little more closely. When looking at older cars, your first area of concern should be the condition of their bodywork:

– The most important structural areas are the sills. Check them by lifting the carpets just inside the doors and looking at the area where the outer edges of the floors join the sills. While you are at it, check the footwells, especially around the edges.

– Look inside the engine bay, if you haven't already done so, checking now for corrosion. Look especially at the tops of struts, where cars use strut-type front suspension. Check inside the boot as well, looking at the outer edges of the boot floor where they join rear wings/inner wings.

– Check for corrosion along the bottoms of wings, the 'skirts' beneath front and rear bumpers and the tops of wing panels. Corrosion that has been covered over with filler will burst through again and be worse than virgin rust. Look out for large blisters of painted filler coming loose.

– In all of these places, ensure that filler hasn't been used to bodge a repair. You can usually tell with a visual check: filled surfaces often appear slightly rippled and edges, especially where they butt up against seams, are often poorly finished. To be on the safe side take a magnet with you. It will 'stick' to steel but not to plastic filler.

– Other crucially important areas are beneath the car. If you don't know what you are doing in this area, or if you don't have the means to get safely beneath the car, leave the check to someone who does. **Never go under a car supported only by a jack.** Jacks are for wheel-changing only. See if you can hire the use of a local garage's hoist and, best of all if you're not expert, have one of their mechanics look around the car with you.

– Check around spring mountings, the joints between floors and sills, all box-section chassis members, and anywhere that suspension components are fixed to the car's body structure.

– Check all brake pipes and hoses. None should show any signs of corrosion.

– Look at the shock absorbers. Any fluid leakage means failure.

– Is the exhaust rusty, patched or holed?

Suspension checks are mostly difficult to carry out unless you know what you are looking for, although a recent MOT certificate should ensure that everything is OK.

– You could try bouncing each corner of the car: if the shock absorbers are good, the car will not bounce up and down after you stop.

– Try jacking up each of the front wheels in turn. Spin them. A 'shot' wheel bearing will produce a graunching sound – but only if it is really quite bad!

– Try grasping each wheel, jacked off the ground. (Keep from under the car, in case it falls off the jack!) Push and pull each wheel, top and bottom. If there is clunking or obvious free movement, expect severe suspension or wheel bearing wear.

– Do examine each wheel very carefully. Any bulges or splits in the sidewalls mean that the tyre will be scrap and not even fit to drive the car home safely or legally. If tyres are badly worn on one side more than the other, it *might* mean that the car's tracking – easily adjustable, although the tyre may be scrap – is out of alignment, or it might indicate suspension damage, maybe from an accident.

– Examine driveshaft (front wheel drive cars only) and steering rack gaiters for splits. If a car has been used with split gaiters, it's best to assume that the rack or driveshaft in question has been running 'dry' and will need replacement.

If you are buying an older car which needs work doing to it – and this may be an excellent way of buying a really cheap set of wheels – try making the owner an offer 'subject to MOT test'. Then, you can have the car tested as an inexpensive (though not necessarily complete) check on the overall condition of the car. You will also know the worst that you can expect and you will know just what you have to do in order to make the car roadworthy. If you shop around, you will also be able to find an MOT testing garage that doesn't charge extra, or only charges a nominal amount, for re-tests, but do check on the time limit between tests.

Mechanical components

At the budget end of the market, the mechanical components are the least vital part of the car in many ways! You can buy parts from the scrapyard at a sufficiently low price to make almost anything repairable at low cost, while 'consumable' items such as shock absorbers, clutches and brake parts can be bought at low cost from motorists' shops. Imported cars can sometimes be an exception to this rule. On the other hand, there are ways around the high cost of parts. In the UK, *Exchange & Mart* has to be the cost-cutter's bible. Some companies that advertise there import engines for most Japanese cars at a cost much lower than that of reconditioning them. They are second-hand but rarely more than a couple of years old, Japan being the ultimate throw-away society. Other companies specialize in supplying parts for cars with high-ticket spares such as BMW and Audi. Without a doubt, before buying a cheap-cheap car of foreign origin, check that cheap spares are available.

Some mechanical checks are best carried out with the engine cold, and there are some tell-tales that you can look for without even hearing the engine running.

— Before starting up, remove the oil filler cap and take a look inside. Grey sludge around the cap is a certain indicator that the engine is on its last legs.

— Pull out the dipstick. Is the oil level very low? Is the oil a dirty black and does it feel gritty between finger and thumb? (*Not* a well-maintained car!) Does it have droplets of water on it? (*Big* problems! Probably a blown head gasket.)

— Check inside the radiator cap (but *only* if the engine is cold!). Do you see the pleasant colour of anti-freeze? Good! Do you see rust? Bad! Do you see droplets of oil? Disastrous! (See previous paragraph.)

— Modern engines have pipes all over the place! Look around the carburettor and distributor in

particular for stubs left bare of their pipes by the engine bodgers. A pipe missing from the exhaust manifold-to-air intake will cause mystery spluttering and stopping on a journey in cold, damp weather; pipes missing from the carburettor may cause the car to run rich or to idle badly, or to accelerate poorly — or who knows *what* some of them are for! But they should all be there.

— Start the car and note whether the starter motor sounds lively or whether it is struggling to keep up. These days a new battery won't come much cheaper than some brands of overhauled starter motor! Then when the engine is running, let checks commence!

— Undo and remove the oil filler cap again. (NB Overhead camshaft engines spray oil around in copious quantities. Ensure that you don't get showered if the filler cap is in the rocker cover!) If you can feel, hear and see oil mist chugging out, the engine bores are badly worn. You will also certainly see smoke from the exhaust (see later)

— Does the oil pressure warning light come on or flicker with engine cold? If not, low oil pressure is likely and an engine rebuild could be near. Or it could be a sign of a very low oil level, and hence poor maintenance.

— Bonnet open. Does the 'top' of the engine rattle on start up? (Mechanical tappets could be out of adjustment, hydraulic tappets worn. Not likely to be expensive in the case of mechanical tappets, but if the rattle continues after the first 30 seconds or so and the car keeps rattling, a more expensive replacement camshaft may be called for.)

— Rev the engine. Does it rattle in a deep, growling way, from low down in the engine? If so, the big end and/or main bearings are gone and it's time for a replacement engine.

— Go to the back of the car. You'll probably see steam, especially in colder weather, and even water dripping out. This is no problem, although it should go away after the car has been driven, except in really cold weather. Rev the engine hard several times, blipping the throttle. If you see anything from puffs to clouds of black smoke (as opposed to grey steam), you have seen another indication that the engine is on the slippery slope.

— Front wheel drive only: Drive the car slowly on

full lock in each direction, room and safety permitting. If you hear a knocking from the area of either driveshaft, it could be worn and in need of replacement.

Static 'running' checks

You can't always take a test drive and if the car is old enough, cheap enough and desirable enough, you may be prepared to put up with that. However, the price would have to be *very* right, because there are always more fish in the sea. But there are certain simulations that you can try out in the drive:

– If the drive is a few yards long, slip the car into first gear, into reverse, and move it as far as you can. Do the gears grind badly? Is the clutch stiff? Does the gear change shift OK? Is the steering wheel or seat loose (ideal time to find out, as you shift your position and push down on the clutch)? Does the brake pedal feel spongy and head for the floorboards? (If you find lots of problems at this stage then, oh dear, you *have* got problems!)

– Pull on the handbrake, put the car into second gear, rev the engine a little and slip the clutch. Does the handbrake work? Does the clutch slip without showing signs of moving the car?

– As the car moves back and forth, try turning the steering as far as possible this way and that. Does it have any tight spots, or is there a lot of free play or graunching sounds? (Worn steering rack or steering box). Does the steering column move from side to side, or is the wheel loose, so that you can move it up and down? (Worn column bushes – not expensive, but an MOT failure and possibly a few hours' work.)

However, far more can be determined by driving the car on the open road.

Interior checks

Disregard this part of the car and you could end up hating it! When a car is running well and looking fairly sound, you forget about its functional qualities. No one ever drove to work humming a happy tune because there is no oil leakage from the shock absorbers! But if the car is fundamentally uncomfortable, it will become your enemy. Be sure to check each of the following:

– Examine the carpets. If they're wet, water is probably leaking in somewhere, unless someone has been getting in with snow on their boots! One of the world's most irritating occurrences is to have a leak that drips cold water on to your accelerator leg – it's always *that* leg. Another is when you turn the heater on and the water inside the car evaporates then condenses on the windscreen, so that you can't see where you are going. Water entering around a windscreen seal can often be cured easily if the car is newish. If it's oldish, the likelihood is that the screen surround steelwork has corroded, making the chances of a tube-based repair just about nil, and requiring some major, awkward and expensive welding repair work. Alternatively, water coming in from beneath suggests that the car's lower structure has as much future as an old car park ticket. Take water leaks seriously! An alternative source of water leaks is the heater radiator (invariably well hidden from view), or the piping or screenwashers. The heater can be expensive and tricky to replace.

– Examine the seats. Rips can be a pain although they are not impossible. Do realize that they will invariably get much worse, although scrap-yard replacements won't cost the earth. Finding the right colour match could be fun, however. Check especially for sagged seats. If your knees come up as your backside goes down, the seat springing has sprung its last. Feel underneath. If you observe the remnants of Pirelli webbing strips, replacement is slightly fiddly but relatively cheap: if there's a split membrane or sheet of rubber, replacements might be impossible. The scrap-yard route is often best.

– Look at the headlining. Can you live with rips or severe discolouration? If it's there, that is more or less what you will have to do because it's almost impossible to clean easily and replacement is usually the sort of job that drives strong men to drink. If you're really keen on a car with scrap headlining, obtain a quote from a trimmer before going ahead.

– Take a *close* look at seat belts and mountings. Pull on inertia reel types – they should lock up when you tug hard – and check that buckles click shut and come free easily. Replacements can be expensive.

– Check that the heater works properly. On a sunny day in June, you forget how damned miserable life can be on a foggy winter's day when the heater doesn't function! Check that the heater controls turn the tap on and off; that the controls direct air where you want it (and in particular that the demister works); that the heater gets really hot when on full; that the fan works. You will want them all to function properly, and on some cars repair can be very time consuming, tricky and expensive, especially on more up-market cars.

You can be sure that the seller already knows about 'odd' faults and things that don't work. He/she probably also knows how much they will cost to put right – could this be why they are selling? To be safe, don't accept lame excuses when things don't work. If things are so easy to fix, why haven't they been done already?

Other expenses spared

Take time to check every accessory and electrical fitting on the car. And if it's fitted with a stereo, ensure that it works and that it is included with the price. If you forget to check that the reversing light works, the car might fail the MOT test. Repair could conceivably require a new lamp unit, if the old one has corroded, or replacement of a particularly difficult-to-reach switch on the gearbox. Or you might even need to call in an auto electrician if there is a more awkward fault. On the other hand, it might just be a bulb...

– With the help of an assistant, check every item of lighting on the car to ensure that all the lamps illuminate as they should. If a fuse has blown, it is important that you know why – it could be because there is a serious and potentially dangerous short somewhere.

– Methodically go through every switch on the dash, the column controls and the centre console. Open every cubby hole and check that everything functions properly.

– Check door seals for bad wear. They are surprisingly expensive to replace.

– Don't forget to check the condition of the spare wheel, the condition (and existence!) of the jack and toolkit, and while you're at it the state of the spare wheel well or spare wheel carrier.

– Open and close all of the windows and the sunroof. (Also look for stains around the sunroof aperture – they can leak unremittingly!) All should function smoothly, without forcing and without grinding noises. Electric windows and central locking should be checked particularly carefully because repair/ replacement costs can be high!

All of this seems like a huge amount to go through, but it is well worth it when you bear in mind the expense you will be committing yourself to, and the potential for problems if you make a bad purchase. And do remember that with a private sale you can buy at the best prices, but you can't take it back if you make a mistake.

Finally, but perhaps most important of all, make sure that the person who is selling you the car actually owns it.

– Ask to see the Registration Document. If it's not available it could be that the 'owner' has (a) lost it; (b) has it but it doesn't show the 'owner's' name because he is a trader masquerading as a private seller; (c) he/she does not have title to the car because it is leased or for some other reason that means the car doesn't properly belong to the seller. If you can't see the Registration Document, *walk away unless satisfied by the following.*

– Ask to see the owner's original purchase receipt.

– Check that the car is owned by the supposed owner rather than being subject to a hire purchase agreement. Your local Citizen's Advice Bureau (see telephone directory) should be able to check it out on your behalf. Also, see P162 – on, Spotting a rogue car.

NB: If you pay for a car that is subsequently found to belong to someone else, you will lose the car as well as having lost your money.

Total checklist

If you want to be as sure as you reasonably can about the condition of your purchase, the following checklist should be taken with you on your car hunt, and the car or cars at the top of your list examined with a fine toothcomb. The following sequence is especially aimed at owners of older cars and was first produced by the author to help prospective purchasers of classic cars. It doesn't claim to be totally exhaustive; the only way you can find out key information on any particular model of car is to talk to a specialist about individual trouble spots. The AA publish information on what to look for when buying specific cars and this can usually be accessed through one of those very expensive telephone lines. Check with the AA for availability.

Checking over a prospective purchase not only can but should be very time consuming if the 'right' car is to be bought rather than a glossed-over heap of trouble. What follows is an elimination sequence in three separate parts, each one taking longer and being more thorough than the last, an approach which has the virtue of saving the purchaser both time and embarrassment. It is always easier to withdraw at an early stage than after an hour spent checking the car over, with the aid of the owner's comments and mugs of coffee! Thus, Stage A aims to eliminate the obvious 'nails' without having to probe too deeply, Stage B takes matters somewhat further for cars that pass the first stage, while Stage C is the 'dirty hands' stage, the one you don't get into on a snowy February evening unless you are really serious.

Wear old, warm clothes (if the ground is cold). An old mat or a board is useful if the ground is wet. In addition, take a bright torch; a pair of ramps; a screwdriver or other probe; copies of the following pages; a notepad and pencil; a bottle; trolley or scissors jack; and axle stands.

> **SAFETY should be carefully considered when inspecting a car, and any necessary steps taken. Never rely on the handbrake to hold a car that is on a slope or up on ramps. Ensure that the wheels are chocked when using jacks or ramps. Use axle stands if you have to inspect the underside of the car. Do not use a naked flame or smoke when inspecting the underside of a car. Wear goggles when probing about beneath a car.**

Using the checklist

The checklist is designed to show step-by-step instructions for virtually all the checks to be made on a car offered for sale. After each check, the fault indicated is shown in brackets. Eg, the instruction: 'Look along wings, door bottoms, wheel arches and sills from front to rear of the car' is followed by the fault, shown in brackets, as '(Ripples indicate filler presence/crash damage – £££.)'. The pound Sterling signs are intended to give a guide to the cost of rectifying the fault if it exists. £ indicates that the cost is likely to be less than the cost of a new tyre, £££ stands for the cost of a new set of tyres, or more, while ££ means that the cost is likely to be between the two. The cost guide relates to the cost of the component/s only, other than in the case of bodywork; allow more if you have the work done for you.

When examining a car you are advised to take this book (or copies of the relevant buying checklists) and a notebook with you. As each item is checked a record can be kept in the notebook. You may wish to record a running cost total for necessary repairs as faults are discovered, as this could be a useful bargaining tool at the end of your examination.

It is strongly recommended that you read the repair and restoration sections of this book, and also the Haynes Owners' Workshop Manual relevant to the car you are examining, so that you are fully familiar with every component being checked.

Stage A – First impressions

1 Is the car square to the ground, and are the bonnet, bumper, grille, and door to hinge-pillar gaps even and level? (Closed-up door gaps and rippled front wings usually indicate poorly repaired crash damage – £££+.) ☐

2 Look along the wings, door bottoms, wheel arches and sills from front to rear of the car. (Ripples indicate filler presence – £££.) ☐

3 Check the quality of chrome work, especially bumpers, where appropriate. (Dents, dings and rust – ££.) ☐

4 Turn on all lights, indicators and reversing lights, and check that they work. (Sidelights/marker lights rust in their sockets

– ££. Rear licence/number plate lamps earthing/ grounding problems plus other specific component problems – £.) ☐

5　Bounce each corner of the car. (Worn shock absorbers allow the corners to feel springy and bounce up and down. Each damper – £.) ☐

6　Check visually for rust – gain an overall impression at this stage. (From cosmetic to dire – £ to £££+. See following sections.) ☐

7　Check for damage to painted or impact resistant bumpers if fitted. (Damage – ££ to £££.) ☐

8　Examine the general condition of the interior at a glance. (Rips, dirt, parts missing – ££ or £££.) ☐

9　Check the fit of the curved part of both bumpers. (Accident damage – Possibly £££.) ☐

10　Check the quality of the paintwork. Does it shine when dry? Are there scratches beneath the shine? Is it chipped? (Neglect and poor-quality, cover-job respray – £££.) ☐

11　Do the seller and his/her surroundings look like those of someone who is likely to have looked after the car? (Maintenance -£££.) ☐

Stage B – Clean hands

If a car doesn't match up to requirements after Stage A, don't be tempted – reject it! There are always more cars to be seen. Stage B decreases the risk of making a mistake without even getting your hands too dirty!

Check hard for body corrosion in all the places shown below. Use a magnet to ensure that no filler is present – magnets will only stick to steel. Work carefully and methodically.

Bodywork

1　Front apron, beneath grille. (Accident damage, corrosion, cheap repair – ££.) ☐

2　Front wing, headlamp area. (Corrosion, filler – £££ if severe.) ☐

3　Lower front wing – continuation of sill line. (Corrosion, filler, damage – £££, if severe because hidden corrosion indicated.) ☐

4　Tops of front wings and joint with main bodywork behind line of bonnet. (Filler – £££.) ☐

5　Sills. (Corrosion, filler, damage – £££ to replace.) ☐

6　Door bottoms. (Corrosion, filler – ££ or £££.

7　Door skins – outer panel. (Corrosion, filler – ££.) ☐

8　If the car is open-topped, measure the fit of the doors along their rear, vertical edges. (Open at bottom, closed at top means sagging bodywork, virtually terminal – £££+.) ☐

9　Rear wheel arch. (Corrosion, filler – £££.) ☐

10　Open each door in turn. Lift up and down and note 'looseness'. (Hinge wear – £. Corroded door – £££.) ☐

11　Check the area along the length of any chrome trim strip and finishings. (Corrosion around trim clips. Unless severe, usually cosmetic – £.) ☐

12　Check the bottom corners of the windscreen apertures. (Corrosion -£££.) ☐

Interior

1　Examine the seat and backrest. (Worn, thin or split covers. Leather – £££, cloth/plastic – ££.) ☐

2　Tip the seat forward on two-door cars. Check for damage. (Scuffing and tears. Leather – £££, cloth/plastic – ££.) ☐

3　Check the dashboard. (Cracks, tears or scratches, 'Wrong' instruments – £ to £££.) ☐

4　Check the condition and cleanliness of the headlining. (If dirty £ to £££ for replacement.) ☐

5　Examine the steering wheel/gear knob. (Incorrect parts fitted – £ to ££.) ☐

6　Test inertia reel seat belts for looseness, fraying, correct operation. (Should hold when tugged sharply – £ to ££.) ☐

7   Check door trim and door/window handles. (Wear and scuffing at bottoms, buckling of hardboard backing, broken handles – £ to ££, if parts available.) ☐

8   Ensure that the seats fold forward (two-door cars), that the 'paddle' allows different backrest positions (where fitted), and that they slide and lock. (Failure to slide easily, especially on the driver's side, is sometimes an indication that the floor is corroded – £££) ☐

9   Wind windows up and down – there should be no restriction. (Usually lack of lubrication – £.) ☐

10 Is the rear parcel shelf there (hatchback cars) and in good condition? (Trimmer to remake/purchase replacement – ££.) ☐

Mechanical

Ask the owner to start up engine. Let it idle – thorough warming-up takes quite a while on the road and this will help. (Does he/she leave it to idle on choke? Harmful practice!) ☐

1   Pull and push the steering wheel and attempt to lift and lower it at right-angles to the steering column. (Clunking indicates: wear in the column bush, loose column connections – £. Wear in steering column universal joint – £.) ☐

2   Pull the bonnet release. Is it stiff? (Seized mechanism or cable – £.) ☐

3   Open the bonnet. Check for non-standard air cleaners, rocker cover, etc. (If originality is important – £ to ££.) ☐

4   Check the engine/engine bay for general cleanliness and presence of oil. (Leaking gasket/lack of detail care – probably £.) ☐

5   Listen to the engine. Top-end tapping. (Anything from tappet adjustment, at no cost of course, to 'shot' camshaft – £££.) Bottom end rumble, timing chain tinkle. (Worn engine. Timing chain and sprockets – ££. Worn crank – £££+.) ☐

6   Is paint peeling around the clutch/brake cylinders? (Carelessly spilt fluid strips paint – £ plus time. Leaking cylinders – ££.) ☐

Stop the engine and leave to cool down.

7   Remove radiator cap slowly with a rag, and beware of spurting, scalding water. Inspect coolant level and its general cleanliness. Orange indicates rust and a long time since coolant was changed. Check for oil on top of water. Remove dipstick. Check for water droplets in oil. (Head gasket problems. Probably – £££.) Check manual for specific cars' safety requirements: hot water may boil and 'blow' out as the pressure is removed. ☐

8   Remove engine oil filler cap. Look for yellow or brown slimy sludge or foaming. (Severe bore/valve guide wear – £££.) Look for white foaming or 'goo' inside cap. (Blocked crankcase ventilation system (where fitted) – £.) ☐

9   Inspect the fins of the radiator. (Exchange radiator – ££.) ☐

10 Examine the engine mountings, if visible, for signs of previous removal. (Engine removal is not necessarily a bad thing, but it would be interesting to know why!) ☐

11 Jack both front wheels off the ground together. Turn the steering wheel from lock-to-lock. (Roughness indicates wear in steering rack or mechanism. Replacement or overhaul – ££-£££.) ☐

Road test

Only carry out the following tests on traffic and pedestrian-free roads. Keep a constant look-out for other road users.

If you as tester are driving, ensure adequate insurance cover. Otherwise simulate the following tests with the owner driving.

1   Start up. Is the starter noisy on engagement? (Worn starter dog – £. Or worn starter – ££ to £££.) ☐

2   Is it difficult to engage first gear? (Worn clutch and/or worn selector mechanism – £££.) ☐

Drive for three or four miles to become familiar with the car and to warm the engine.

3   Drive at 30 mph. Brake gently to a halt. (a) Does the car pull to one side? (Worn pads or shoes – £. Seized callipers – ££.) (b) Do the brakes rub or grind? (Worn pads or shoes – £, but more if discs or drums ruined.) ☐

4   Drive at 30 mph in third gear. Apply then release the accelerator four or five times. Listen for transmission 'clunk'. (Worn universal joint – £. Worn differential – £££. Worn halfshaft/driveshaft – ££. Worn wire wheel splines, when fitted – ££.) ☐

5   Drive at 40 mph. Lift off the accelerator. Listen for differential whine. (Worn differential – £££, if severe or unbearably noisy.) ☐

6   Accelerate hard in second gear to 40 mph, then lift off. Listen for engine knocking. (Worn engine bearings – £££.) ☐

7   Also, does the gearbox jump out of gear? (Worn internal selector mechanism – £.) ☐

8   Drive as in 6 and 7 above, but lift off in third gear. Does the gearbox jump out of gear? (Worn internal selector mechanism – £.) ☐

9   Drive at 50 mph in fourth gear. Change into third gear. Does the gearbox 'crunch'? (Worn synchromesh – £. Faulty/worn clutch -££) ☐

10   Drive at 30 mph in third gear. Change into second gear. Does the gearbox 'crunch'? (Worn synchromesh – ££ to £££. Faulty/worn clutch – ££) ☐

11   Do the front wheels flutter or shake at 40 mph? (Wheels out of balance – £. Worn front suspension – ££ to £££.) ☐

12   Check that road conditions are suitable. With the ratchet knob or button depressed (don't let it go!) pull the handbrake on whilst travelling at 10 mph maximum. Don't risk a skid! (Car pulls to one side – faulty handbrake on that side. – See 20 below. If handbrake has no discernible effect, rear brakes probably oiled or worn – ££.) ☐

13   In second gear at about 30 mph, accelerate hard, then decelerate hard, but don't brake. If the car veers to left or right, a rear-wheel drive car's rear axle may be loose or the springs are faulty or subframe mountings (front or rear wheel drive cars) are loose, soft or corroded. (New axle U-bolts – £. New rear springs – ££. Mountings – £ to £££++, if bad corrosion). Also, check tyre pressure and tyre types. ☐

14   When stationary, operate the brake pedal. Apply light pressure in repeated strokes. (If the pedal slowly works its way to the floor – even over a minute. The master cylinder may be faulty. Dangerous fault – ££.) ☐

15   Accelerate from about 1,000 rpm in top gear, full throttle. (Pinking/spark knock probably indicates maladjusted timing. Can cause piston damage over a long period – ££ or £££.) ☐

16   At highway speeds climb a slight hill with a very light throttle. (Hesitation, coughing, snapping or spitting indicates over-lean carburettor setting. Can cause valve damage over a long period – ££.) ☐

17   If the car is an automatic, does the gearbox clunk heavily going into Drive or change up and down very slowly/lazily? (Clogged filter, low oil level – £, unless damage has occurred. Worse faults need investigating – up to £££+, although not that common.) ☐

18   Front wheel drive cars – when it is safe to do so, drive slowly in tight circles, first in one direction and then in the other. Listen for knocking or clunking noises coming from the driveshafts. (New joint, if available separately, £ or ££; new driveshaft if not, ££ or £££.) ☐

19   Stop the car. Apply the parking brake firmly. Engage second gear. Gently let out the clutch – but depress again as soon as car shows any signs of distress. (If car pulls away, worn rear brakes – £. Oil in brake drum – ££. If car remains stationary but engine continues to run, worn clutch – ££+.) ☐

Boot/trunk inspection

1   Is the spare tyre inflated and with a good tread? (Replacement – £, obviously!) ☐

2   Does the jack work? (Replacement – £, or lubrication.) ☐

3   Is the door key the same as the ignition key? (Ask why, if not. Can be inconvenient!) ☐

4   Is there a separate key for the boot lock? (Replacement key if right number can be found, or even replacement lock – £.) ☐

5   Does the boot light work (if fitted)? (Switch, bulb or wiring fault – £.) ☐

Stage C – Dirty hands

This is the level at which the car – by now being seriously considered – is given the sort of checks that make as sure as possible that there are no serious hidden faults which could still make the purchaser change his or her mind. It might also throw up a few minor faults to use as bargaining points with the seller!

While Stage A took only a minute or so and Stage B took quite a while longer, Stage C involves a lot more time, inconvenience and effort, but if you want to be sure, it's the most vital stage of all.

> SAFETY: Ensure that wheels are chocked when using jacks or ramps. Never go under a car supported only by a jack.

1 Jack the rear wheels off ground, one at a time. Grasp wheel, twist sharply back and forth – list   for 'clunks'. If wire wheels are fitted, do they move relative to the brake drum? (Worn splines on hubs/wheels – £££. Otherwise worn differential – £££.) ☐

2 Jack up the front wheel at the wishbone, partially compressing the front suspension. Spin the wheel and listen for roughness in the wheel bearings. (Imminent wheel bearing failure – £ to ££.) ☐

3 Grip the roadwheel at the top and bottom – ensuring that the car weight cannot fall on to your hand – and rock in the vertical plane. (Play indicates: wear in wire wheel splines – £££; wear in wheel bearing – £; wear in kingpin or suspension joints (see manual) – ££ to £££.) N.B. Check Chapter 1, 'Checking front suspension', page 73 on for the different types of checks applicable to different front suspension set-ups. ☐

4 From beneath the car, examine the back of the rear brake drums and the insides of the wheels for oil contamination. (Failed oil seal/block differential breather – £.) ☐

5 Lift the carpets and check the floor for rusting, particularly adjacent to the inner sills in footwell. (Significant corrosion – possibly £££.) ☐

6 Feel inside the front inner wings for corrosion, especially at the front and rear. (Severe corrosion – £££.) ☐

7 Remove mud, if present, from around the rear suspension mountings. Probe for corrosion with a screwdriver. (Significant corrosion - £££.) ☐

8 Examine and probe around inside of rear wheel arches and area inside boot/trunk in line with rear wheels. (Corrosion – £££.) ☐

9 Sniff around the fuel tank from beneath and look for evidence of fuel staining, especially from the front of the tank and from around the sender unit. (Most tanks corrode from above, from outside. Replacement – ££ to £££.) ☐

10 Probe around jacking point/s, chassis sections and under-sill area with a screwdriver. Check visually for distorted jack points and supports and general corrosion. (Severe corrosion – £££.) ☐

11 Examine the insides of the front apron, particularly at the ends. (Corrosion – ££.) ☐

12 Examine the insides of the rear apron, particularly at the ends. (Corrosion – ££.) ☐

13 Inspect the engine for oil leaks. NB: There will almost invariably be some with an older car!

Front seal on timing chain cover. – £; front seal leaking onto timing belt – ££ (new belt also required). ☐

Rear seal. – Leaking oil usually comes through gearbox bell housing drain hole. Sometimes gearbox oil leak to blame (Engine and/or gearbox removal required; may be £££. ☐

Side covers – tappet inspection plates – on side of engine. Around the oil filter. (Spin-on canisters can come loose as can bolt-mounted type. Badly fitted rubber seal on bolt-mounted type – £.) ☐

Camshaft/rocker cover on top of engine. (Usually – £) ☐

14 Front wheel drive models: examine driveshaft boots for splits or other damage. Damage to outboard boots may show up as grease thrown round inside of wheel arch. (Boot replacement – £; if neglected, new joint or driveshaft – ££ or £££). ☐

15 Examine the rear axle for oil leakage and oil thrown on to the body. (Slight leakage not uncommon. Heavy leakage suggests a faulty seal, clogged vent or overfilled differential casing – £.) ☐

16 Grasp each shock absorber in turn and twist and shake. (Worn bushes, linkages or shock-absorbers – £ each.) ☐

17 Look for evidence of grease on grease points in the few instances where used. (Lack of servicing – £ to £££.) ☐

18 Condition of the exhaust system and exhaust mountings. (Replacement exhaust – ££ or £££.) ☐

19 Check brake discs for deep scoring. (Replacement or reground discs – £ to ££.) ☐

20 Check visually the condition of the battery from above and battery mountings, from below. (New battery/batteries – £ – ££. Corroded mountings – ££ to £££.) ☐

21 Determine the free play of the clutch pedal. (If more than 1 in (2.5 cm) or so, the clevis pin in the pedal/master cylinder pushrod is worn – hydraulically operated clutches only. – £.) Excessive free play with cable clutch can mean that cable needs adjusting (free), cable or self-adjusting mechanism needs renewing (£), or internal fault in clutch mechanism (££) NB: Springs should usually be attached to both pedals. Move the pedals from side to side. (More than slight movement indicates worn pedal bushes or the bolt holding the pedals is loose – £.) ☐

22 Check the steering wheel for excessive free play by attempting to rotate it lightly with the car stationary and the front wheels on the ground. Normally, more than 1 to 2 in (2.5 to 5 cm) at the circumference of the wheel is excessive (check manual). (Severe wear in steering mechanism – £££.) ☐

Diesel engines supplement
by David Bowler

1 Disregard the colour of the oil – it is designed to hold particles of engine dirt in suspension and discolours very quickly. ☐

2a Try to hear engine start from cold. Note the cranking speed of engine: if low (below 125 rpm) a new battery could be needed. ☐

2b If the engine does not start quickly, are the cold starting aids working? These are usually glow or heater plugs, which are easily changed, but replacement injection pumps and injectors are very expensive. ☐

3 Is there much smoke coming from the exhaust pipe? White smoke on initial start up is OK, but should disappear when engine warms up. If not the engine is overcooled, possibly one or more cylinders are low on compression – this can also be expensive. Blue smoke indicates worn bores, pistons or valve stems and guides as with a petrol engine. Black/grey smoke indicates faulty fuel-injection equipment – the very least of which will involve removal and overhaul of the injectors, a rather expensive and specialist operation. ☐

4 Look at the fuel-injection pump whilst someone is moving the accelerator pedal (with the engine stationary). The stop at the position of maximum movement should have a lead seal wired on to it to prevent tampering with the maximum engine speed. If this seal is broken, forget buying the vehicle. ☐

5 If there is much smoke from the exhaust, bear in mind this is now part of the MOT test and must fall within legal limits. Therefore although the diesel has many advantages, initial 'sorting out' bills can be high. ☐

NB: Black smoke from a diesel engine can be due to nothing more serious than a blocked fuel filter or air filter (£) – though it is best for the novice to err on the side of caution.

Buying at auction

If you're feeling brave, this could be the place where you can buy at the prices that traders pay. But if you get it wrong, you could be in trouble! The biggest problem with buying at auction is the risk of getting drawn in and buying the wrong car *and* paying too much for it. There's no need to think that the auctioneer will sell you a Bentley Mulsanne just because you have blown your nose at the wrong moment. But there is *every* risk that you will be carried away by the excitement unless you are well prepared.

The key to successful buying at auction is to go at least once and preferably more often without intending to buy, just so that you can learn the ropes. Familiarize yourself with the auction procedure. Stand at the back and just keep your eyes open. You will note that many cars have a reserve price and that the auctioneer makes it clear which are which. He may even have a means, such as with coloured lights, of letting everyone know when the reserve has been reached. If the car fails to reach its reserve, no sale will be made there and then. If it does reach it, the person who has made the winning bid has to go to register the purchase, usually to an office to one side of the room. If the car has failed to reach its reserve, you may still have a chance to make an offer for the car at the office, but this is the sort of thing you may best find out about by telephoning in advance.

In many ways, an auction can seem a somewhat intimidating event. Approach it in the right spirit, however, and it can be the best free entertainment for miles around. The sight of corralled motor traders *en masse* is amusing in itself − if you see one smile, it's probably because he has got wind − and the range of cars and their prices can be fascinating. Also, look out for the private 'punter' bidding more than a car is worth − and make a mental note that you won't be in that category when the serious stuff starts. But it's not difficult, provided that you have a little self-control.

It is essential to have bought a price guide magazine in advance, and to have narrowed down the field so that you know precisely the sort of car you are looking for. It's also important to know the sorts of cars that appear in auctions, week in and week out. They are the sorts of cars that medium and large companies have bought for company use and the cars that hire firms have bought, now being sold off for whatever price the market will bear. There are also cars that have been 'snatched back' by finance houses from people unable or unwilling to pay their bills, and those sent out by receivers from companies that have gone bankrupt. At the bottom end of the ladder are the cars that main dealer garages won't sell themselves and can't

sell through the trade, for whatever reason. If you're looking for the best in the bracket, the auction is probably not the best place to go: too much pressure and too little chance of finding the right sort of car. If you want a car that is only two or three years old, with bodywork that will be as sound as a bell but possibly a little travel worn, and the sort of mechanics that you can expect at high mileage, this might be the place for you. Most cars in this category have been given the sort of treatment that you would expect under the circumstances: servicing has been done, but without anyone having to be answerable to an owner; drivers have been those you have seen thrashing up and down the motorway, flat out; interiors are likely to be stale and weary. On the credit side, modern cars are made to take punishment and mechanical components could still have a lot of life left in them while you may consider that the potential cost savings will be worthwhile.

The other reason for attending before intending to buy is to ensure that the auction you are visiting appears sound. Some are right at the bottom end of the motor traders' ladder (subterranean, in other words) and are places where you may be ripped off. Avoid them like the plague; stick with the reputable establishments approved by the Society of Motor Auctions (SMA).

Some cars are sold 'with warranty'. This means − don't get too excited − that you have one hour after the end of the auction to return the car for a full refund, if the need arises. (Just try doing that at a disreputable auction: you could find that the auction had closed earlier than you thought!) If you buy a 'warranty' car:

− Test drive it *straight away*: find out from the office beforehand how long you have got and what time they go home.

− Check out the major mechanical components as described earlier in this chapter.

− If you find a major fault or if you just have any doubts, take the car back *straight away*.

It is important to note that cars can be inspected visually before they are sold and that while they can sometimes be started up, they can never be driven. The only 'road test' you will get will be to watch the car being driven from parking lot to sale point. Use it to listen for odd noises from clutch, gearbox and engine, and look out for black smoke on start-up.

When the car reaches the auction ring, the

auctioneer will describe it. This information may well have been displayed with the vehicle: number of owners, length of MOT certificate, service history (if there is one) and – rather important, this – whether it is 'direct from seller'. If it is not, it is being sold through the trade and you may be expected to pay for polished tyres and covered-up faults. 'Sellers' are usually companies selling their own fleet or individual cars, such as when a rep or director leaves the company.

Before you have got this far, make sure that you have:

– Ensured that you know which model or models of car you will consider.

– Written down and taken with you the 'trade book' value of cars in each year and registration letter category you are contemplating, looking with mileage taken into consideration, as this has a big effect on value.

– Established a concrete limit to what you are prepared to pay.

You should stay mum at the start of the bidding. The auctioneer may try to start the bidding at a high level; the will of the people may force him to start lower. They may be told all manner of tales by the auctioneer in connection with their ability to see a bargain when one is staring them in the face. It may be that no one will smile. Wait until a few bids are in and a kind of traders 'floor' level has been set, and only then make your own bid. Just raise your arm clearly so that the auctioneer can see you: no need to jump or shout! If the car comes your way, that's fine. If it doesn't because someone wants to bid more than you, that's also fine. You must bear in mind that an auction is *not* a game show. If you go storming ahead, trying to beat that so-and-so to the car of your dreams, you will stand the chance of losing a lot of money.

Your previous visit should have given you some indication of how far below book values auction prices are pitched; after all, that's why you have gone there. Set your price targets, perhaps pitching them a hundred or two higher in order to have a realistic chance of buying the car ahead of a seasoned trader, but whatever happens, *go no higher!*

The right choice

You can save a lot of money by buying one make of car rather than another. East European cars, for instance, and some Italian cars can be far cheaper to buy than the Fords and Vauxhalls that fill our roads. But what is the catch?

The biggest catch of all, if you intend buying a car that is just a year or two old, is that cheaper cars will continue to depreciate very rapidly and you might save a lot of money but you might also lose a lot. If you intend keeping the car for many years that may not matter, of course, and all cars seem to be valued at next-to-nothing by the garage when you come to trade them in. However, some cars do achieve a notably better price than others, so make a point of carrying out your homework. Hondas, Subarus and Toyotas tend to hold value quite well, reflecting the fact that they are currently the most reliable three models of car on British roads. Datsuns do less well (although still holding their value better than most), while some German cars have had a reputation for clinging on to value better than most. British cars have improved beyond measure in the last few years, and even Jaguars, after showing the hefty initial drop in value suffered by most luxury cars in their first two years, are currently holding their values extremely well – but that is the sort of situation that is prone to change and you must monitor the market for yourself. French cars tend to depreciate more than average, although there are notable exceptions, small Peugeots maintaining their value quite well. There are virtually no exceptions to the current rule that Italian mass-produced cars depreciate faster than average, although there are signs that this will change in the coming years; they last much better than they used to, but perceptions are slow to change. Biggest droppers of all have traditionally been East European cars, although even that is likely to change over a period of years. It is essential to bear in mind the cruel fact that *depreciation is the biggest single cost in motoring.*

Quality is still important but less so than it used to be, as the big manufacturers have got their hands on all aspects of car manufacturing the world over. From The West Coast of the USA to the Eastern-most part of Europe, Japanese work and quality practices are having their effect. Standards have been improving steadily for a number of years and cheaper cars are not always worse cars. This gives the buyer of an older car a tremendous opportunity to make a saving, provided that he or she buys an unconventional model with eyes wide open.

Among the cheapest of second cars have been

older Skodas and Ladas. If you buy one of these – and you will be able to for a fraction of the cost of their Western European counterparts – you will have to be prepared to live with drawbacks. One of them is that the cars are relatively unsophisticated; another is that spares may be erratic in their supply; a third is that the quality of their dealers has sometimes been poor and it might be difficult obtaining a satisfactory level of service or parts supply. The answer is to:

– Visit your local dealer and see what sort of service appears to be on offer. If they appear tatty and slovenly, give them a miss.

– See if you can find someone who owns or who has owned the model of car you are interested in and ask if they have had problems.

– Test drive the car even more thoroughly and critically than you might otherwise do.

There are other ways of buying older cars at lower than average prices. As I have said, older Italian cars lose money at a frightening rate – which is really good news for those who want to buy a car that is five years old or more. Mechanically, Italian cars have always been fine if a little quirky for British tastes. Bodily they used to be unmitigated disasters, although they have improved beyond measure in this respect. But if you feel unsure, just try looking around you in a city car park. How does the bodywork on the cars that you are interested in compare with the benchmark Fords and Vauxhalls of the same age?

Larger cars are often cheaper to buy than their smaller brethren, and if you only drive low mileages you might consider one of them. A Senator may end up with a value no higher than an Astra, but it would give a lot more pleasure in use – except when expensive repair bills come in, and it has to be said that there is a lot more to go wrong on a larger car!

One major factor to bear in mind before buying any second-hand car is that you must check out insurance costs. Foreign cars and all GTis, for instance can cost an arm and a leg to insure, especially if you want fully comprehensive insurance. But there are ways in which you can save money on insurance;

– Obtain quotes from both brokers and direct-sell companies advertising in the motoring press.

– If the car is over 10 years old (and sometimes when younger), you might be able to take out classic car insurance. This gives you a lower premium, but *only* if you agree to drive no more than a certain nominated mileage. You might also gain the extra benefit that the insurers may give an 'Agreed Value', so that in the event of total loss, they pay out that sum.

– Consider not taking out fully comprehensive cover, especially if the car has a very low value and you could afford to replace it.

It seems scandalous that there should be a need for such a thing as Agreed Value policies. Unfortunately insurance companies are notorious for offering sometimes derisory payments when a total loss occurs and certainly less than the value of the car. Those who are prepared to fight the insurance company usually obtain a higher offer, but this is rare, it seems. Do bear this in mind when taking out comprehensive cover. The pay out in the event of theft or write-off will possibly only be three-quarters of what you will need to spend in order to replace the car, and it may be much less.

One last way of saving money by carefully directing your choice, is by buying a model without too many letters stuck on the boot or tailgate lid. Models with names such as 'GLSxi' invariably cost a considerable amount more than those with a simple name. You pay a disproportionate more for the extras! Unless, that is, the car has once again reached 'a certain age'. Then its age is deemed to count for more than the sexy attractions of electric windows and central locking, while the addition of certain add-ons, such as a turbo, can actually count against the car. If you are lucky enough to buy a car with a full service history – and those cars with the greatest potential for trouble should *always* have one – the add-ons should provide you with more pleasure than trauma. But if all you want is a set of reliable wheels, a car that starts on a frosty morning and gets you to work, in which the heater and rear screen demister works; a car with simple, reliable, manual everything, one *without* a line of 'alphabetti spaghetti' across the tailgate would be a better buy. And if you're really going to take account of the advice in this book and do your own maintenance, your life will remain much simpler!

How to spot a clocked car

Two groups of people are most responsible for 'clocking' cars' milometers to make them appear that they have done a lower mileage: our dear friends, the down-market or unscrupulous motor traders, and – surprise, surprise – private owners.

Cars with conventional milometers are easily 'clocked', once you know how, by taking out the speedometer although, I once heard of someone who lay beneath a car all one Sunday afternoon with an electric drill winding the thousands away – and this man is now a highly respected, highly paid accountant!

All you can do is look for tell-tale signs that a car has been clocked or concrete evidence that it has not; and if that isn't forthcoming and you have the slightest doubt, assume the worst. Clues that a car's milometer has been tampered with include:

– Numbers that don't line up (although it is true that this can happen even if the thing has never been tweaked in its life, so don't take it as conclusive proof).

– Scratches on the numbers, as if from a small screwdriver – pretty conclusive!

– Finger prints and marks on the inside of the speedo glass.

– Check service records. Where there aren't any, assume the worst.

– Look for signs of wear that seem excessive for the car's mileage: a worn or sagging driver's seat; carpet worn beneath throttle pedal; pedal rubber worn through. A car that has done 125,000 miles will show these signs of wear, while one that has only done 25,000 miles certainly should not. Also take great care to go through the mechanical checks described elsewhere in this article; a smoking engine and a low mileage almost certainly don't belong together.

Buy it – and keep it!

If you buy a stolen car, you could lose both the car *and* the cash, and remember that this applies even though you may have bought the car in good faith and were quite unaware that the car was stolen. While the majority of used car sales don't involve dodgy vehicles, it is always worth taking the simple precautions outlined below. Not only will you be saving yourself a lot of trouble, but you will also be closing another avenue for a car thief.

If you buy a used car from a reputable dealer and it turns out to be stolen, there should be no problem obtaining a full refund, especially if he or she is a member of the Retail Motor Industry Federation (or, in Scotland, the Scottish Motor Trade Association).

If you buy your car through a small ad, for instance in a newspaper, you should make the following checks:

1   Be cautious about advertisements which specify times to phone. Sometimes these phone numbers turn out to be those of a public call box, or the houses of friends or acquaintances who are not involved in the sale.
2   When you respond to an advert, don't specify the vehicle that you are interested in. Instead say, 'I'm calling about the car that you advertised for sale.' The person answering will then have to be honest about whether he has more than one car to sell, in which case he may be a dealer.
3   Never allow the seller to bring the vehicle to you. Always insist on going to where the vehicle is on sale. Anyone who is less than honest will be put off by this approach.
4   Before you go, make sure that you know how to find the chassis and engine numbers on the vehicle in which you are interested.
5   When you arrive at the seller's house, try to find an excuse to go inside, to establish in your own mind whether the person actually lives there.
6   Look out for signs of casual car dealing, for

instance if the person selling the car to you has other vehicles lying around in various states of repair, or there are lots of spare parts scattered around the garage or drive.

7 Remember when you examine the vehicle to check that the chassis and engine numbers match with the numbers on the documents.

8 Ask to see the Registration document. In particular, check how long the car has been in the owner's possession. Be cautious if it has only been in the particular ownership for a short time. If the owner does not have the Registration Document, ask how long he has had the vehicle. If he has owned it for some time, ask why there is no Registration document.

9 Check the Registration Document for watermarks, typeface, spelling mistakes and overtyping. Irregularities could indicate a forgery.

10 If you buy through auctions, take advantage of any indemnity clauses which will protect you in the event of your buying a stolen vehicle. It will cost a nominal sum, but could save you a lot of money, time and embarrassment.

11 Don't forget to look out for the obvious: for instance, a vehicle that has the badges and trimmings of a top of the range model, but does not have the level of performance to match.

12 If you buy from an advertisement, keep a copy of it. Also, try to keep a note of what the person selling the car tells you.

See *Chapter 4 Keeping your car* for information on the security steps you can take to ensure that the hyenas don't get your vehicle.

Raising the readies

Most people take out a loan in order to buy their car. But if it is at all possible avoid doing so, because if you borrow money, it is usually true that the cost of a loan is greater than the cost of running the car!

For the person truly interested in running a car at the lowest possible cost, this has to be one of the strongest reasons of all for running an old car: one that can be purchased outright for cash. When manufacturers offer special finance deals on new cars, they are obliged by law to show the total cost of paying for the car. Even when loans are available at 'special' low rates, owners often end up paying 20 per cent – and often much

more – over and above the cost price of the car. On a £10,000 car, an extra £2,000 has to be found just to service the loan. Many owners would be more than happy to purchase a whole car for that sort of money and good, reliable vehicles *are* available in that price range.

In reality, only one term can be used to compare interest charges between different types of lender. It is almost always shown in advertisements for credit as Annual Percentage Rate or APR. If rates were shown quarterly or monthly as opposed to annually, there would be no way of comparing like with like, since a rate of 2 per cent a month is not necessarily the same as 24 per cent per annum. It all depends on whether the interest is being charged on the capital at the start of the loan, or on the value of the loan as it is being paid off. In the end, all you, the borrower should be interested in is:

– The bottom line. How much money in total will the loan have cost by the time it is paid off? Don't be intimidated or afraid to ask. *Don't* sign up for a loan deal without having taken away the agreement for inspection. If it seems a bit hard going, pop along to your bank, show them the deal and ask if they can do anything better. They would love to lend you the money – that's what they exist for – and they will be the first to tell you if the loan you are being offered looks dodgy or extortionate. Better still, take any loan offers you receive along to your local Citizens' Advice Bureau. You'll find them a great help and on no one's side but yours. And they won't charge you anything!

– Is the interest rate fixed or variable? Make sure it is fixed. If you can afford to pay now, it won't be the end of the world if rates go down; it might be if they go up and you can't afford to pay. If they go down a lot, you may be able to take out a new loan at lower rates to replace the old one, especially from the bank, where they expect you to be canny with your money.

– Insurance. Can you protect yourself against sickness or job loss through paying a small extra amount? (Bear the amount of extra in mind when comparing loans, but peace of mind can be valuable.)

Do remember that, when the seller or the bank offers you a loan, they are doing it for their own benefit. No one is doing you a favour by offering you a loan; they are doing so in order to make more profit. Car dealers make a high level of profit from selling you a loan package, as do high street banks. So shop around for the best deal, just as you would with any other purchase.

Selling your car

Before buying a car, most people need to sell the one they have already got. There is absolutely no need to join the ranks of the dishonest minority in order to obtain the best price when selling. Your car is one among thousands and so you want it to be acceptable, attractive and known about. Here are a few tips to help you get the best price:

- Gather together all the service history, bills and useful paperwork that will encourage a buyer to part with the money. Don't wait until they have bought the car; use these selling points to help you to clinch the deal.

- For cars that need it, a full MOT test certificate is a huge selling incentive, even more so than a period of unexpired road fund licence.

- Be prepared to give up at least one and probably two days of work in preparing the appearance of your car. It is undoubtedly true that a car that has been polished until it gleams, the wheels and tyres clean and buffed, the interior as clean as you can make it, and the engine bay shining will sell ten times more easily and be worth more money than a car that is ankle deep in cigarette ash. Spend on – or rather invest in – cleaners and engine degreaser. Put an air freshener in the car and scrub out the ashtray if you're a fan of the weed.

- Ensure that nothing relatively minor, such as a headlamp or interior light, is left broken. It looks terrible, no matter how good the rest of the car might be.

- Place your advertisement with care: family and everyday cars in the local paper; specialist cars in *Exchange & Mart* ; anything you like in a local auto trader advertising paper.

- Remember to give the name, model and engine size, the colour, and mileage. It is a big mistake to leave out the price in the hope that someone will make an offer. In a national advert or one covering a wide area, be sure to show the area in which you live along with the telephone STD code.

- Spend enough money on your ad to give all the key selling points (there must be some!) such as low mileage, good mechanical, body and interior condition, service history or whatever.

- Avoid 'smart' motor traders terms like the plague, such as 'must be seen', 'beautiful condition' or 'one of the best around'. They serve no useful purpose and suggest that you have nothing positive to say about the car.

- Stay with anyone who wants to look over your car although couples often need to discuss things privately if they are getting seriously interested. Be polite, move out of earshot if requested, but *take the keys with you*. Be prepared to be open, honest and helpful (it is actually reassuring to the potential buyer), while not afraid to point out the good points

- If your car is in huge demand and the phone red hot, don't accept a low offer (and never accept a low offer immediately after – or before! – the advert officially appears), but remember that usually the incentive of a little cash knocked off can clinch a deal.

- If you accept an offer, take a deposit. From that point on, the deal is legally binding on both parties.

- *Don't* let anyone take your car out for a test drive unless (a) you are certain that they are fully insured (and how **can** you be?), and (b) you go with them.

- *Don't* part with the car unless you have either the cash or a banker's draft in your hands, or you have allowed sufficient time for a cheque to clear. (Special clearance can take one day and costs extra – always telephone the bank to make sure it has gone through; they won't always remember to call you...)

- When the buyer calls to take the car, ensure that you tear off the bottom of the V5 Registration Document and send it to DVLC notifying them of change of ownership. You don't want to receive someone else's speeding ticket!

Appendix 1
Workshop procedures
and safety first

Professional motor mechanics are trained in safe working procedures, whereas the onus is on you, the home mechanic, to find them out for yourself and act upon them. However enthusiastic you may be about getting on with the job in hand, do take the time to ensure that your safety is not put at risk. A moment's lack of attention can result in an accident, as can failure to observe certain elementary precautions.

There will always be new ways of having accidents, and the following points do not pretend to be a comprehensive list of all dangers; they are intended rather to make you aware of the risks and to encourage a safety-conscious approach to all work you carry out on your vehicle.

Be sure to consult the suppliers of any materials and equipment you may use, and to obtain and read carefully operating and health and safety instructions that they may supply.

Essential DOs and DON'Ts

DON'T rely on a single jack when working underneath the vehicle. Always use reliable additional means of support, such as axle stands, securely placed under a part of the vehicle that you know will not give way.

DON'T attempt to loosen or tighten high-torque nuts (e.g. wheel hub nuts) while the vehicle is on a jack; it may be pulled off.

DON'T start the engine without first ascertaining that the transmission is in neutral (or 'Park' where applicable) and the parking brake applied.

DON'T suddenly remove the filler cap from a hot cooling system – cover it with a cloth and release the pressure gradually first, or you may get scalded by escaping coolant.

DON'T attempt to drain oil, automatic transmission fluid, or coolant until you are sure it has cooled sufficiently to avoid scalding you.

DON'T grasp any part of the engine, exhaust or catalytic converter without first ascertaining that it is sufficiently cool to avoid burning you.

DON'T allow brake fluid or antifreeze to contact vehicle paintwork.

DON'T syphon toxic liquids such as fuel, brake fluid or antifreeze by mouth, or allow them to remain on your skin.

DON'T inhale dust — it may be injurious to health (see Asbestos below).

DON'T allow any spilt oil or grease to remain on the floor — wipe it up straight away, before someone slips on it.

DON'T use ill-fitting spanners or other tools which may slip and cause injury.

DON'T attempt to lift a heavy component which may be beyond your capability — get assistance.

DON'T rush to finish a job, or take unverified short cuts.

DON'T allow children or animals in or around an unattended vehicle.

DON'T park vehicles with catalytic converters over combustible materials such as dry grass, oily rags, etc. if the engine has recently been run. As catalytic converters reach extremely high temperatures, any such materials in close proximity may ignite.

DON'T run vehicles equipped with catalytic converters without the exhaust system heat shields fitted.

DO wear eye protection when using power tools such as an electric drill, sander, bench grinder etc., and when working under the vehicle.

DO use a barrier cream on your hands prior to undertaking dirty jobs — it will protect your skin from infection as well as making the dirt easier to remove afterwards; but make sure your hands aren't left slippery. Note that long term contact with used engine oil can be a health hazard.

DO keep loose clothing (cuffs, tie etc.) and long hair well out of the way of moving mechanical parts.

DO remove rings, wrist watch etc., before working on the vehicle — especially the electrical system.

DO ensure that any lifting tackle used has a safe working load rating adequate for the job, and is used precisely as recommended by the manufacturer.

DO keep your work area tidy — it is only too easy to fall over articles left lying around.

DO get someone to check periodically that all is well, when working alone on the vehicle.

DO carry out work in a logical sequence and check that everything is correctly assembled and tightened afterwards.

DO remember that your vehicle's safety affects that of yourself and others. If in doubt on any point, get specialist advice.

IF, in spite of following these precautions, you are unfortunate enough to injure yourself, seek medical attention as soon as possible.

Fire

Remember at all times that petrol (gasoline) is highly flammable. Never smoke, or have any kind of naked flame around, when working on the vehicle. But the risk does not end there — a spark caused by an electrical short-circuit, by two metal surfaces contacting each other, by a central heating boiler in the garage 'firing up', or even by static electricity built up in your body under certain conditions, can ignite petrol vapour, which in a confined space is highly explosive.

Always disconnect the battery earth (ground) terminal before working on any part of the fuel system, and never risk spilling fuel on to a hot engine or exhaust.

It is recommended that a fire extinguisher of a type suitable for fuel and electrical fires is kept handy in the garage or workplace at all times. Never try to extinguish a fuel or electrical fire with water.

Fumes

Certain fumes are highly toxic and can quickly cause unconsciousness and even death if inhaled to any extent. Petrol (gasoline) vapour comes into this category, as do the vapours from certain solvents such as trichloroethylene and those from many adhesives. Any draining or pouring of such volatile fluids should be done in a well-ventilated area.

When using cleaning fluids and solvents, read the instructions carefully. Never use any materials from unmarked containers — they may give off poisonous vapours.

Never run the engine of a motor vehicle in an enclosed space such as a garage. Exhaust fumes contain carbon monoxide which is extremely poisonous. If you need to run the engine, always do so in the open air or at least have the rear of the vehicle outside the workplace.

If you are fortunate enough to have the use of an inspection pit, never drain or pour petrol, and never run the engine, while the vehicle is standing over it; the fumes, being heavier than air, will concentrate in the pit with possibly lethal results.

The battery

Never cause a spark, or allow a naked light, near the vehicle battery. It will normally be giving off a certain amount of hydrogen gas, which is highly explosive.

Always disconnect the battery earth (ground) terminal before working on the fuel or electrical systems.

If possible, loosen the filler plugs or cover when charging the battery from an external source. Do not charge at an excessive rate or the battery may burst.

Take care when topping up and when carrying the battery. The acid electrolyte, even when diluted, is very corrosive and should not be allowed to contact the eyes or skin.

If you ever need to prepare electrolyte yourself, always add the acid slowly to the water, and never the other way round. Protect against splashes by wearing rubber gloves and goggles.

Mains electricity

When using an electric power tool, inspection light etc., which works from the mains, always ensure that the appliance is correctly connected to its plug and that, where necessary, it is properly earthed (grounded). Do not use such appliances in damp conditions and, again, beware of creating a spark or applying excessive heat in the vicinity of fuel or fuel vapour.

Also, before using any mains powered electrical equipment, take one more simple precaution – use an RCD (Residual Current Device) circuit breaker. Then, if there is a short, the RCD circuit breaker minimises the risk of electrocution by instantly cutting the power supply. Buy from any electrical store or DIY centre. RCDs fit simply into your electrical socket before plugging in your electrical equipment.

Ignition HT voltage

A severe electric shock can result from touching certain parts of the ignition system, such as the HT leads, when the engine is running or being cranked, particularly if components are damp or the insulation is defective. Where an electronic ignition system is fitted, the HT voltage is much higher and could prove fatal. Consult your handbook or main dealer if in any doubt. Risk of injury while working on running engines, e.g. adjusting the timing, can arise if the operator touches a high voltage lead and pulls his hand away on to a projection or revolving part.

Welding and bodywork repairs

It is so useful to be able to weld when carrying out restoration work, and yet there is a good deal that could go dangerously wrong for the uninformed — in fact more than could be covered here. **For safety's sake** you are strongly recommended to seek tuition, in whatever branch of welding you wish to use, from your local evening institute or adult education classes. In addition, all of the information and instructional material produced by the suppliers of materials and equipment you will be using must be studied carefully. You may have to ask your stockist for some of this printed material if it is not made available at the time of purchase.

In addition, it is strongly recommended that *The Car Bodywork Repair Manual*, published by Haynes, is purchased and studied before carrying out any welding or bodywork repairs. Consisting of 292 pages, around 1,000 illustrations and written by Lindsay Porter, the author of this book, *The Car Bodywork Repair Manual* picks the brains of specialists from a variety of fields, and covers arc, MIG and 'gas' welding, panel beating and accident repair, rust repair and treatment, paint spraying, glass-fibre work, filler, lead loading, interiors and much more besides. Alongside a number of projects, the book describes in detail how to carry out each of the techniques involved in car bodywork repair with safety notes where necessary. As such, it is the ideal complement to this book.

Compressed gas cylinders

There are serious hazards associated with the storage and handling of gas cylinders and fittings, and standard precautions should be strictly observed in dealing with them. Ensure that cylinders are stored in safe conditions, properly maintained and always handled with special care and make constant efforts to eliminate the possibilities of leakage, fire and explosion.

The cylinder gases that are commonly used are oxygen, acetylene and liquid petroleum gas (LPG). Safety requirements for all three gases are: Cylinders must be stored in a fire resistant, dry and well-ventilated space, away from any source of heat or ignition and protected from ice, snow or direct sunlight. Valves of cylinders in store must always be kept uppermost and closed, even when the cylinder is empty. Cylinders should be handled with care and only by personnel who are reliable, adequately informed and fully aware of all associated hazards. Damaged or leaking cylinders should be immediately taken outside into the open air, and the supplier and fire authorities should be notified immediately. No one should approach a gas cylinder store with a naked light or cigarette. Care should be taken to avoid striking or dropping cylinders, or knocking them together. Cylinders should never be used as rollers. One cylinder should never be filled from another. Every care must be taken to avoid accidental damage to cylinder valves. Valves must be operated without haste, never fully opened hard back against the back stop (so that other users know the valve is open) and never wrenched shut but turned just securely enough to stop the gas. Before removing or loosening any outlet connections, caps or plugs, a check should be made that the valves are closed. When changing cylinders, close all valves and appliance taps, and extinguish naked flames, including pilot jets, before disconnecting them. When reconnecting ensure that all connections and washers are clean and in good condition and do not overtighten them. Immediately a cylinder becomes empty, close its valve.

Safety requirements for acetylene: Cylinders must always be stored and used in the upright position. If a cylinder becomes heated accidentally or becomes hot because of excessive backfiring, immediately shut the valve, detach the regulator, take the cylinder out of doors well away from the building, immerse it in or continuously spray it with water, open the valve and allow the gas to escape until the cylinder is empty. If necessary, notify the emergency fire service without delay.

Safety requirements for oxygen are: No oil or grease should be used on valves or fittings. Cylinders with convex bases should be used in a stand or held securely to a wall.

Safety requirements for LPG are: The store must be kept free of combustible material, corrosive material and cylinders of oxygen.

Cylinders should only ever be carried upright, securely strapped down, preferably in an open vehicle or with windows open. Carry the suppliers safety data with you. In the event of an accident, notify the Police and Fire services and hand the safety data to them.

Dangerous liquids and gases

Because of flammable gas given off by batteries when on charge, care should be taken to avoid sparking by switching off the power supply before charger leads are connected or disconnected. Battery terminals should be shielded, since a battery contains energy and a spark can be caused by any conductor which touches its terminals or exposed connecting straps.

When internal combustion engines are operated inside buildings the exhaust fumes must be properly discharged to the open air. Petroleum spirit or mixture must be contained in metal cans which should be kept in a store. In any area where battery charging or the testing of fuel injection systems is carried out there must be good ventilation, and no sources of ignition. Inspection pits often present serious hazards. They should be of adequate length to allow safe access and exit while a car is in position. If there is an inspection pit, petrol may enter it. Since petrol vapour is heavier than air it will remain there and be a hazard if there is any source of ignition. All sources of ignition must therefore be excluded.

Lifting equipment

Special care should be taken when any type of lifting equipment is used. Lifting jacks are for raising vehicles; they should never be used as supports while work is in progress. Jacks must be replaced by adequate rigid supports before any work is begun on the vehicle. Risk of injury while working on running engines, e.g. adjusting the timing, can arise if the operator touches a high voltage lead and pulls his hand away on to a projection or revolving part. On some vehicles the voltage used in the ignition system is so high as to cause injury or death by electrocution. Consult your handbook or main dealer if in any doubt.

Work with plastics

Work with plastic materials brings additional hazards into workshops. Many of the materials used (polymers, resins, adhesives and materials acting as catalysts and accelerators) readily produce very dangerous situations in the form of poisonous fumes, skin irritants, risk of fire and explosions. Do not allow resin or 2-pack adhesive hardener, or that supplied with filler or 2-pack stopper to come into contact with skin or eyes. Read carefully the safety notes supplied on the tin, tube or packaging.

Jacks and axle stands

Special care should be taken when any type of lifting equipment is used. Any jack is made for lifting the car, not for supporting it. NEVER even consider working under your car using only a jack to support the weight of it. Jacks are only for raising vehicles, and must be replaced by adequate supports before any work is begun on the vehicle; axle stands are available from many discount stores, and all auto parts stores. These stands are absolutely essential if you plan to work under your car. Simple triangular stands (fixed or adjustable) will suit almost all of your working situations. Drive-on ramps are very limiting because of their design and size.

When jacking the car from the front, leave the gearbox in neutral and the brake off until you have placed the axle stands under the frame. Make sure that the car is on level ground first! Then put the car into gear and/or engage the handbrake and lower the jack. Obviously DO NOT put the car in gear if you plan to turn over the engine! Leaving the brake on, or leaving the car in gear while jacking the front of the car will necessarily cause the jack to tip (unless a good quality trolley jack with wheels is being used). This is unavoidable when jacking the car on one side, and the use of the handbrake in this case is recommended.

If the car is older and if it shows signs of weakening at the jack tubes while using the factory jack, it is best to purchase a good scissors jack or hydraulic jack — preferably trolley-type (depending on your budget).

Workshop safety — summary

1. Always have a fire extinguisher at arm's length whenever welding or when working on the fuel system — under the car, or under the bonnet.
2. NEVER use a naked flame near the petrol tank.
3. Keep your inspection lamp FAR AWAY from any source of dripping petrol (gasoline); for example, while removing the fuel pump.
4. NEVER use petrol (gasoline) to clean parts. Use paraffin (kerosene) or white (mineral) spirits.
5. NO SMOKING!

If you do have a fire, DON'T PANIC. Use the extinguisher effectively by directing it at the base of the fire.

Paint spraying

NEVER use 2-pack, isocyanate-based paints in the home environment. Ask your supplier if you are not sure which is which. If you have use of a professional booth, wear an air-fed mask. Wear a charcoal face mask when spraying other paints and maintain ventilation to the spray area. Concentrated fumes are dangerous!

Spray fumes, thinners and paint are highly flammable. Keep away from naked flames or sparks.

Paint spraying safety is too large a subject for this book. See Lindsay Porter's *The Car Bodywork Repair Manual* (Haynes) for further information.

6.1 *Invest in a workshop-sized extinguisher. Choose the carbon dioxide type or preferably, dry powder but never a water type extinguisher for workshop use. Water conducts electricty and can make worse an oil or petrol-based fire, in certain circumstances.*

6.1

Fluoroelastomers –
Most Important! Please Read This Section!

Many synthetic rubber-like materials used in motor cars contain a substance called fluorine. These substances are known as fluoroelastomers and are commonly used for oil seals, wiring and cabling, bearing surfaces, gaskets, diaphragms, hoses and 'O' rings. If they are subjected to temperatures greater than 315°C, they will decompose and can be potentially hazardous. Fluoroelastomer materials will show physical signs of decomposition under such conditions in the form of charring of black sticky masses. Some decomposition may occur at temperatures above 200°C, and it is obvious that when a car has been in a fire or has been dismantled with the assistance of a cutting torch or blow torch, the fluoroelastomers can decompose in the manner indicated above.

In the presence of any water or humidity, including atmospheric moisture, the by-products caused by the fluoroelastomers being heated can be extremely dangerous. According to the Health and Safety Executive, 'Skin contact with this liquid or decomposition residues can cause painful and penetrating burns. Permanent irreversible skin and tissue damage can occur.' Damage can also be caused to eyes or by the inhalation of fumes created as fluoroelastomers are burned or heated.

If you are in the vicinity of a vehicle fire or a place where a vehicle is being cut up with cutting equipment, the Health and Safety Executive recommend the following action:

1. Assume unless you know otherwise that seals, gaskets and 'O' rings, hoses, wiring and cabling, bearing surfaces and diaphragms are fluoroelastomers.
2. Inform firefighters of the presence of fluoroelastomers and toxic and corrosive fume hazards when they arrive.
3. All personnel not wearing breathing apparatus must leave the immediate area of a fire.

After fires or exposure to high temperatures

1. Do not touch blackened or charred seals or equipment.
2. Allow all burnt or decomposed fluoroelastomer materials to cool down before inspection, investigation, tear-down or removal.
4. Preferably, don't handle parts containing decomposed fluoroelastomers, but if you must, wear goggles and PVC (polyvinyl chloride) or neoprene protective gloves whilst doing so. Never handle such parts unless they are completely cool.
5. Contaminated parts, residues, materials and clothing, including protective clothing and gloves, should be disposed of by an approved contractor to landfill or by incineration

according to national or local regulations. Original seals, gaskets and 'O' rings, along with contaminated material, must not be burned locally.

Symptoms and clinical findings of exposure:

A Skin/eye contact
Symptoms may be apparent immediately, soon after contact or there may be considerable delay after exposure. Do not assume that there has been no damage from a lack of immediate symptoms; delays of minutes in treatment can have severe consequences:

1. Dull throbbing ache.
2. Severe and persistent pain.
3. Black discolouration under nails (skin contact).
4. Severe, persistent and penetrating burns.
5. Skin swelling and redness.
6. Blistering.
7. Sometimes pain without visible change.

B Inhalation (breathing) – immediate
1. Coughing.
2. Choking.
3. Chills lasting one to two hours after exposure.
4. Irritation.

C Inhalation (breathing) – delays of one to two days or more
1. Fever.
2. Cough.
3. Chest tightness.
4. Pulmonary oedema (congestion).
5. Bronchial pneumonia.

First aid

A Skin contact
1. Remove contaminated clothing immediately.
2. Irrigate affected skin with copious amounts of cold water or limewater (saturated calcium hydroxide solution) for 15 to 60 minutes. Obtain medical assistance urgently.

B Inhalation
Remove to fresh air and obtain medical supportive treatment immediately. Treat for pulmonary oedema.

C Eye contact
Wash/irrigate eyes immediately with water followed by normal saline for 30 to 60 minutes. Obtain immediate medical attention.

Appendix 2
Tools and working facilities

Introduction

A selection of good tools is a fundamental requirement for anyone contemplating the maintenance and repair of a motor vehicle. For the owner who does not possess any, their purchase will prove a considerable expense, offsetting some of the savings made by doing-it-yourself. However, provided that the tools purchased are of good quality, they will last for many years and prove an extremely worthwhile investment.

To help the average owner to decide which tools are needed to carry out the various tasks detailed in this manual, we have compiled three lists of tools under the following headings: Maintenance and minor repair tool kit, Repair and overhaul tool kit, and Special tools. The newcomer to practical mechanics should start off with the Maintenance and minor repair tool kit and confine himself to the simpler jobs around the vehicle. Then, as his confidence and experience grows, he can undertake more difficult tasks, buying extra tools as, and when, they are needed. In this way, a Maintenance and minor repair tool kit can be built up into a Repair and overhaul tool kit over a considerable period of time without any major cash outlays. The experienced do-it-yourselfer will have a tool kit good enough for most repairs and overhaul procedures and will add tools from the Special tools category when he feels the expense is justified by the amount of use these tools will be put to.

Maintenance and minor repair tool kit

The tools given in this list should be considered as a minimum requirement if routine maintenance, servicing and minor repair operations are to be undertaken.

Ideally, purchase sets of open-ended and ring spanners, covering similar size ranges. That way, you will have the correct tools for loosening nuts from bolts having the same head size, for example, since you will have at least two spanners of the same size.

Alternatively, a set of combination spanners (ring one end, open-ended the other), give the advantages of both types of spanner. Although more expensive than open-ended spanners, combination spanners can often help you out in tight situations, by gripping the nut better than an open-ender.

Combination spanners — ⅜, ⁷⁄₁₆, ½, ⁹⁄₁₆, ⅝, ¹¹⁄₁₆, ¾, ¹³⁄₁₆, ⅞, ¹⁵⁄₁₆ in. AF.

Combination spanners — 8, 9, 10, 11, 12, 14, 15, 17, 19 mm.

Adjustable spanner — 9 in

Engine sump/gearbox/rear axle drain plug key (where applicable)

Spark plug spanner (with rubber insert)

Spark plug gap adjustment tool

Set of feeler gauges

Brake adjuster spanner (where applicable)

Brake bleed nipple spanner

Screwdriver — 4 in long x ¼ in dia (crosshead)

Combination pliers — 6 in

Hacksaw, junior

Tyre pump

Tyre pressure gauge

Grease gun (where applicable)

Oil can

Fine emery cloth (1 sheet)

Wire brush (small)

Funnel (medium size)

Repair and overhaul tool kit

These tools are virtually essential for anyone undertaking any major repairs to a motor vehicle, and are additional to those given in the Basic list. Included in this list is a comprehensive set of sockets. Although these are expensive they will be found invaluable as they are so versatile — particularly if various drives are included in the set. We recommend the ½ in square-drive type, as this can be used with most proprietary torque wrenches. On the other hand, ⅜ in drive are better for working in confined spaces and, if of

good quality will be amply strong enough for work inside the engine bay. If you cannot afford a socket set, even bought piecemeal, then inexpensive tubular box spanners are a useful alternative.

The tools in this list will occasionally need to be supplemented by tools from the Special list.

Sockets (or box spanners) to cover range in previous list

Reversible ratchet drive (for use with sockets)

Extension piece, 10 in (for use with sockets)

Universal joint (for use with sockets)

Torque wrench (for use with sockets)

'Mole' wrench — 8 in

Ball pein hammer

Soft-faced hammer, plastic or rubber

Screwdriver — 6 in long x ⁵⁄₁₆ in dia (plain)

Screwdriver — 2 in long x ⁵⁄₁₆ in square (plain)

Screwdriver — 1½ in long x ¼ in dia (crosshead)

Screwdriver — 3 in long x ⅛ in dia (electrician's)

Pliers — electrician's side cutters

Pliers — needle nosed

Pliers — circlip (internal and external)

Cold chisel — ½ in

Scriber

Centre punch

Pin punch

Hacksaw

Valve grinding tool

Steel rule/straight-edge

Allen keys

Selection of files

Wire brush (large)

Axle stands

Jack (strong scissor or hydraulic type)

Special tools

The tools in this list are those which are not used regularly, are expensive to buy, or which need to be used in accordance with their manufacturers' instructions. Unless relatively difficult mechanical jobs are undertaken frequently, it will not be economic to buy many of these tools. Where this is the case, you could consider clubbing together with friends (or a motorists' club) to make a joint purchase, or borrowing the tools against a deposit from a local garage or tool hire specialist.

The following list contains only those tools and instruments freely available to the public, and not those special tools produced by the vehicle manufacturer specifically for its dealer network.

Valve spring compressor

Piston ring compressor

Ball joint separator

Universal hub/bearing puller

Impact screwdriver*

Micrometer and/or vernier gauge

Carburettor flow balancing device (where applicable)

Dial gauge

Stroboscopic timing light

Dwell angle meter/tachometer

Universal electrical multimeter

Cylinder compression gauge

Lifting tackle

Trolley jack*

Light with extension lead*

Rivet gun*

* An increasing number of so-called specialist tools are coming onto the market at low cost, particularly but not exclusively those asterisked above. But do take care! Some – especially those currently made in China – are of very poor quality.

Buying tools

Tool factors can be a good source of implements, due to the extensive ranges which they normally stock. On the other hand, accessory shops usually offer excellent quality goods, often at discount prices, so it pays to shop around.

The old maxim 'buy the best tools you can afford' is a good general rule to go by, since cheap tools are seldom good value, especially in the long run. Conversely, it isn't always true that the MOST expensive tools are best. There are plenty of good tools available at reasonable prices, and the shop manager or proprietor will usually be very helpful in giving advice on the best tools for particular jobs.

Care and maintenance of tools

Having purchased a reasonable tool kit, it is necessary to keep the tools in a clean serviceable condition. After use, always wipe off any dirt, grease and metal particles using a clean, dry cloth, before putting the tools away. Never leave them lying around after they have been used. A simple tool rack on the garage or workshop wall, for items such as screwdrivers and pliers is a good idea. Store all normal spanners and sockets in a metal box. Any measuring instruments, gauges, meters, etc. must be carefully stored where they cannot be damaged or become rusty.

Take a little care when the tools are used. Hammer heads inevitably become marked, and screwdrivers lose the keen edge on their blades from time to time. A little timely attention with emery cloth or a file will soon restore items like this to a good serviceable finish.

Working facilities

Not to be forgotten when discussing tools, is the workshop itself. If anything more than routine maintenance is to be carried out, some form of suitable working area becomes essential.

It is appreciated that many an owner mechanic is forced by circumstance to remove an engine or similar item without the benefit of a garage or workshop. Having done this, any repairs should always be done under the cover of a roof, if feasible.

Wherever possible, any dismantling should be done on a clean, flat workbench or table at a suitable working height. Engine dismantling, though, is safer carried out on an engine stand (they can be hired sometimes) or on a large cardboard box opened out to give a clean surface on the workshop floor.

Any workbench needs a vice — the larger the better — and one with a jaw opening of 4 in (100 mm) is suitable for most jobs. As mentioned previously, some clean dry storage space is also required for tools, as well as for lubricants, cleaning fluids, touch-up paints and so on, which soon become necessary.

Another item which may be required, and

Spanner jaw gap comparison table

AF size	Actual size	Nearest metric size	Metric size in inches
4BA	0.248 in	7 mm	0.276 in
2BA	0.320 in	8 mm	0.315 in
7/16 in	0.440 in	11 mm	0.413 in
1/2 in	0.500 in	13 mm	0.510 in
9/16 in	0.560 in	14 mm	0.550 in
5/8 in	0.630 in	16 mm	0.630 in
11/16 in	0.690 in	18 mm	0.710 in
3/4 in	0.760 in	19 mm	0.750 in
13/16 in	0.820 in	21 mm	0.830 in
7/8 in	0.880 in	22 mm	0.870 in
15/16 in	0.940 in	24 mm	0.945 in
1 in	1.000 in	26 mm	1.020 in

Whitworth size	Actual size	Nearest AF size	AF Actual size	Nearest Metric size	Metric size in inches
3/16 in	0.450 in	7/16 in	0.440 in	12 mm	0.470 in
1/4 in	0.530 in	1/2 in	0.500 in	14 mm	0.500 in
5/16 in	0.604 in	9/16 in	0.560 in	15 mm	0.590 in
3/8 in	0.720 in	11/16 in	0.690 in	18 mm	0.710 in
7/16 in	0.830 in	13/16 in	0.820 in	21 mm	0.830 in
1/2 in	0.930 in	7/8 in	0.880 in	24 mm	0.945 in
9/16 in	1.020 in	1 in	1.010 in	26 mm	1.020 in

Appendix 3
British and American
technical terms

English	American	English	American
Accelerator	Gas pedal	Leading shoe (of brake)	Primary shoe
Aerial	Antenna	Locks	Latches
Alternator	Generator (AC)	Motorway	Freeway, turnpike
Anti-roll bar	Stabilizer or sway bar	Number plate	License plate
Battery	Energizer	Paraffin	Kerosene
Bodywork	Sheet metal	Petrol	Gasoline
Bonnet (engine cover)	Hood	Petrol tank	Gas tank
Boot (luggage compartment)	Trunk	'Pinking'	'Pinging'
Boot lid	Trunk lid	Propeller shaft	Driveshaft
Bottom gear	First gear	Quarterlight	Quarter window
Bulkhead	Firewall	Retread	Recap
Cam follower or tappet	Valve lifter or tappet	Reverse	Back-up
Carburettor	Carburetor	Rocker cover	Valve cover
Catch	Latch	Roof rack	Car-top carrier
Choke/venturi	Barrel	Saloon	Sedan
Clearance	Lash	Seized	Frozen
Crownwheel	Ring gear (of differential)	Side indicator lights	Side marker lights
Disc (brake)	Rotor/disk	Side light	Parking light
Drop arm	Pitman arm	Silencer	Muffler
Drophead coupé	Convertible	Sill panel	Rocker panel
Dynamo	Generator(DC)	Spanner	Wrench
Earth (elec)	Ground	Split cotter (for valve spring cap)	Lock (for valve spring retainer)
Engineer's blue	Prussian blue	Split pin	Cotter pin
Estate car	Station wagon	Steering arm	Spindle arm
Exhaust manifold	Header	Sump	Oil pan
Fast back	Hard top	Tab washer	Tang; lock
Fault finding/ diagnosis	Trouble shooting	Tailgate	Liftgate
Float chamber	Flat bowl	Tappet	Valve lifter
Free-play	Lash	Thrust bearing	Throw-out bearing
Freewheel	Coast	Top gear	High
Gudgeon pin	Piston pin or wrist pin	Trackrod (of steering)	Tie-rod (or connecting rod)
Gearchange	Shift	Trailing shoe (of brake)	Secondary shoe
Gearbox	Transmission	Transmission	Whole drive line
Halfshaft	Axleshaft	Tyre	Tire
Handbrake	Parking brake	Van	Panel wagon/van
Hood	Soft top	Vice	Vise
Hot spot	Heat riser	Wheel nut	Lug nut
Indicator	Turn signal	Windscreen	Windshield
Interior light	Dome lamp	Wing/mudguard	Fender
Layshaft (of gearbox)	Countershaft		

which has a much more general usage, is an electric drill with a chuck capacity of at least 5/16 in (8 mm). This, together with a good range of twist drills, is virtually essential for fitting accessories such as wing mirrors and reversing lights. Cordless drills are far more convenient to use and don't carry any electrical risks in use.

Last, but not least, always keep a supply of old newspapers and clean, lint-free rags available, and try to keep any working areas as clean as possible.As this book has been written in England, it uses the appropriate English component names, phrases and spelling. Some of these differ from those used in America. Normally, these cause no difficulty, but to make sure, a glossary is printed opposite. In ordering spare parts remember the parts list will probably use these words:

Miscellaneous points

An 'oil seal' is fitted to components lubricated by grease!

A 'damper' is a 'shock absorber'. It damps out bouncing, and absorbs shocks of bump impact. Both names are correct, and both are used haphazardly.

Note that British drum brakes are different from the Bendix type that is common in America, so different descriptive names result. The shoe end furthest from the hydraulic wheel cylinder is on a pivot; interconnection between the shoes as on Bendix brakes is most uncommon. Therefore the phrase 'Primary' or 'Secondary' shoe does not apply. A shoe is said to be 'Leading' or 'Trailing'. A 'Leading' shoe is one on which a point on the drum, as it rotates forward, reaches the shoe at the end worked by the hydraulic cylinder before the anchor end. The opposite is a 'Trailing' shoe, and this one has no self-servo from the wrapping effect of the rotating drum.

Appendix 4
Specialist suppliers featured in this book

BOC Ltd, The Priestley Centre, 10 Priestley Road, The Surrey Research Park, Guildford, Surrey, GU2 5XY.
Tel: 0483 579857.
Welding gases and DIY 'Portapak' gas welding equipment.

Bosch, Robert Bosch Ltd, PO Box 98, Broadwater Park, North Orbital Road, Denham, Uxbridge, Middlesex, UB9 5HJ.
Tel: 0895 834466.
Very wide range of high quality DIY and professional power tools (and large range of Bosch automotive parts and accessories).

Champion Sparking Plug Co Ltd, Arrowebrook Road, Upton, Wirral, Merseyside, L49 0UQ.
Tel: 051 678 7070.
Suppliers of sparking plugs, leads, engine filters and windscreen wiper blades used in this book.

Comma Oils & Chemicals, Comma Works, Denton Industrial Area, Lower Range Road, Gravesend, Kent, DA12 2QX.
Tel: 0474 564311.
CopperEase, X – stream corrosion resistant coolant and a wide range of auto products.

'Dis-Car-Nect', Richbrook International Ltd, Dept Cr, 2 Munro Terrace, 112 Cheyne Walk, London, SW10 0DL.
Tel: 071 351 9333.
Car battery isolator.

Hammerite Products Ltd, Prudhoe, Northumberland, NE42 6LP.
Tel: 0661 830000.
Waxoyl, Hammerite hammered and smooth metal finishes, available from all high street auto. accessory stores.

Holt Lloyd, Lloyds House, Alderley Road, Wilmslow, Cheshire.
Tel: 0625 526838.
Aerosol tyre sealant.

HPI Autodata, HP Information plc, Dolphin House, PO Box 61, New Street, Salisbury, Wiltshire, SP1 2TB.
Tel: 0722 422422.

Michelin Tyre Plc, Public Relations, Davy House, Lyon Road, Harrow, Middlesex, HA1 2DQ.
Tel: 081 861 2121.

'The Minder', Portland Marketing Ltd, Hernes Estate, Greys Road, Henley on Thames, RG9 4NT.
Tel: 0491 411 510.
Security steering wheel clamp: AA tested and approved.

Mintex Don, PO Box 18, Cleckheaton, West Yorkshire, BO19 3UJ.
Tel: 0274 875711.
High quality replacement and performance brake and clutch friction materials.

Partco, See *Yellow Pages* for your local Partco centre (look under Motor Factors). Suppliers of almost every type of consumable and component used in automotive repair.

Plastic Padding Ltd, Wooburn Industrial Park, Wooburn Green, High Wycombe, Bucks, HP10 0PE.
Tel: 0628 527912.
Fibreglass, filler and car body repair products.

Potters Vehicle Dismantlers, Sandy Lane, Titton, Stourport-on-Severn, Worcestershire.
Tel: 0299 823134.
The author's favourite car dismantlers!

PP Video, The Storehouse, Little Hereford Street, Bromyard, Hereford, HR7 4DE
Tel: 0885 488800.
The author, Lindsay Porter's, other hat! 'Video Skill-Guide to Gas Welding' produced with BOC. 1 hour. £14.99. Plus around 50 classic car and motorsport tapes.

'Radio-Cassette Lock', Metro Products, see 'Stoplock'.

'Rimlok', Deltalease Vehicle Management Ltd, Unit 5, Maling Street, Ouseburn, Newcastle Upon Tyne, NE6 1LP.
Tel: 901 265 7744.
High security wheelclamps.

SATA, Minden Industrial Ltd, 16 Greyfriars Road, Moreton Hall, Bury St Edmunds, Suffolk, IP32 7DX.
Tel: 0284 702156.
Rust-prevention injection equipment.

Sparkrite, Brenda Road, Hartlepool, Cleveland, TS25 2BQ.
Tel: 0429 862616.
Wide range of car alarms.

SP Tyres UK Ltd, Fort Dunlop, Erdington, Birmingham, B24 9QT.
Tel: 021 384 4444.
Manufacturers of Dunlop tyres.

'Stoplock', Metro Products (Accessories and Leisure) Ltd, Eastman House, 118 Station Road East, Oxted, Surrey, RH8 0QA.
Tel: 0883 717644.
Universal steering immobilizer, radio-cassette lock, trailer tow ball lock and range of other auto. products.

Sykes-Pickavant Ltd, Kilnhouse Lane, Lytham St Annes, Lancashire, FY8 3DU.
Tel: 0253 721291.
Manufacturers and suppliers of the complete range of high quality workshop hand tools.

Valvoline Oil Co Ltd, Dock Road, Birkenhead, Merseyside, L41 1DR.
Tel: 051 652 1551.
Manufacturers of a wide range of automotive lubricants, many of which are featured through the pages of this book.

Vintage Supplies, Folgate Road, North Walsham, Norfolk, NR28 0AJ.
Tel: 0692 406343.
'Slosh Tank' fuel tank sealant.

Wurth UK Ltd, 1 Centurion Way, Erith, Kent, DA18 4AF.
Tel: 081 310 6666.
Zinc-rich primer and other workshop equipment.

XL Components, Unit 3, Weststone, Berryhill Industrial Estate, Droitwich, Worcestershire.
Tel: 0905 795795.
Specialist in reconditioned steering and suspension components of all types and a full range of reconditioned distributors.